HISTORICAL AND LITERARY STUDIES
PAGAN, JEWISH, AND CHRISTIAN

NEW TESTAMENT TOOLS AND STUDIES

EDITED BY

BRUCE M. METZGER, Ph.D., D.D., L.H.D.

Professor of New Testament Language and Literature
Princeton Theological Seminary

VOLUME VIII

LEIDEN
E. J. BRILL
1968

HISTORICAL AND LITERARY STUDIES

PAGAN, JEWISH, AND CHRISTIAN

BY

BRUCE M. METZGER

With 20 plates

LEIDEN
E. J. BRILL
1968

TO
MY WIFE

CONTENTS

LIST OF PLATES

PREFACE

The chapters included in the present volume are concerned with a variety of subjects, some more closely and some less closely related to the New Testament and the early Church. Whatever unity the collection may have arises from the effort of the author to apply the historical method, in its broadest sense, to a number of tasks and problems that have engaged his attention over the past quarter of a century.

In gathering these studies together for republication the author has taken the opportunity to incorporate in each chapter additional material and to introduce a variety of other modifications. In some cases (for example, in the chapters that deal with the Mystery Religions and with the question when scribes began to use writing desks) the additions are considerable both in number and extent.

The following is a list of the journals, Festschriften, and series in which the chapters were originally published.

Chap. I from *The Harvard Theological Review*, XLVIII (1955), 1-20.

Chap. II from *American Journal of Philology*, LXVI (1945), 225-233.

Chap. III from *Journal of Near Eastern Studies*, XV (1956), 18-26.

Chap. IV from *Journal of Biblical Literature*, LXXVI (1957), 153-156.

Chap. V from *ib.*, LXX (1951), 297-307.

Chap. VI from *Verbum Domini*, XXXIV (1956), 349-350, and from *The Expository Times*, LXIX (1957), 52-54.

Chap. VII from *New Testament Studies*, V (1958-59), 299-306.

Chap. VIII from *New Testament Studies in Memory of Raymond T. Stamm*, edited by J. M. Myers, H. N. Bream, and Otto Reimherr (E. J. Brill, Leiden, 1968), pp. 118-128.

Chap. IX from *Biblical and Patristic Studies in Memory of Robert Pierce Casey*, edited by J. Neville Birdsall and Robert W. Thomson (Herder Verlag, Freiburg im Breisgau, 1963), pp. 78-95.

Chap. X from *Studies in the History and Text of the New Testament in Honor of Kenneth Willis Clark*, edited by Boyd L. Daniels and M. Jack Suggs in *Studies and Documents*, XXIX (University of Utah Press, Salt Lake City, 1967), pp. 89-94.

Chap. XI from *Studia Patristica*, VII, Part I, edited by F. L. Cross (= *Texte und Untersuchungen zur Geschichte der altchristlichen Literatur*, XCII; Akademie-Verlag, Berlin, 1966), pp. 531-542.

Chap. XII in part from *Akten des XI. internationalen Byzantinisten-Kongresses 1958* (Verlag C. H. Beck, Munich, 1960), pp. 356-362, and in part from *Revue de Qumran*, I (1958-59), 509-515.

Chap. XIII from *New Testament Studies*, VIII (1961-62), 72-77.
Chap. XIV from *The Expository Times*, LXXVIII (1966-67), 324–327, 372–375.

The author expresses his gratitude to the several editors and publishers for granting him permission to reissue the articles mentioned above. He is also deeply indebted to Professor Carl Nordenfalk of the National Museum, Stockholm, for making valuable suggestions concerning material in Chapter XII, particularly concerning the dates assigned to several of the Carolingian miniatures.

In reading the proofs assistance was rendered by Miss Margaret A. Schatkin and Mr. Carl Bremer. The index is the work of my son, James B. Metzger.

Princeton, New Jersey   BRUCE M. METZGER

CHAPTER ONE

METHODOLOGY IN THE STUDY OF THE MYSTERY RELIGIONS AND EARLY CHRISTIANITY

From the days of the Renaissance and Reformation to the present, the Mystery Religions of antiquity have engaged the attention of classical scholars and theologians alike.[1] During what may be called the precritical stage of the study of this subject, it was commonly believed that by the Mysteries a constant succession of priests or hierophants transmitted from age to age an esoteric doctrine, better and nobler than that of the popular religion.[2] Whether this recondite science had been derived originally from the hidden wisdom of India or Egypt, or from the Old Testament, or even from a primitive revelation to all mankind, was debated with characteristic disregard for historical methodology.

The first scholar who made an exhaustive and critical examination of the statements of ancient authors regarding the Mysteries was Christian August Lobeck.[3] Although Lobeck confined his attention to the Eleusinian, the Orphic, and the Samothracian Mysteries, his monograph, published in 1829, was of the greatest importance in the inauguration of a new era in the scientific study of the subject in general. A great deal of rubbish and pseudo-learning was swept aside, and it became possible to discuss intelligently the rites and teachings of the Mysteries.[4]

Furthermore, it was also during the nineteenth century that ar-

---

[1] Perhaps the first from the standpoint of classical scholarship as well as Protestant theology to give serious consideration to the Mysteries was Isaac Casaubon. In his *De rebus sacris et ecclesiasticis exercitationes* (London, 1614) he attempted to show that sacramental ceremonies in the early Roman Catholic Church were influenced by the ancient Mystery religions. For an account of the preceding period, see Edgar Wind, *Pagan Mysteries in the Renaissance* (New Haven, 1958).

[2] E.g., G. E. J. de Sainte Croix, *Recherches historiques et critiques sur les mystères du paganisme* (Paris, 1784), and F. Creuzer, *Symbolik und Mythologie der alten Völker* (Leipzig, 1810).

[3] C. A. Lobeck, *Aglaophamus, sive de theologiae mysticae Graecorum causis*, 2 vols. (Königsberg, 1829).

[4] For a brief summary of some of the earlier discussions of the question of the relation of the Mysteries to Christianity, see Samuel Cheetham, *The Mysteries, Pagan and Christian* (London, 1897), pp. ix sqq.

chaeology began to make quite significant additions to what was known of the beliefs and practices of devotees of the Mysteries. Excavations of places of worship supplemented the evidence from classical and patristic authors with thousands of inscriptions, mosaics, gems, statues, altars, lamps, sacrificial instruments, and the like.

It thus became increasingly possible to make scientific comparisons between the Mysteries and early Christianity. From the latter part of the nineteenth century to the present, many scholars have expressed their opinion regarding the relationship between the Church and the competing religions in the Roman Empire.[1] As would be expected in view of the fragmentary and occasionally ambiguous evidence, different investigators have arrived at quite divergent results. On the one hand, some scholars believe that only a minimum of outside influence came to bear upon primitive Christianity (e.g., Anrich,[2] Cheetham,[3] Clemen,[4] Kennedy,[5] Machen,[6] Fracassini,[7] Boulanger,[8] Jacquier,[9] Nock,[10] Heigl,[11] Prümm,[12] Rahner,[13]

---

[1] Besides the scores of monographs published during the past century which deal exclusively with the relation of the Mysteries to Christianity, there are hundreds of volumes which devote one or more chapters to this question, not to speak of hundreds of additional studies in which the authors more briefly express their opinion on the problem. In addition, there is an enormous bibliography on the Mysteries *per se*. A. D. Nock remarks with subtle sarcasm, " 'Savior-gods' and mysteries probably did not bulk so large in the life of the first century A.D. as in modern study"; see his "Early Gentile Christianity and its Hellenistic Background," in *Essays on the Trinity and the Incarnation*, ed. A. E. J. Rawlinson (London, 1928), p. 81; reprinted in Nock's *Early Gentile Christianity and its Hellenistic Background* (New York, 1964), p. 29.

[2] Gustav Anrich, *Das antike Mysterienwesen in seinem Einfluss auf das Christentum* (Göttingen, 1894).

[3] *Op. cit.*

[4] Carl Clemen, *Religionsgeschichtliche Erklärung des Neuen Testaments. Die Abhängigkeit des ältesten Christentums von nichtjüdischen Religionen und philosophischen Systemen* (Giessen, 1909); Eng. trans., *Primitive Christianity and Its Non-Jewish Sources* (Edinburgh, 1912); and *Der Einfluss der Mysterienreligionen auf das älteste Christentum* (*Religionsgeschichtliche Versuche und Vorarbeiten*, XIII; Giessen, 1913).

[5] H. A. A. Kennedy, *St. Paul and the Mystery Religions* (London, 1913).

[6] J. Gresham Machen, *The Origin of Paul's Religion* (New York, 1921), pp. 211-290.

[7] Umberto Fracassini, *Il misticismo greco e il Cristianesimo* (Città di Castello, 1922).

[8] André Boulanger, *Orphée, rapports de l'orphisme et du Christianisme* (Paris, 1925).

[9] Ernst Jacquier, "Mystères païens (les) et Saint Paul," *Dictionnaire apologétique de la foi catholique*, ed. A. d'Alès, III (1926), 964-1014.

Zwart,[1] and Wagner[2]). Others, on the other hand, believe not only that the amount of influence was relatively large but also that it made itself felt in the formulation of central doctrines and rites of the Church (e.g., Hatch,[3] Wobbermin,[4] Gardner,[5] Soltau,[6] Brückner,[7] Reitzenstein,[8] Perdelwitz,[9] Loisy,[10] Bousset,[11] Böhlig,[12] Glasse,[13]

---

[10] A. D. Nock's essay mentioned above, p. 2, note 1; and his articles on "Le religioni di mistero," *Ricerche religiose*, VI (1930), 392-403, and "Mysteries," *Encyclopædia of the Social Sciences*, XI (1937), 172-175.

[11] Bartholomäus Heigl, *Antike Mysterienreligionen und Urchristentum* (Münster, 1932).

[12] Karl Prümm, *Der christliche Glaube und die altheidnische Welt*, 2 vols. (Leipzig, 1935); *Das antike Heidentum nach seinem Grundströmmungen. Ein Handbuch zur biblischen und altchristlichen Umweltkunde* (Münster, 1942); *Religionsgeschichtliches Handbuch für den Raum der altchristlichen Umwelt* (Rome, 1954); and "Mystères," *Dictionnaire de la Bible, Supplément*, VI, fasc. 30 (Paris, 1957), cols. 1-225.

[13] Hugo Rahner, "Das christliche Mysterium und die heidnischen Mysterien," *Eranos-Jahrbuch*, 1944 (Band XI), *Die Mysterien* (Zürich, 1945), 347-449.

[1] Alb. Zwart, *Heidensche en christelijke mysteriën; de theologische grondslagen der mysteriënliturgie* (Brussels/Amsterdam, 1947).

[2] Günter Wagner, *Das religionsgeschichtliche Problem von Römer 6, 1-11* (*Abhandlungen zur Theologie des Alten und Neuen Testaments*, 39; Zurich/Stuttgart, 1962); Eng. trans., *Pauline Baptism and the Pagan Mysteries* (Edinburgh and London, 1967).

[3] Edwin Hatch, *The Influence of Greek Ideas and Usages upon the Christian Church* (London, 1890).

[4] Georg Wobbermin, *Religionsgeschichtliche Studien zur Frage der Beeinflussung des Urchristentums durch das antike Mysterienwesen* (Berlin, 1896).

[5] Percy Gardner, *The Origin of the Lord's Supper* (London, 1893); *The Growth of Christianity* (London, 1907); and *The Religious Experience of St. Paul* (London, 1911).

[6] Wilhelm Soltau, *Das Fortleben des Heidentums in der altchristlichen Kirche* (Tübingen, 1906).

[7] Martin Brückner, *Der sterbende und auferstehende Gottheiland in den orientalischen Religionen und ihr Verhältnis zum Christentum* (Tübingen, 1908).

[8] Richard Reitzenstein, *Die hellenistischen Mysterienreligionen* (Leipzig, 1910; 3rd ed., 1927).

[9] Richard Perdelwitz, *Die Mysterienreligionen und das Problem des I Petrusbriefes* (Giessen, 1911).

[10] Alfred Loisy, "The Christian Mystery," *Hibbert Journal*, X (1911-12), 45-64; and *Les mystères païens et le mystère chrétien* (Paris, 1914; 2e éd., 1930).

[11] Wilhelm Bousset, "Christentum und Mysterienreligionen," *Theologische Rundschau*, XV (1912), 41-61; "Die Religionsgeschichte und das Neue Testament," *ibid.*, 251-278; *Kyrios Christos* (Göttingen, 1913); and *Jesus der Herr* (Göttingen, 1916).

[12] Hans Böhlig, *Die Geisteskultus von Tarsos im augusteischen Zeitalter mit Berüchsichtigung der paulinischen Schriften* (Göttingen, 1913).

[13] John Glasse, *The Mysteries and Christianity* (Edinburgh, 1921).

Elderkin,[1] Macchioro,[2] Weigall,[3] Case,[4] Schütze,[5] Holland,[6] Hyde[7] Vassall,[8] Prentice,[9] and Schneider[10]).

Such widely divergent opinions are due, at least in part, to differences in methodology in dealing with the evidence. In what follows an attempt is made to outline some considerations which, it is suggested, must be taken into account in estimating the amount of influence of the Mysteries upon early Christianity.

I. First of all, a distinction is to be made between the faith and practice of the earliest Christians and that of the Church during subsequent centuries. One cannot deny that post-Constantinian Christianity, both Eastern and Western, adopted not a few pagan rites and practices.[11] From Asclepius came the practice of incubation in churches for the cure of diseases.[12] The functions of more than

---

[1] George W. Elderkin, *Kantharos; Studies in Dionysiac and Kindred Cult* (Princeton, 1924).

[2] Vittorio Macchioro, *Orfismo e Paolinismo, studi e polemiche* (Montevarchi, 1922); and *From Orpheus to Paul, a History of Orphism* (New York, 1930).

[3] Arthur Weigall, *The Paganism in our Christianity* (London, c. 1928).

[4] Shirley Jackson Case, *Experience with the Supernatural in Early Christian Times* (New York, 1929), pp. 106-145, and *The Origins of Christian Supernaturalism* (Chicago, c. 1946).

[5] A. Schütze, *Mithras-Mysterien und Urchristentum* (Stuttgart, 1937).

[6] A. Holland, *Les cultes de mystères; l'ancienne rédemption païenne et le Christianisme* (Paris, 1938).

[7] W. W. Hyde, *Paganism to Christianity in the Roman Empire* (Philadelphia, 1946), and *Greek Religion and its Survivals* (New York, 1963).

[8] William F. Vassall, *The Origin of Christianity, Brief Study of the World's Early Beliefs and their Influence on the Early Church* (New York, 1952).

[9] William K. Prentice, *The Gospel of the Kingdom of God* (Boston, 1953), pp. 139-162.

[10] Carl Schneider, *Geistesgeschichte des antiken Christentums*, I (Munich, 1954), pp. 84ff. and 256ff.

[11] Cf. the following statement in a letter which Flavius Vopiscus attributes to Hadrian: "The land of Egypt ... I have found to be wholly light-minded, unstable, and blown about by every breath of rumour. There those who worship Serapis are, in fact, Christians, and those who call themselves bishops of Christ are, in fact, devotees of Serapis ... Even the patriarch himself, when he comes to Egypt, is forced by some to worship Serapis, by others to worship Christ," *Scriptores historiae Augustae, Firmus*, viii (*Loeb Classical Library*, III, 399f., ed. and trans. by David Magie). The fact that this letter is an obvious forgery does not detract from its value in reflecting the opinion of a fourth century non-Christian author who wrote perhaps during the Julian revival. Christian syncretism in Egypt emerged at least as early as the second half of the second century when certain Gnostics established a Larium (in Alexandria?) where they venerated images of Jesus, Pythagoras, Plato, Aristotle, and other philosophers (Irenaeus, *Adv. haer.* I, xxv, 6 [I, 210, Harvey]).

[12] See L. Deubner, *De incubatione capita quattuor* (Leipzig, 1900); Mary

one local demi-god were taken over by Christian saints whose names even, in some cases, remind one of the original pagan prototypes.[1] Statues of Isis holding the infant Harpocrates (Horus),[2] as well as the exalted hymns in honor of the Egyptian Queen of Heaven, find their obvious counterparts in the growth of the cult of Mary.[3] Just as Sabazios with characteristic gesture—three fingers raised, the thumb and other finger bent down—blessed his adherents, so the Catholic bishop of the West gave (and still gives) his blessing to the faithful.[4] Through various paths the ancient idea of "refrigerium"

Hamilton, *Incubation, or the Cure of Disease in Pagan Temples and Christian Churches* (London, 1906); and E. J. and L. Edelstein, *Asclepius*, 2 vols. (Baltimore, 1945).

[1] See Ernst Lucius, *Die Anfänge des Heiligenkults* (Tübingen, 1904); W. W. Hyde, *Greek Religion and Its Survivals* (Boston, 1923), pp. 41-85; Hippolyte Delehaye, *Les légendes hagiographiques*, 3ᵉ éd. (Brussels, 1923), pp. 140-201; G. J. Laing, *Survivals of Roman Religion* (Boston, 1931); *idem*, "Roman Religious Survivals in Christianity," in *Environmental Factors in Christian History*, ed. by J. T. McNeill (Chicago, 1939), pp. 72-90; and L. J. van der Lof, "Die Mysterienkulte zur Zeit Augustins," *Zeitschrift für die neutestamentliche Wissenschaft*, LIII (1962), 245-251.

[2] For influence in apocryphal literature, see G. Klameth, "Harpokrato motivai apokrifų pasakojimuose apie Jėsans vaikystę," ["Quomodo Aegyptii mythi de divino infante Harpocrate influxerint in narrationes apocryphas de infantia Christi Domini"], *Soter, religijos mokslo laikraštis*, IV (1927), 62-67.

[3] While it is doubtless true that the earliest artistic representations of Mary with the infant Jesus do not portray her nursing the child, as was customary in the representation of Isis and Horus (so G. A. S. Snijder, *De forma matris cum infanto sedentis apud antiquos* [Vienna, 1923], p. 69), it is equally true that subsequent Christian art and cultus betray decided borrowings in this and other respects from the cult of Isis (and perhaps also the cult of Astarte); see W. Drexler, s.v. "Isis," in W. H. Roscher's *Ausführliches Lexikon der griechischen und römischen Mythologie*; Theodor Trede, "Die Himmelskönigin," in his *Das Heidentum in der römischen Kirche*, II (Gotha, 1890), 338-371; Francis Legge, *Forerunners and Rivals of Christianity*, I (Cambridge, 1915), 84-89; Werner Peek, *Der Isishymnus von Andros und verwandte Texte* (Berlin, 1930); E. O. James, *Cult of the Mother-Goddess* (New York, 1959), pp. 201-227; G. A. van Wellen, *Theotokos, Eine Ikonographische Abhandlung über das Gottesmutterbild in frühchristlicher Zeit* (Utrecht/Antwerp, 1961); R. Merkelbach, *Isisfeste in griechisch-römischer Zeit. Daten und Riten* (Meisenheim am Glan, 1963); and R. E. Witt, "Isis-Hellas," *Proceedings of the Cambridge Philological Society*, No. 192 (1966), 48-69, especially pp. 65ff. for parallels with practices in the Greek Orthodox Church. On Isis and Greek patristic writers, see Witt, "The Importance of Isis for the Fathers," in *Studia Patristica*, vol. VIII, ed. F. L. Cross (= *Texte und Untersuchungen*, Band XCIII; Berlin, 1966), 135-145. Concerning influence from the cult of Astarte, see Gustav Rösch, "Astarte-Maria," *Theologische Studien und Kritiken*, LXI (1888), 265-299; cf. Trede, *op. cit.*, "Die grosse Mutter," pp. 85-121.

[4] Chr. Blinkenberg, "Darstellungen des Sabazios und Denkmäler seines Kultus" in his *Archaeologische Studien* (Copenhagen, 1904), pp. 66-128, and

entered both popular and official circles of the Church.[1] Processions
in which sacred objects are carried for display to the on-lookers,
the tonsure of priests, certain funeral rites, the use of lighted tapers,
popular ideas regarding the geography of Hades—all these have
quite generally acknowledged pagan prototypes.[2] The real difference
of opinion, however, arises with regard to the relation of nascent
Christianity to its pagan rivals.

II. The nature and amount of the evidence of the Mysteries create
certain methodological problems. Partly because of a vow of secrecy
imposed upon the initiates, relatively little information concerning
the teaching imparted in the Mysteries has been preserved. Furthermore, since a large part of the scanty evidence regarding the Mysteries dates from the third, fourth, and fifth Christian centuries, it
must not be assumed that beliefs and practices current at that time
existed in substantially the same form during the pre-Christian era.
In fact, that pagan doctrines would differ somewhat from place to
place and from century to century is not only what one should have
expected, but also what the sources reveal to be a fact. For example,
the grades of Mithraic initiation in the West apparently included

---

F. Cumont, *Comptes rendus de l'Académie des inscriptions et belles-lettres*, 1906,
pp. 72-79.

[1] See A. M. Schneider, *Refrigerium nach literarischen Quellen und Inschriften*, Inaug. Diss. (Freiburg im B., 1928); E. Buonaiuti, "Refrigerio pagano e
refrigerio cristiano," *Ricerche religiose*, v (1929), 160-167; A. Perrot, *Le
"Refrigerium" dans l'au delà* (Paris, 1937); Mircea Eliade, "Locum refri-
gerii...," *Zalmoxis, revue des études religieuses*, 1 (1938), 203-208; and J.
Quasten, " 'Vetus superstitio et nova religio,' the Problem of *Refrigerium* in
the Ancient Church of North Africa," *Harvard Theological Review*, XXXIII
(1940), 253-266.

[2] See Gerhard Loeschcke, *Jüdisches und Heidnisches im christlichen Kult*
(Bonn, 1910), pp. 16-36; A. Dieterich, *Nekyia*, 2te Aufl. (Leipzig, 1913);
Andrew Alföldi, *A Festival of Isis in Rome under the Christian Emperors of
the Fourth Century* (Budapest, 1937); M. P. Nilsson, "Pagan Divine Services
in Late Antiquity," *Harvard Theological Review*, XXXVIII (1945), 63-69; and
Hugo Rahner, *Griechische Mythen in christlicher Deutung* (Zürich, 1945).

For a classical statement of the multifarious influence of paganism on the
early and the medieval Church, see Charles Reade, *The Cloister and the
Hearth*, chap. 74 (Everyman's Library edition, chap. 72). No little research
went into this chapter of Reade's historical novel; for his sources, see Albert
M. Turner, *The Making of the Cloister and the Hearth* (Chicago, 1938), pp. 186-
188.

Some consideration of the earlier period is also given in Jean Seznec, *La
survivance des dieux antiques* (*Studies of the Warburg Institute*, XI [London,
1940]), Eng. trans. and revision, *The Survival of the Pagan Gods; The Mythological Tradition and its Place in Renaissance Humanism and Art* (New York,
1953).

that of "Cryphius"; in the East (in its stead?) was that of "Nymphus."[1] Again, over the years the efficacy of the rite of the taurobolium differed in what was promised to the initiate.[2] Methodologically, therefore, it is extremely hazardous to assume, as has sometimes been done, that a pagan rite or belief which a Christian author cites must have existed in the same form in pre-Christian days.

III. Another methodological consideration, often overlooked by scholars who are better acquainted with Hellenistic culture than with Jewish, is involved in the circumstance that the early Palestinian Church was composed of Christians from a Jewish background, whose generally strict monotheism and traditional intolerance of syncretism must have militated against wholesale borrowing from pagan cults.[3] Psychologically it is quite inconceivable that the Judaizers, who attacked Paul with unmeasured ferocity for what they considered his liberalism concerning the relation of Gentile converts to the Mosaic law, should nevertheless have acquiesced in what some have described as Paul's thoroughgoing contamination of the central doctrines and sacraments of the Christian religion. Furthermore, with regard to Paul himself, scholars are coming once again to acknowledge that the Apostle's prevailing set of mind was rabbinically oriented, and that his newly-found Christian faith ran in molds previously formed at the feet of Gamaliel.[4]

---

[1] See pp. 26ff. below.

[2] According to epigraphical evidence, the taurobolium was efficacious for twenty years (*Corpus Inscriptionum Latinarum*, VI, 504, of A.D. 376, and 152, of A.D. 390), for eternity (*CIL*, VI, 510, of A.D. 376), and, possibly, for twenty-eight years (so an inscription discussed by Cumont in *Comptes rendus de l'Académie des inscriptions*, 1923, pp. 253ff.). See Clifford H. Moore, "The Duration of the Efficacy of the Taurobolium," *Classical Philology*, XIX (1924), 363-365. For convenient lists of inscriptions commemorating the taurobolium (a) "pro salute imperatoris" and (b) for private individuals, see H. Graillot, *Le Culte de Cybèle, mère des dieux* (Paris, 1912), pp. 159ff. and 167ff.

[3] For a balanced essay on the general immunity of Jews from influences of the Mysteries, see S. H. Hooke's chapter, "Christianity and the Mystery Religions," in the symposium, *Judaism and Christianity*, vol. I, *The Age of Transition*, ed. by W. O. E. Oesterley (London, 1937), pp. 235-250. Despite its useful contribution in the assembly of widely scattered materials, E. R. Goodenough's *Jewish Symbols in the Greco-Roman Period*, 12 vols. (New York, 1953-65) falls short of proving that pre-Christian, Palestinian Judaism had been influenced by the Mysteries *per se*; see trenchant critiques by Morton Smith in *Anglican Theological Review*, XXXVI (1954), 218-220, in *Journal of Biblical Literature*, LXXXVI (1967), 53-68, and by R. M. Grant in *Gnomon*, XXXVIII (1966), 423f.

[4] Noteworthy examples of this change of emphasis in Pauline studies are

IV. In estimating the degree of opportunity afforded the early Palestinian Church of being influenced by the Mysteries, it is certainly a significant fact that, unlike other countries bordering the Mediterranean Sea, Palestine has been extremely barren in yielding archaeological remains of the paraphernalia and places of worship connected with the Mysteries.[1]

V. That there *are* parallels between the Mysteries and Christianity has been observed since the early centuries of the Church, when both Christian[2] and non-Christian[3] alike commented upon certain similarities. In evaluating the significance of alleged parallels in certain crucial matters (i.e., the sacraments and the motif of a dying

---

found in W. D. Davies, *Paul and Rabbinic Judaism*; *Some Rabbinic Elements in Pauline Theology* (London, 1948; 2nd ed., 1955), and H. J. Schoeps, *Paul, the Theology of the Apostle in the Light of Jewish Religious History* (Philadelphia, 1961). On the question of Paul's early training in Jerusalem, see the careful exegesis of Acts 22.3 by W. C. van Unnik, *Tarsus or Jerusalem; the City of Paul's Youth?* trans. by G. Ogg (London, 1962).

[1] According to the map prepared by Nicola Turchi (in his *Le religioni misteriosofiche del mondo antico* [Rome, 1923]), showing the diffusion of the Mysteries of Cybele, dea Syria, Isis, Mithra, Orpheus-Dionysius, and Samothrace in the Roman Empire, the only cult which penetrated Palestine proper was the Isiac cult. Evidence (is it merely numismatic?) for this cult was found at Aelia Capitolina, i.e., subsequent to Hadrian's rebuilding of Jerusalem *c.* A.D. 135. By this time the fundamental doctrines and sacraments of the Church had been fixed. Similar maps for the cults of Isis, Mithra, and Cybele, which Herbert Preisker includes in his *Neutestamentliche Zeitgeschichte* (Berlin, 1937), likewise indicate no archaeological remains of these cults within Palestine during the first century. It is significant that in an early second century invocation to Isis (P. Oxy. 1380) containing a detailed list of places at which Isis was worshipped (67 places in Egypt, and 55 outside Egypt) the only place within Palestine that is mentioned (lines 94f.) is Strato's Tower, the site on the Palestinian coast just south of Syria chosen by Herod the Great for the building of Caesarea, the capital of Roman Palestine.

Jerome provides literary evidence that at Bethlehem the cult of Adonis found a foothold as a result of Hadrian's attempt to paganize Jerusalem and its environs; *Epistola* lviii *ad Paulinum*, 3, "Bethleem, nunc nostram et augustissimum orbis locum, ... lucus inumbrabat Thamuz, id est Adonidis, et in specu, ubi quondam Christus paruulus uagiit, Ueneris amasius plagebatur" (*Corpus Scriptorum Ecclesiasticorum Latinorum*, LIV, 532, 4-8 Hilberg). See also Wolf Wilhelm von Baudissin, *Adonis und Esmun* (Leipzig, 1911), p. 83 and p. 522, note 5.

[2] E.g., Justin Martyr, *Apol.* 1, lxvi, 4 and *Dial.*, lxx, 1; and Tertullian, *de Corona*, xv (*Corpus Scriptorum Ecclesiasticorum Latinorum*, LXX, 186-188 Kroymann) and *de Praescript.*, xl (*ib.*, 51f.).

[3] E.g., apparently Celsus, *ap.* Origen, *Contra Celsum*, vi, 22 (*Griechische Christliche Schriftsteller*, Orig., II, 91-93 Klostermann) and, no doubt with exaggeration, Flavius Vopiscus, *Firmus*, viii (quoted above, p. 4, note 11).

and rising savior-god), consideration must be given to the following.

(A) Some of the supposed parallels are the result of the modern scholar's amalgamation of quite heterogeneous elements drawn from various sources. As Schweitzer pointed out, "Almost all the popular writings fall into this kind of inaccuracy. They manufacture out of the various fragments of information a kind of universal Mystery-religion which never actually existed, least of all in Paul's day."[1]

Even reputable scholars have succumbed to the temptation to be more precise than the existing state of information will permit. Commenting on this temptation, Edwyn R. Bevan says caustically: "Of course if one writes an imaginary description of the Orphic mysteries, as Loisy, for instance, does, filling in the large gaps in the picture left by our data from the Christian eucharist, one produces something very impressive. On this plan, you first put in the Christian elements, and then are staggered to find them there."[2]

It goes without saying that alleged parallels which are discovered by pursuing such methodology evaporate when they are confronted with the original texts. In a word, one must beware of what have been called "parallels made plausible by selective description."

(B) Even when the parallels are actual and not imaginary, their significance for purposes of comparison will depend upon whether they are genealogical and not merely analogical parallels.[3] That is to say, one must inquire whether the similarities have arisen from more or less equal religious experience, due to equality of what may be called psychic pitch and equality of outward conditions, or whether they are due to borrowing one from the other. Interesting

---

[1] A. Schweitzer, *Geschichte der Paulinischen Forschung* (Tübingen, 1911), pp. 151f. (Eng. trans., *Paul and his Interpreters* [London, 1912], pp. 192f.). In a similar vein F. C. Conybeare refers to "the untrained explorers [who] discover on almost every page connections in their subject matter where there are and can be none, and as regularly miss connections where they exist" (*The Historical Christ* [London, 1914], p. vii). For a critique of the supposed influence of the Iranian Primeval-Man and Redeemer mythology on Johannine theology, see Carsten Colpe, *Die religionsgeschichtliche Schule. Darstellung und Kritik ihres Bildes vom gnostischen Erlösermythus* (*Forschungen zur Religion und Literatur des Alten und Neuen Testaments*, LXXVIII; Göttingen, 1961).

[2] Edwyn R. Bevan, in the symposium, *The History of Christianity in the Light of Modern Knowledge* (Glasgow, 1929), p. 105; reprinted by Thomas S. Kepler, *Contemporary Thinking about Paul, An Anthology* (New York, 1940), p. 43.

[3] For this distinction, see Adolf Deissmann, *Licht vom Osten*, 4te Aufl. (Tübingen, 1923), pp. 226ff. (Eng. trans., *Light from the Ancient East* [New York, 1927], pp. 265ff.).

as the parallels are which Sir James G. Frazer collected from the four corners of the earth in his monumental work, *The Golden Bough*, by no means all of them are to be regarded as the result of demonstrable borrowing. In seeking connections it is not enough (as F. C. Conybeare pointed out) "for one agent or institution or belief merely to remind us of another. Before we assert literary or traditional connection between similar elements in story and myth, we must satisfy ourselves that such communication was possible."[1]

It is a fact that in various spheres close similarities even in phraseology have been discovered which are related to each other by nothing more direct than analogy. For example, in a letter published in *The* (London) *Times* at the end of July, 1938, the late Professor Harold Temperley pointed out two quite remarkable parallels between speeches made by Canning in 1823 and 1826 and their modern couterparts in Neville Chamberlain's utterances on July 26, 1938. In a subsequent letter, the Prime Minister disclaimed having previously read either of Canning's speeches, and concluded that the parallels "indicate simply the continuity of English thought in somewhat similar circumstances, even after an interval of more than a hundred years."[2] Or, to take an example from ancient times, a close parallel to the docetism expressed in the apocryphal *Acts of John* has been discovered in Ovid's *Fasti*.[3] It would be vain, however, to imagine that Greek Christian writers were indebted to Ovid for their docetic interpretation of Christ's sufferings. So too, as Toynbee points out in his *Study of History*,[4] the uniformity of human

---

[1] Conybeare, *op. cit.*, p. viii.

[2] The text of the two letters is given by E. G. Selwyn in the introduction of his commentary on *The First Epistle of St. Peter* (London, 1949), pp. 8f.

[3] The parallel is discussed by R. L. P. Milburn in *Journal of Theological Studies*, XLVI (1945), 68f.

[4] Arnold J. Toynbee, *A Study of History*, VI (Oxford, 1939), 276ff., and 376-539. On anthropological and cultural parallels in general, see M. P. Nilsson in Gercke-Norden's *Einleitung in die Altertumswissenschaft*, 4te Aufl., II, iv (Leipzig, 1933), 58ff.; H. J. Rose, *Concerning Parallels* (*Frazer Lecture*, 1934) (Oxford, 1934); and A. D. Nock in *Gnomon*, xv (1939), 18f., and in *American Journal of Philology*, LXV (1944), 99ff. In a celebrated Inaugural Lecture at Oxford Prof. R. C. Zaehner reminded his hearers of the considerable difference in substance there may be in religious teachings (like the doctrines of release or incarnation in various religions) which may appear superficially very similar (*Foolishness to the Greeks* [Oxford, 1953], pp. 14ff.). For a needed warning against extravagant and exaggerated deductions from literary parallels, see Samuel Sandmel's comments entitled "Parallelomania," *Journal of Biblical Literature*, LXXXI (1962), 1-13. For several most curious historical parallels between St. John Colombini, the founder of the Order of

nature sometimes produces strikingly similar results in similar situations where there can be no suspicion of any historical bridge by which the tradition could have been mediated from one culture to the other.[1]

(C) Even when parallels are genealogical, it must not be uncritically assumed that the Mysteries always influenced Christianity, for it is not only possible but probable that in certain cases the influence moved in the opposite direction. In what T. R. Glover aptly called "the conflict of religions in the Early Roman Empire," it was to be expected that the hierophants of cults which were beginning to lose devotees to the growing Church should take steps to stem the tide. One of the surest ways would be to imitate the teaching of the Church by offering benefits comparable with those held out by Christianity. Thus, for example, one must doubtless interpret the change in the efficacy attributed to the rite of the taurobolium. In competing with Christianity, which promised eternal life to its adherents, the cult of Cybele officially or unofficially raised the efficacy of the blood bath from twenty years to eternity.[2]

---

the Jesuates, and Ignatius Loyola, the founder of the Jesuits, see Marc Bloch, *The Historian's Craft* (New York, 1953), pp. 223f.

[1] The two facts that all human beings eat and that most of them seek companionship with one another and with their god account for a large percentage of similarities among the examples from around the world gathered by Fritz Bammel in his interesting study of *Das heilige Mahl im Glauben der Völker. Eine religionsphänomenologische Untersuchung* (Gütersloh, 1950). For a discussion of certain parallels between the Osiris cult and Christianity, where "any theory of borrowing on the part of Christianity from the older faith is not to be entertained, for not only can it not be substantiated on the extant evidence, but it is also intrinsically most improbable," see S. G. F. Brandon, "The Ritual Perpetuation of the Past," *Numen*, VI (1959), 112-129 (quotation is from p. 128).

[2] So, e.g., Hugo Hepding, *Attis, seine Mythen und sein Kult* (Giessen, 1903), p. 200, note 7, and Rahner, *Eranos-Jahrbuch*, XI (1944), 397f.; cf. also P. Lambrechts, *Aspecten van het onsterfelijkheidsgeloof in de Oudheid*, in *Handelingen der Zuidnederlands Maatschappij voor Taal- en Letterkunde en Geschiedenis*, X (1956), 13-49. On the other hand, Moore thinks that "*in aeternam renatus* represents rather the enthusiastic hopes of the devotee than any dogma" (*op. cit.*, p. 363), and Nilsson regards the phrase as reflecting "a heightening which was easy to make in an age when so many spoke of eternity" (*Geschichte der griechischen Religion*, II [München, 1950], 626; 2te Aufl. [1961], p. 653); but they have apparently forgotten that Augustine tells of having known a priest of Cybele who kept saying, "Et ipse Pilleatus christianus est" ("and even the god with the Phrygian cap [i.e. Attis] is a Christian"), *In Ioannis evangelium tractatus*, vii, 1, 6 (Migne, *Patrologia Latina*, XXXV, 1440). The imitation of the Church is plain in the pagan reforms attempted by the Emperor Julian, a devoted adherent to the cult of Cybele.

VI. Finally, in arriving at a just estimate of the relation of the Mysteries to Christianity as reflected in the New Testament, attention must be given to their differences as well as resemblances. These differences pertain both to language and ideas.

(A) It is instructive to consider what words are missing from the vocabulary of the earliest Christian writers. Many ordinary, everyday words of contemporary pagan religions are conspicuous by their absence from the New Testament; words such as μύστης, μυστικός, μυσταγωγός, or the religious terms καθαρμός, καθάρσια, κάθαρσις. Christians are never called ἱεροί, nor are ἱερόν and ναός ever used of their place of meeting. One seeks in vain for τελεῖν in the sense "to initiate" and its compounds, τέλος in the same sense, as well as τελετή,[1] ἀτέλεστος, and such common words in the Mysteries as ἱεροφάντης, ὄργια, κάτοχος, ἔνθεος, ἐνθουσιάζειν and its correlates, which, as Nock says, "might so well have been used to describe possession by the Spirit." The important point to observe, as Nock continues, is that "these are not recondite words; they belonged to the everyday language of religion and to the normal stock of metaphors. It almost seems that there was a deliberate avoidance of them as having associations which were deprecated. Certainly there is no indication of an appropriation of pagan religious terms."[2]

The few words which are common to the New Testament and the texts of the Mysteries either are so infrequent in the New Testament as to be inconclusive in establishing religious affinities (e.g., μυεῖν, ἐμβατεύειν, ἐπόπτης, each of which appears only once), or have an entirely different meaning in the two corpora of sources (e.g., μυστήριον).[3]

In general see Carl Clemen, *Der Einfluss des Christentums auf andere Religionen* (Giessen, 1933), especially pp. 22-29. See also p. 7, note 2 above.

[1] Cf. C. Zijderveld, Jr., Τελετή. *Bijdrage tot de kennis der religieuze terminologie in het Grieksch* (Purmerend, 1934).

[2] A. D. Nock, "The Vocabulary of the New Testament," *Journal of Biblical Literature*, LII (1933), 134, who cites still other words common in popular religions but absent from the New Testament. See also Nock, "Hellenistic Mysteries and Christian Sacraments," *Mnemosyne*, 4th Ser., v (1952), 177-213, esp. 200, "Any idea that what we call the Christian sacraments were in their origin indebted to pagan mysteries or even to the metaphorical concepts based upon them, shatters on the rock of linguistic evidence" (reprinted in Nock's *Early Gentile Christianity and its Hellenistic Background* [New York, 1964], p. 132).

[3] See Nock, "Mysterion," *Harvard Studies in Classical Philology*, LX (1951), 201-204, and R. E. Brown, "The Semitic Background of the New Testament *Mysterion*," *Biblica*, XXXIX (1958), 426-448; XL (1959), 70-87; also *Catholic Biblical Quarterly*, XX (1958), 417-443.

(B) In the nature of the case a most profound difference between Christianity and the Mysteries was involved in the historical basis of the former and the mythological character of the latter. Unlike the deities of the Mysteries, who were nebulous figures of an imaginary past, the Divine Being whom the Christian worshipped as Lord was known as a real Person on earth only a short time before the earliest documents of the New Testament were written. From the earliest times the Christian creed included the affirmation that Jesus "was crucified under Pontius Pilate." On the other hand, Plutarch thinks it necessary to warn the priestess Clea against believing that "any of these tales [concerning Isis and Osiris] actually happened in the manner in which they are related."[1]

(C) Unlike the secretiveness of those who guarded the Mysteries, the Christians made their sacred books freely available to all.[2] Even when the *disciplina arcani* was being elaborated in the fourth and fifth centuries (whether as a diplomatic and paedagogic technique and/or as a Christian borrowing from the Mysteries, need not be determined now),[3] it was still possible to contrast the simplicity and openness of Christian rites with the secrecy of pagan Mysteries.[4]

---

[1] Plutarch, *de Iside et Osiride*, xi (*Loeb Classical Library*, p. 29); see also lviii, "We must not treat legend as if it were history" (*op. cit.*, p. 139). On other differences between Christianity and the Mysteries, see E. O. James, *In the Fulness of Time* (London, 1935), pp. 87f.

[2] Apuleius refers to "quosdam libros litteris ignorabilibus praenotatos, partim figuris cuiuscemodi animalium concepti sermonis compendiosa verba suggerentes, partim nodosis et in modum rotae tortuosis capreolatimque condensis apicibus a curiosa profanorum lectione munita," *Metamorphoses*, xi, 22. On the contrary, Christians not only made available the Greek Scriptures, but prepared versions in the principal vernaculars as well. On the contrast in general, see Harnack, *Bible Reading in the Early Church* (London, 1912), pp. 28f. and 146f.

[3] For the history of views regarding the *disciplina arcani* down to the beginning of the present century, see Heinrich Gravel, *Die Arcandisciplin*, I Theil: *Geschichte und Stand der Frage*, Diss. Münster (Lingen a/Ems, 1902). For more recent summaries, see A. Jülicher in Pauly-Wissowa, *Real-Encyclopädie*, v, 1175f.; L. Schindler, *Altchristliche Arkandisziplin und die antiken Mysterien*, Program. Tetschen (1911); E. Vacandard, "Arcane," *Dictionnaire d'histoire et de géographie ecclésiastiques*, III (1924), 1497-1513; O. Perler, "Arkandisziplin," *Reallexikon für Antike und Christentum*, I (1950), 667-676; and S. Laeuchli, *Mithraism in Ostia* (Evanston, 1967), pp. 93-100.

[4] E.g., Pseudo-Augustine, *Quaestiones veteris et novi Testamenti*, cxiv, 6 (*CSEL*, L, 305 Souter): Hinc est unde nihil apud nos in tenebris, nihil occulte geritur. Omne enim, quod honestum scitur, publicari non timetur; illud autem, quod turpe et inhonestum est, prohibente pudore non potest publicari. Quam ob rem pagini mysteria sua in tenebris celebrant, uel in eo prudentes.

(D) The differences between the Christian sacraments of baptism and the Eucharist and corresponding ceremonies in the Mysteries are as profound as their similarities are superficial. Both of the Christian sacraments, in their earliest phase, were considered to be primarily *dona data*, namely blessings conveyed to those who by nature were unfit to participate in the new order inaugurated by the person and work of Jesus Christ.[1] Pagan sacraments, on the contrary, conveyed their benefits *ex opere operato* by "the liberating or creating of an immortal element in the individual with a view to the hereafter, but with no effective change of the moral self for the purposes of living."[2]

Methodologically it is begging the question to assume that every lustral rite or communal meal in the Mysteries possessed sacramental significance. Actually it is only in Mithraism, of all the cults, that one finds evidence that washing with water was part of the ritual by which a new member was admitted to one or other of the grades in the Mithraic system.[3] Similarly with respect to sacramental meals reserved for those who had been initiated into the community of devotees, there is singularly little evidence.[4] Nothing is heard of sacramental meals in Orphism. The drinking of the *kykeon* in the rites at Eleusis,[5] which has sometimes been thought to be the prototype of Paul's teaching and practice regarding the Lord's Supper,[6] is as different as possible from the Christian Communion. The latter was the privilege of the τέλειοι, or fully initiated; but

---

Erubescunt enim palam inludi; turpia enim, quae illic uice legis aguntur, nolunt manifestari, ne qui prudentes se dicunt hebetes his uiceantur, quos stultos appellant.

[1] So, *inter alia*, I Cor. 10 and the Fourth Gospel. See Nock's discussion of "Baptism and the Eucharist as 'Dona Data,' " in *Mnemosyne*, 4th Ser., v (1952), 192-202; reprinted in Nock's *Early Gentile Christianity and its Hellenistic Background* (New York, 1964), pp. 109-145.

[2] A. D. Nock, "Mystery," *Encyclopædia of the Social Sciences*, XI (1937) 174.

[3] Tertullian, *De baptismo*, v (*CSEL*, XX, 204, 29ff. Reifferscheid and Wissowa). Probably because of its great expense, the taurobolium appears never to have been required for membership in the cult of Magna Mater.

[4] Albrecht Dieterich's generalization, "It is remarkable that a sacramental meal should play so large a part in the dominant cults of later antiquity" (*Eine Mithrasliturgie*, 3te Aufl. [Leipzig and Berlin, 1923], p. 102), exceeds all bounds of legitimate inference from the actual evidence.

[5] Clement of Alexandria, *Cohortatio ad gentes*, ii (*GCS*, Clem., I, 16, 19 Stählin), and Arnobius, *Adversus nationes*, v, 26 (*CSEL*, IV, 197, 24 Reifferscheid).

[6] So, e.g., Gardner; see p. 3, note 5 above.

the drinking of the *kykeon* was a preliminary ceremony, prescribed for the candidate prior to his initiation. Furthermore, in the Eleusinian rite there was no table-fellowship, nor was the ceremony continually repeated.[1]

The Attis cult practiced a rite involving eating something out of the timbrel and drinking something out of the cymbal,[2] but whether these actions of eating and drinking had any significance beyond that of a number of other symbolical acts involved in the initiation, is not known. Nor is there any suggestion that all the initiates participated in this ceremony as the central act of worship subsequent to their incorporation into the community—if there was a community—of devotees of Attis.

The supposition that the Samothracian Mysteries included a sacred meal rests upon an interpretation (proposed, e.g., by Dieterich[3] and Hepding[4]) of a fragmentary inscription discovered at Tomi on the Black Sea.[5] Unfortunately, however, the meaning of the inscription depends so largely upon editorial reconstruction of the missing portions that Hemberg in his magisterial treatment of the cult finds no reason even to mention the inscription.[6]

Mithraism alone among the Mystery cults appears to have had something which looked like the Christian Eucharist. Before the initiate there were set a piece of bread and a cup of water, over which the priest uttered a ritual formula. In such a case of obvious resemblance, the Church Fathers took note of it, ascribing it to the ingenuity of demons.[7] It is fair to urge that had there been other

---

[1] S. Eitrem, "Eleusinia—les mystères et l'agriculture," *Symbolae osloenses*, XX (1940), 140ff. See also the strictures of G. E. Mylonas, *Eleusis and the Eleusinian Mysteries* (Princeton, 1961), pp. 271f., against the view that the Eleusinian Mysteries involved a sacramental meal.

[2] Clement of Alexandria, *Protrepticus*, ii, 15 (*GCS*, Clem., I, 13, 12 Stählin), and Firmicus Maternus, *De errore profanorum religionum*, xviii, 1 (43, 17 Ziegler). It may be pointed out, for whatever it is worth, that Firmicus makes a point of contrasting the Christian and Phrygian rites; see also William M. Groton, *The Christian Eucharist and the Pagan Cults* (New York, 1914), pp. 8 1ff.

[3] *Op. cit.*, pp. 104f.

[4] *Op. cit.*, pp. 185f.

[5] Edited by Gregor G. Točilescu in *Archäologisch-epigraphische Mitteilungen aus Oesterreich*, VI (1882), 8f.

[6] Bengt Hemberg, *Die Kabiren* (Uppsala, 1950).

[7] Justin Martyr, *Apol.* I, lxvi, 4; cf. *Dial.*, lxx, 1; and Tertullian, *de Praescr.*, xl. On the question of the testimony of Justin concerning the elements used in the Eucharist, see A. von Harnack's provocative monograph, *Brod und Wasser, die eucharistischen Elemente bei Justin* (= *Texte und Untersuchungen*,

parallels between the Christian sacraments and pagan rites, one should expect that contemporary Christian writers would have noticed them and given the same explanation.

The problems connected with the formation and transmission of the words of institution of the Lord's Supper are too complicated for discussion here,[1] but on almost any view of this matter the Jewishness of the setting, character, and piety expressed in the rite is overwhelmingly pervasive in all the accounts of the origin of the Supper.[2] Moreover, unlike what have been called the sacred meals in the cults of Eleusis and of Attis, the Christian sacrament is not a seasonal rite, but is celebrated quite independently of the time of year. Furthermore, the eucharistic elements are set apart by prayer;

VII, 11; 1891), 117-144, and the rebuttals by Zahn, Jülicher, Veil, and, most recently, L. W. Bernard, *Justin Martyr, his Life and Thought* (Cambridge, 1967), pp. 177-179.

[1] See, e.g., Hans Lietzmann, *Messe und Herrenmahl* (Tübingen, 1926), Eng. trans. by Dorothea H. G. Reeve, *Mass and the Lord's Supper, A Study in the History of the Liturgy*, fasc. 1—(Leiden, 1953—); N. P. Williams, "The Origins of the Sacraments," in *Essays Catholic and Critical*, ed. by E. G. Selwyn, 3rd ed. (London, 1929), pp. 367-423; August Arnold, *Der Ursprung des christlichen Abendmahl im Lichte der neuesten liturgiegeschichtlichen Forschung* (Freiburg, 1937); Joachim Jeremias, "The Last Supper," *Journal of Theological Studies*, L (1949), 1-10; A. J. B. Higgins, *The Lord's Supper in the New Testament* (London, 1952); and J. Jeremias, *The Eucharistic Words of Jesus*, trans. by N. Perrin (New York, 1966).

[2] On the Jewish background of the Lord's Supper, see especially Blasius Ugolini, "Dissertatio de ritibus in Cœna Domini ex antiquitatibus paschalibus illustratis," in his monumental *Thesaurus antiquitatum sacrarum*, XVII (Venice, 1755), 1127-1188; Georg Beer's introduction, "Zur Geschichte des Paschafestes," in his ed. of *Die Mischna*, II Seder, *Moëd*, 3. Traktat, *Pesachim* (Giessen, 1912), pp. 1-109, especially pp. 92-109 which deal with the Lord's Supper; Paul Billerbeck's excursus, "Das Passamahl," in H. L. Strack and Billerbeck, *Kommentar zum Neuen Testament aus Talmud und Midrasch*, IV, i (München, 1928), 41-76; Gregory Dix, *The Shape of the Liturgy*, 2nd ed. (London, 1949), pp. 48ff.; and the contributions of Jeremias mentioned in the preceding footnote.

Whether the Prayer of Aseneth (otherwise called Joseph and Asenath) preserves indications of a Jewish religious meal distinct from the Passover and similar to the Lord's Supper has no immediate bearing upon the present inquiry, for the date of this apocryphon may well be post-Christian, and in any case it is basically Jewish in its outlook. See G. D. Kilpatrick in *Expository Times*, LXIV (1952), 4-8, and J. Jeremias's reply, *ibid.*, pp. 91-92; see also R. D. Richardson's essay in the Eng. trans. of Lietzmann, *op. cit.*, pp. 343-347.

The resemblance between the Lord's Supper and certain Mithraic ceremonies, which Justin Martyr explained (see p. 15, note 7 above) as due to the work of demons in anticipation of the Christian sacrament, may be regarded either as fortuitous or as the result of adaptation by Mithraic priests of an impressive rite in the Christian cultus.

in fact, the giving of thanks is so central in the sacrament that this provides a name for the rite itself (εὐχαριστία).[1]

Finally, the differences of cultic vocabulary between primitive Christianity and the Mysteries (see VI (A) above) are nowhere more obvious than in the case of baptism.[2] That the antecedents of Christian baptism are to be sought in the purificatory washings mentioned in the Old Testament and in the rite of Jewish proselyte baptism, is generally acknowledged by scholars today.[3]

---

[1] Nock observes that although paganism expressed gratitude for blessings received, "we cannot imagine copious impromptu prayer in a pagan rite," *Mnemosyne*, 4th Ser., v (1952), 201; reprinted in Nock's *Early Gentile Christianity and its Hellenistic Background* (New York, 1964), p. 133. In this connection reference may be made to a third century papyrus edited by Theodor Schermann, *Frühchristliche Vorbereitungsgebete zur Taufe*, in *Münchener Beiträge zur Papyrusforschung*, III (München, 1917).

[2] With regard to the Christian terminology of baptism, Erich Fascher concludes: "Aufs Grosse und Ganze gesehen haben die ersten Christen also schon durch die Wortwahl (Wörter, die selten und weder in der Profangräcität noch in LXX kultisch bestimmt sind) ihr Eigentümliches zum Ausdruck gebracht," article "Taufe," Pauly-Wissowa, *Real-Encyclopädie*, Zweite Reihe, 8te Halbband (IV, A, ii; 1932), 2504, 12-17; for Nock's judgment on the difference of sacramental terminology, see p. 12, note 2 above. See also the extensive analysis made by Günter Wagner, *op. cit.* (see p. 3, note 2 above).

[3] See, among many monographs on the subject, Konstantin Hartte, *Zum semitischen Wasserkultus (vor Ausbreitung des Christentums)*, Diss. Tübingen (Halle, 1912); Gottfried Polster, "Der kleine Talmudtraktat über die Proselyten," *Angelos, Archiv für neutestamentliche Zeitgeschichte und Kulturkunde*, II (1926), 2-38; J. Leipoldt, *Die urchristliche Taufe im Lichte der Religionsgeschichte* (Leipzig, 1928); J. Coppens, "Baptême," *Dictionnaire de la Bible, Supplément*, I (1928), 852-924, especially "Rapports entre les mystères païens et le baptême chrétien," 911-920; J. Jeremias, "Der Ursprung der Johannestaufe," *Zeitschrift für die neutestamentliche Wissenschaft*, XXVIII (1929), 312-320; Louis Finkelstein, "The Institution of Baptism for Proselytes," *Journal of Biblical Literature*, LII (1933), 203-211; H. H. Rowley, "Jewish Proselyte Baptism and the Baptism of John," *Hebrew Union College Annual*, XV (1940), 313-334; and H. G. Marsh, *The Origin and Significance of New Testament Baptism* (Manchester, 1941).

Reitzenstein's conclusions in his *Die Vorgeschichte der christlichen Taufe* (Leipzig and Berlin, 1929), rest upon the very dubious methodology of appealing to evidence from the Mandaic literature, which dates in its present form from the seventh and eighth centuries, and is itself partly dependent on Christianity. Recent evaluations of the limited usefulness of Mandaism in accounting for elements in Christian origins include those by W. L. Knox, *St. Paul and the Church of the Gentiles* (Cambridge, 1939), pp. 212-219, and C. H. Dodd, *The Interpretation of the Fourth Gospel* (Cambridge, 1953), pp. 115-130. For a guide to the extensive literature on the subject, see S. A. Pallis, *Essay on Mandæan Bibliography, 1560-1930* (Copenhagen and London, 1933); for more recent studies, see Kurt Rudolph, *Die Mandäer*, 2 vols. (Göttingen, 1960-1961); Rudolf Macuch, "Zur Frühgeschichte der Mandäer," *Theologische Literaturzeitung*, XC (1965), cols. 649-660; and Edwin M. Yamau-

(E) The motif of a dying and rising savior-god has been frequently supposed to be related to the account of the saving efficacy of the death and resurrection of Jesus Christ. The formal resemblance between the two, however, must not be allowed to obscure the great differences in content.

(1) In all the Mysteries which tell of a dying deity, the god dies by compulsion and not by choice, sometimes in bitterness and despair, never in a self-giving love. But according to the New Testament, God's purpose of redeeming-love was the free divine motive for the death of Jesus, who accepted with equal freedom that motive as his own.

(2) Christianity is *sui generis* in its triumphant note affirming that even on the Cross Jesus exercised his kingly rule (*Dominus regnat ex ligno*). Contrary to this exultant mood (which has been called the *gaudium crucis*), the pagan devotees mourn and lament in sympathy with a god who has unfortunately suffered something imposed on him. As Nock points out, "In the Christian commemoration the only element of mourning is the thought that *men* have betrayed and murdered Jesus. His death is itself triumph."[1]

(3) In all strata of Christian testimony concerning the resurrection of Jesus Christ, "everything is made to turn upon a dated experience of a historical Person,"[2] whereas nothing in the Mysteries points to any attempt to undergird belief with historical evidence of the god's resurrection. The formulation of belief in Christ's resurrection on the third day was fixed prior to Paul's conversion (*c.* A.D. 33-36), as the choice of technical phraseology in I Cor. 15.3 indicates,[3] and

chi, "The Present Status of Mandæan Studies," *Journal of Near Eastern Studies*, xxv (1966), 88-96.

[1] A. D. Nock, "A Note on the Resurrection," in *Essays on the Trinity and the Incarnation*, ed. A. E. J. Rawlinson (London, 1928), p. 48; reprinted in Nock's *Early Gentile Christianity and its Hellenistic Background* (New York, 1964), p. 106.

[2] The phrase is Nock's, *ibid.*, p. 49. See also George C. Ring, S.J., "Christ's Resurrection and the Dying and Rising Gods," *Catholic Biblical Quarterly*, VI (1944), 216-229, and G. Bertram, "Auferstehung (des Kultgottes)," *Reallexikon für Antike und Christentum*, I (Stuttgart, 1950), 919-930.

[3] Of no little significance is Paul's choice of the pair of verbs with which he begins this account of the institution of the Lord's Supper, παρέλαβον and παρέδωκα. These correspond exactly to קִבֵּל and מָסַר, the *termini technici* with which Pirke Aboth, the heart of the Mishnah, opens ("Moses *received* the Torah from Sinai and *delivered* it to Joshua, and Joshua to the Elders, and the Elders to the Prophets," etc.). Among other monographs dealing with Paul's *tanna*-like role in receiving and delivering tradition concerning Jesus, see G. Kittel, *Die Probleme des palästinischen spätjudentums und das Ur-*

was proclaimed openly as part of the general apostolic *kerygma* from the very earliest days of the Church, as the evidence in all strata of Acts makes abundantly clear.[1] Moreover, the proclamation of the Resurrection by the members of the Christian community at Jerusalem was not merely a means of confusing their opponents; it was the presupposition of their own communal life.

What shall be said of parallels to the tradition that the Resurrection of Christ took place "on the third day?" The devotees of Attis commemorated his death on March 22, the Day of Blood, and his coming to life four days later, March 25, the Feast of Joy or *Hilaria*. According to one account of the Egyptian cult, the death of Osiris took place on the 17th of Athyr (a month corresponding to the period from October 28 to November 26), the finding and re-animation of his body in the night of the 19th.[2] When Adonis rose is not certain, but the reconstruction of a papyrus text has been thought to make the third day probable.[3]

---

christentum (Stuttgart, 1926), pp. 26f.; Adolf Schlatter, *Paulus der Bote Jesu* (Stuttgart, 1934), p. 320; W. D. Davies, *Paul and Rabbinic Judaism* (London, 1948; 2nd ed., 1955), pp. 248f.; B. Gerhardsson, *Memory and Manuscript, Oral Tradition and Written Transmission in Rabbinic Judaism and Early Christianity* (Uppsala, 1961; 2nd ed., 1964), pp. 288-323; and J. Jeremias, *The Eucharistic Words of Jesus*, trans. by Norman Perrin (New York, 1966), pp. 101f.

The fact that occasionally either παραδιδόναι and *tradere* or παραλαμβάνειν, *accipere*, and *percipere*, were used with reference to the Mysteries (for examples see Lobeck, *op. cit.*, I, 39, note; Anrich, *op. cit.*, p. 54, notes 4 and 5; Dieterich, *Eine Mithrasliturgie*, pp. 53f.) cannot be supposed to throw significant light upon Paul's usage in I Cor. 11.23 (*pace* Eduard Norden, *Agnostos Theos* [Berlin, 1913], pp. 288f.) in view of the facts that (1) no pagan example has been found which employs both verbs side by side, and (2) as a rabbi trained at Jerusalem, Paul would not only have known *verbatim* the phraseology embedded in Aboth, but would have frequently heard the pair of verbs used in the course of rabbinical debate.

[1] See C. H. Dodd, *The Apostolic Preaching and Its Developments* (London, 1936), and A. M. Hunter, *Paul and his Predecessors*, rev. ed. (London, 1961).

[2] On the diversity and reticence of the several accounts of the Osiris legends, see Georges Nagel, "The 'Mysteries' of Osiris in Ancient Egypt," *The Mysteries, Papers from the Eranos Yearbooks*, ed. by Joseph Campbell (New York, 1955): "The various episodes of the legend are not attested in the same way and with the same frequency. The texts often speak of the battles of Horus and Seth for the heritage of Osiris, and often they mention the laments of Isis over her husband's death. But with regard to the actual death and resurrection of Osiris they are always quite reticent and usually give us no more than brief allusions" (p. 123).

[3] Gustave Glotz, "Les fêtes d'Adonis sous Ptolémée II," *Revue des études grecques*, XXXIII (1920), 169-222, especially 213. For a convincing demolition of Glotz's reconstruction and interpretation, see pp. 230f. of Lambrechts' study mentioned in note 2 on p. 21 below.

In evaluating such parallels, the first thing that the historian must do is to sift the evidence. In the case of Attis, the evidence for the commemoration of the *Hilaria* dates from the latter part of the second Christian century.[1] There are, in fact, no literary or epigraphical texts prior to the time of Antonius Pius (A.D. 138-161) which refer to Attis as the divine consort of Cybele,[2] much less any that speak of his resurrection.[3] With good grounds, therefore, it has been argued that the festival of the *Hilaria* was not introduced into the cultus of Cybele until the latter part of the second Christian century or even later.[4]

In the case of Osiris, after his consort Isis had sought and reassembled thirteen of the fourteen pieces into which his body had been dismembered by his wicked brother Typhon (otherwise known as Set), through the help of magic[5] she was enabled to reanimate his corpse. Thereafter Osiris became "Lord of the Underworld and Ruler of the Dead," in which role he presides at the bar of judgment and assigns to the souls of the departed their proper reward for virtue

---

[1] Cf. Duncan Fishwick, "The *Cannophori* and the March Festival of Magna Mater," *Transactions and Proceedings of the American Philological Association*, XCVII (1966), 193-202.

[2] Certainly Catullus' poem, *Attis*, provides no hint of any such depiction of Attis, even though one may not agree with Elder's view that the poet intended to confine his attention to the psychological revulsion felt by "an ordinary man who by emasculation became a priest of Cybele" (John P. Elder, "Catallus' *Attis*," *American Journal of Philology*, LXVIII [1947], 395).

[3] Pierre Lambrechts, *Attis, van herdersknaap tot God* (*Verhandelingen van de koninklijke Vlaamse Academie voor wetenschappen, letteren en schone kunsten van België*, Kl. der Letteren, No. 46; Brussels, 1962), pp. 8 and 26ff.; cf. G. Wagner, *op. cit.* (see above p. 3, note 2), pp. 228-235 (Eng. trans., pp. 217-229). For the ambiguous and extremely limited iconographic representations of the periodic resurrection of Attis, see M. J. Vermaseren, *The Legend of Attis in Greek and Roman Art* (Leiden, 1966), p. 40.

[4] Pierre Lambrechts, "Les fêtes 'phrygiennes' de Cybèle et d'Attis," *Bulletin de l'Institut historique belge de Rome*, XXVII (1952), 141-170, and "Attis à Rome," *Mélanges Georges Smets* (Brussels, 1952), pp. 461-471. On the reform of the cult of Magna Mater under Antoninus Pius, see Jean Beaujeu, *La Religion romaine à l'apogée de l'Empire*; I, *La Politique religieuse des Antonins (96-192)* (Paris, 1955), pp. 312ff., who supports his arguments with numismatic evidence. Cf. also Th. Köves, "Zum Empfang der Magna Mater in Rom," *Historia*, XII (1963), 321-347, who draws attention to the supplanting of the old "Roman" rites celebrated in April (the Megalesia) under the Republic by the Phrygian rites celebrated in March.

[5] Johannes Leipoldt appropriately calls attention to the feature of magical incantations as a significant difference between pagan and Christian account of the resurrection of the cult-god ("Zu den Auferstehungs-Geschichten," *Theologisches Literaturzeitung*, LXXIII [1948], col. 738 (= *Von den Mysterien zur Kirche. Gesammelte Aufsätze* [Leipzig, 1961], pp. 200f.).

or punishment for wrongdoing. Whether this can be rightly called a resurrection is questionable, especially since, according to Plutarch,[1] it was the pious desire of devotees to be buried in the same ground where, according to local tradition, the body of Osiris was still lying.

In the case of Adonis, there is no trace of a resurrection in pictorial representations or in any texts prior to the beginning of the Christian era.[2] In fact, the only four witnesses that refer to the resurrection of Adonis date from the second to the fourth century (Lucian,[3] Origen,[4] Jerome[5] (who depends upon Origen), and Cyril of Alexandria[6]) and none of these mentions the *triduum*.

The attempt to link the Adonis and Attis cults to the worship of Tammuz and his alleged resurrection[7] rests, as Kramer put it, on "nothing but inference and surmise, guess and conjecture."[8] Still more remote from the rise of Christianity is the Sumerian epic involving Inanna's descent to the Nether World.[9]

---

[1] Plutarch, *de Iside et Osiride*, 359B (20). No fewer than twenty-three locations, identified by classical authors and Greek inscriptions, claimed to be the place where Osiris's body lay; for a list, see Theodor Hopfner, *Plutarch über Isis und Osiris*; 1. Teil, *Die Sage* (*Monographien des Archiv Orientální*, IX; Prague, 1940), pp. 160f. The cult of Osiris, in fact, involved not so much a genuine "mystery" initiation, open to devotees, as a funerary service for the departed; see Georges Nagel, "Les 'mystères' d'Osiris dans l'ancienne Égypte," *Eranos-Jahrbuch 1944* (Band XI), *Die Mysterien* (Zurich, 1945), pp. 164ff.; Eng. trans., "The 'Mysteries' of Osiris in Ancient Egypt," *The Mysteries, Papers from the Eranos Yearbooks*, ed. by Joseph Campbell (*Bollingen Series*, XXX. 2; New York, 1955), pp. 132ff.; for the distinction cf. also Gustave Jéquier, "Drames, mystères, rituels dans l'ancienne Égypte," *Mélanges offerts à M. Niedermann* ... (Neuchatel, 1944), pp. 37ff. On the question of the so-called parallels between the cult of Osiris and Christianity, see G. Bertram, "Auferstehung (des Kultgottes)," *Reallexikon für Antike und Christentum*, 1 (1950), cols. 921f., and the quotation from Brandon, p. 11 above, note 1.

[2] See, e.g., P. Lambrechts' survey of the evidence in his "La 'resurrection' d'Adonis," *Mélanges Isidore Lévy* (*Annuaire de l'Institut de philologie et d'histoire orientales et slaves*, XIII [1953]; Brussels, 1955), pp. 207-240.

[3] *De dea Syria*, vi.

[4] *Selecta in Ezek.* (Migne, *PG*, XIII. 797).

[5] *In Ezek.*, viii. 13f. (Migne, *PL*, XXV. 82).

[6] *In Isaiam*, ii. 3 (Migne, *PG*, LXX. 440f.).

[7] E.g., Wilfred H. Schoff, "Tammuz, Pan, and Christ," *The Open Court*, XXVI (1912), 513-532.

[8] S. N. Kramer, ed., *Mythologies of the Ancient World*, p. 10. Cf. G. Wagner, *op. cit.* pp. 149-167 (Eng. tr., pp. 136ff.), and E. M. Yamauchi, "Tammuz and the Bible," *Journal of Biblical Literature*, LXXXIV (1965), 283-290, and *idem*, "Descent of Ishtar," *The Biblical World, a Dictionary of Biblical Archaeology*, ed. by Charles F. Pfeiffer (Grand Rapids, 1966), p. 200.

[9] Contrary to W. F. Albright's statement that in the Sumerian original of the epic of Inanna's Descent to the Nether World the goddess "is explicitly

There is, however, no need to go so far afield as these beliefs to account for the Christian conviction that Jesus rose the third day. It was a widely prevalent belief among the Jews that the soul of a dead man hovered near the corpse for three days, hoping to return to the body, but that on the fourth day, when decomposition set in, the soul finally departed, a belief that seems to be reflected in Martha's comment regarding her brother Lazarus (John 11.39).[1] Moreover, apart from such parallels, it might be urged that the phrase "on the third day" or "after three days" occurs so often in the Old Testament with reference to the normal interval between two events in close succession that the dating of the Resurrection "on the third day" was both appropriate and inevitable.

Apart from these considerations, however, it remains a fact that the notation of the *third* day is so closely intertwined within all the New Testament accounts of Jesus' resurrection as to point to the conclusion that the Christian witnesses began to experience the living presence of Jesus Christ on the third day after his crucifixion, and thereafter it was recalled that he had promised on more than one occasion that, after his death, he would in three days rise again.[2]

---

said to remain three days and three nights in the underworld" (*From Stone Age to Christianity*, 2nd ed. [Baltimore, 1946], pp. 341f., note 81), a careful examination of the epic (conveniently edited by J. B. Pritchard, *Ancient Near Eastern Texts* [Princeton, 1950], pp. 52-57) indicates that it is "after three days and three nights had passed" (line 169) that Ninshubur, perceiving that his mistress, Inanna, has not returned from the Nether World, proceeds to make the rounds of the gods, lamenting before each of them in accord with a formula which Inanna had previously given him. Then Father Enki devises a plan to restore the goddess to life; he fashions two sexless creatures and instructs them to proceed to the Nether World and to sprinkle the "food of life" and the "water of life" upon Inanna's impaled body. This they do, and the goddess subsequently revives. The time of the reanimation is not disclosed, but doubtlessly the mythographer conceived it to be consideraby later than the period of three days and three nights. On this point also see F. Nötscher, "Zur Auferstehung nach drei Tagen," *Biblica*, xxxv (1954), 313-319. Accepting a reading proposed by Adam Falkenstein (*Bibliotheca Orientalis*, xxii [1965], 279f.) S. N. Kramer made a correction to his earlier interpretation of Inanna's Descent, concluding that "Dumuzi, according to Sumerian mythographers, rises from the dead annually, and after staying on earth for half a year, descends to the Nether World for the other half" ("Dumuzi's Annual Resurrection: An Important Correction to 'Inanna's Descent,' " *Bulletin of the American Schools of Oriental Research*, no. 183 [Oct. 1966], p. 31).

[1] Among many discussions of this belief, see especially Emil Freistedt, *Altchristliche Totengedächtnistage und ihre Beziehung zum Jenseitsglauben und Totenkultus der Antike* (Münster, 1928), pp. 53ff.

[2] For an interesting suggestion why Jesus emphasized the importance of

(4) Finally, Christianity and the Mystery cults differ in what may be called their views regarding the philosophy of history.

(a) It is generally acknowledged that the rites of the Mysteries, which commemorate a dying and rising deity, represent the cyclical recurrence of the seasons. In other words, such myths are the expression of ancient nature-symbolism; the spirit of vegetation dies every year and rises every year. According to popular expectation, the world-process will be indefinitely repeated, being a circular movement leading nowhere. For the Christian, on the other hand, as heir to the Hebraic view of history, the time-process comprises a series of unique events, and the most significant of these events was the death and resurrection of Jesus Christ. Unlike the recurrent death and reanimation of the cultic deities symbolizing the cycle of nature, for the Christians the importance of Jesus' work was related just to this "once-for-all" character of his death and resurrection.[1]

(b) In another respect besides that of repetition, the Mysteries differ from Christianity's interpretation of history. The speculative myths of the cults lack entirely that reference to the spiritual and moral meaning of history which is inextricably involved in the experiences and triumph of Jesus Christ. In fact, not until the fourth century, when doubtless this stark contrast between the two became increasingly apparent to thoughtful pagans, is there any indication of an attempt to read moral values into certain cultic myths.[2]

---

the third day after his death, see Sir Edwyn Hoskyns, *The Fourth Gospel*, 2nd ed. (London, 1947), pp. 199-200. Hoskyns points out that, according to customs of hospitality prevailing in the East, three days constitute a temporary habitation, and the fourth day implies permanent residence. When therefore, in accord with Hosea's promise that the Lord had not permanently humiliated his people but would raise them up on the third day (Hosea 6.2), "it is said in the Gospels that Jesus emphasized the importance of the third day after His death, what is meant is that He assured to His disciples that death could not permanently engulf Him ... He would be but a visitor to the dead, not a permanent resident in their midst" (p. 200).

[1] It must not be supposed that the recurring annual festival of Easter belies what has just been said regarding the particularity of the Christian message. It has been proved that the celebration of Easter did not arise at once out of belief in the Resurrection, but developed later by gradual stages out of the Jewish Passover; see E. Schwartz, "Osterbetrachtungen," *Zeitschrift für neutestamentliche Wissenschaft*, VII (1906), 1-33.

[2] Notably into the cult of Attis by Iamblichus (died A.D. 330), as reported by Julian, *Oration* v, and by Sallustius, *Concerning the Gods and the Universe*, iv.

The main purpose of the foregoing study has been to deal with problems of methodology and to raise questions regarding the correctness of certain assumptions which, in some circles, are generally accepted as valid. Lest the argument concerning methodology be merely theoretical, the discussion has necessarily involved certain beliefs and doctrines, but these, so far from being exhaustive, are to be regarded only as selected examples. If any conclusions can be drawn from the preceding considerations of methodology, they must doubtless be, first, that the evidence requires that the investigator maintain a high degree of caution in evaluating the relation between the Mysteries and early Christianity; and, second, that the central doctrines and rites of the primitive Church appear to lack genetic continuity with those of antecedent and contemporary pagan cults.

CHAPTER TWO

THE SECOND GRADE OF MITHRAIC INITIATION

Among the numerous Mithraic texts and testimonies collected by Franz Cumont[1] there is only one which supplies the sequence of the seven grades of initiation in the Mithraic religion. This is the testimony of St. Jerome in his *Epistula ad Laetam*, which, according to the critical edition by Hilberg,[2] reads:

> Ante paucos annos propinquus uester Graccus nobilitatem patriciam nomine sonans, cum praefecturam regeret urbanam, nonne specu Mithrae et omnia portentuosa simulacra, quibus corax, cryphius, miles, leo, Perses, heliodromus, pater initiantur subuertit, fregit, exussit et his quasi obsidibus ante praemissis inpetrauit baptismum Christi?

Now, it is a remarkable fact that not one of the six manuscripts of St. Jerome which Hilberg collated reads *cryphius*. One manuscript reads *nymphus*;[3] two others, *nimphus*;[4] a fourth, *nimplus*,[5] which is corrected to read with the remaining two, *nimfus*.[6] Likewise three other manuscripts, which had been collated earlier by Cumont but whose evidence Hilberg did not use, support the testimony of the six manuscripts which Hilberg emends. One of these reads *nunphus*; the other two, *nymphus*.[7] In the face of such documentary evidence it would seem presumptuous to set aside St. Jerome's testimony unless very strong reasons unequivocally demand it. Such counterevidence has been thought to be supplied in several inscriptions

---

[1] *Textes et Monuments figurés relatifs aux Mystères de Mithra*, II (Brussels, 1896), 1-184, 457-476.

[2] *Epistula*, cvii, 2, edited by Isidor Hilberg in *Corpus Scriptorum Ecclesiasticorum Latinorum*, LV (Vienna, 1912), 292, 2-7.

[3] Vaticanus lat. 355 and 356, saec. ix-x.

[4] Caroliruhensis Augiensis 105, saec. ix-x, and Berolinensis lat. 18, saec. xii.

[5] Turicensis Augiensis 41, saec. ix.

[6] Spinaliensis 68, saec. viii, and Augustodunensis 17 A, saec. x.

[7] Parisinus lat. 1867, saec. ix (*nunphus*); Parisini latt. 1871, saec. x, and 1872, saec. xi (*nymphus*). Cumont (*op. cit.*, II, p. 18) rejects their testimony in favor of the emendation *cryphius*. (It may be noted that Cumont's statement [*op. cit.*, I, p. 316, n. 7] that "the mss. of St. Jerome give *gryphus* or *nymphus*" is made without the citation of any evidence and must be accounted an error as respects *gryphus*).

from a Mithraeum found in the Piazza S. Silvestro in Rome.[1] These incriptions provide corroborative evidence for five of the grades in St. Jerome's list, viz., *hierocoracica* (no. 751[b]), *leontica* (nos. 749, 752 [*bis*], 753), *persica* (no. 750), [*h*]*eliaca* (no. 750), and *patrica* (no. 751[a]).[2] Thus there are lacking grades corresponding to St. Jerome's *nymphus* and *miles*. In two of these inscriptions, however, are found two expressions which suggested the emendation that now is printed as the text of St. Jerome. These two inscriptions are, in part:

> ... consulibus s(upra) s(criptis) ostenderunt cryfios
> VIII kal(endas) mai(as) felic(iter)   (no. 751[a], A.D. 358).

> ... cons(ulibus) s(upra) s(criptis) tradiderunt chryfios
> VI idu(s) apr(iles) felic(iter)   (no. 753, A.D. 362).

From *cryfios* and *chryfios* Cumont and Hilberg produce *cryphius* and introduce it into St. Jerome's text in the place of *nymphus*.

But some evidence has rather recently come to light to prove that one of the regular Mithraic grades of initiation was that of νύμφος. Excavations at Dura-Europos have unearthed a Mithraeum whose graffiti supply parallels for all of St. Jerome's grades except *heliodromus*.[3] The disputed rank of νύμφος is found more than a dozen times, sometimes with the epithet ἀγαθός.[4] The manuscript tradition of St. Jerome concerning *nymphus* is therefore correct and modern scholars—down to the most recent (1955) editor of the

---

[1] *Corpus Inscriptionum Latinarum*, VI, 749-753 (= Hermann Dessau, *Inscriptionum Latinarum selectae*, 4267f.).

[2] Each of these neuter adjectives is the object of *tradere*, "to confer (the degree)."

[3] The reading *Helios, Dromo* in Migne's *Patrologia Latina*, XXII, col. 869, is an arbitrary emendation by Vallarsi (cf. the note by Dom John Martin, *ibid.*, col. 1264). The only parallel to *Heliodromus* which Ernst Wüst cites in Pauly-Wissowa, *Real-Enc.*, XV, *s. v.* "Mithras," col. 2142, is a half-Christian, half-pagan inscription at Otourah dated A.D. 314 (published by Sir William M. Ramsay in *Journal of Hellenic Studies*, IV [1883], 420) where ['Η]λιοδρόμος Διός occurs. He might have cited also the phonetically equivalent Εἰλειοδρόμος, which appears five times in some magic tablets discovered in Rome (Richard Wünsch, *Sethianische Verfluchtungstafeln aus Rom* [Leipzig, 1898], tablet 21, lines 5 and 15; tablet 22, line 6; and tablet 27, lines 6 and 38).

[4] *The Excavations at Dura-Europos, Conducted by Yale University and the French Academy of Inscriptions and Letters; Preliminary Report of the Seventh and Eighth Seasons of Work, 1933-1934 and 1934-1935*, edited by M. I. Rostovtzeff, F. E. Brown, and C. B. Welles (New Haven, 1939), p. 123. Cf. also Rostovtzeff in *Römische Mittheilungen*, XLIX (1934), 206.

Latin text of St. Jerome's letters, Jérôme Labourt[1]—are wrong.

But what did *nymphus* or νύμφος mean to the Mithraic initiate? The suggestion by Vallarsi[2] that *nymphus* is Νύμφη, the sign of *Virgo* in the zodiac, has *prima facie* plausibility by reason of the presence of zodiacal signs in much of Mithraic art. In accord with this interpretation, the grade may have involved the inculcation of chastity and perhaps imposed on the initiate vows of continence.[3] If, however, the grade were derived from the zodiac, one would expect not only that others of the seven grades would disclose a similar derivation,[4] but also that instead of seven there would have been twelve grades.

The obvious meaning of νύμφος is "the grade of the Bridegroom," equating the word with νυμφίος and perhaps involving a mystic marriage (with the deity?) for which the initiate may have been clad in a wedding garment.[5]

Cumont objects to this interpretation on the score that such a grade would be rather inappropriate in a religion which admitted only men to its membership. He is inclined to think that, as νύμφη meant properly a young woman of marriageable age, so νύμφος, in

---

[1] *Saint Jérôme, Lettres*, texte établi et traduit par Jérôme Labourt, v (Paris, 1955), 146. The reconstructed text of Jerome is also cited in *Thesaurus Linguae Latinae*, vi, 3 (1936-42), col. 2594, line 62, *s. v.* "heliodromus."

[2] *Op. cit.*, col. 869. The difference in gender is not a serious obstacle to such identification.

[3] My colleague, Professor Otto A. Piper, has suggested to me that this would then be the positive doctrine of sexual continence corresponding to the negative symbolism which he believes to be represented in the tauroctony by the scorpion attacking the genitals of the bull. Mention may be made, too, of an Ostian dedication (*C.I.L.*, xiv, 66) which seems to indicate that a man could follow Mithras not only as leader but also as moral exemplar. It is, in part: C. Valerius Heracles pater *et* an*tis*/tes dei iu*b*enis inconrupti so*l*is invicti Mithra*e* ... (see A. D. Nock in *Journal of Roman Studies*, xxvii [1937], 112).

[4] Vallarsi's attempt (Migne, *P.L.*, xxii, col. 869) to equate five of the other grades with stars or signs of the zodiac is not convincing.

[5] Pseudo-Augustine, *Quaestiones veteris et novi testamenti*, cxiv, 11 (*C.S.E.L.*, l, p. 308, 19ff., ed. Souter) and the Konjica relief (Cumont, *op. cit.*, i, p. 175, fig. 10) indicate that each initiate, wearing the insignia appropriate to his degree, would attempt to imitate the animal or person involved. Thus, donning a mask of a crow or a lion, they would flap their wings and imitate the cry of a crow or growl like a lion. Although there is no literary evidence that the Mithraic *nymphus* wore a *velum* (the veil or the *flammeum* of the Roman marriage ceremony), Vermaseren interprets a figure on the Santa Prisca murals (see p. 31, note 1 below) as a Mithraic (male) initiate wearing a bridal veil (M. J. Vermaseren, *Mithras, de geheimzinnige god* [Amsterdam and Brussels, 1959], p. 116, Engl. trans., *Mithras, the Secret God* [London, 1963], p. 142).

religious terminology, may have been applied to an "adolescent."
The initiation to this degree would then be, according to Cumont,
a relic of the *rites de passage* which are observed among many
peoples at the time of puberty, when the child is admitted to the
society of full-grown men.[1]

Against Cumont's interpretation, however, and in favor of the
meaning of "bridegroom" is a liturgical formula[2] preserved by
Firmicus Maternus which, in the Teubner text of Firmicus, reads:
***δε νυμφίε, χαῖρε νυμφίε, χαῖρε νέον φῶς.[3] It is significant that the
only manuscript of Firmicus has in both instances ΝΥΝΦΕ [= νύμφε],
which was corrected in each case to νυμφίε. Now, from the context
immediately following it can be seen that Firmicus understood
νύμφος to mean *sponsus*.[4]

So much for νύμφος, *nymphus*. Whether the term *cryfios* (*chryfios*)

---

[1] *Comptes rendus de l'Académie des inscriptions et belles-lettres*, 1934, p. 108.
Also, to the same effect, Joseph Bidez and Franz Cumont, *Les Mages hellé-
nisés; Zoroastre, Ostanès et Hystaspe d'après la tradition grecque*, II (Paris,
1938), 154.

[2] This formula has been generally referred to the Eleusinian mysteries;
e.g., by Theodorus Friedrich, *In Iulii Firmici Materni de errore profanorum
religionum libellum quaestiones* (Diss. Giessen, 1905), pp. 25 and 44ff., and
J. Coman, *Revista Clasica*, IV-V (Bucharest, 1933), 93. But other scholars
hold other opinions; e.g., Gillis P:son Wetter, *Phōs; eine Untersuchung über
hellenistische Frömmigkeit* (Uppsala and Leipzig, 1915), p. 19, thinks that
νυμφίε is Attis; Albrecht Dieterich, *Eine Mithrasliturgie*, 3te Aufl., herausg.
Otto Weinreich (Leipzig and Berlin, 1923), pp. 122f., 214, and 256f., refers
it to Dionysus; and more recently, in his edition of Firmicus, Gilbert Heuten
(*Travaux de la Faculté de Philosophie et Lettres de l'Université de Bruxelles*,
VIII [1938], 179) has revived—apparently without his knowing its ancestry—a
suggestion made long ago by Bishop Münter (in his edition of Firmicus
[Hauniae, 1826], p. 76, adn. 1) that the formula pertains to the Mithraic cult.
Whether any of these theories is true or not must remain uncertain because
the immediately preceding context of Firmicus is corrupt. (Ziegler, the editor
of the Teubner text, believes that a whole leaf was lost from the archetype
of the only extant manuscript). But, to whatever cult this formula be
referred—and it is not necessary for the present argument that it be Mithraic
—it seems to the present writer that the way Firmicus opens the following
chapter, which clearly refers to Mithraism, almost precludes the Mithraic
origin of the formula involving νύμφε. The following chapter begins: Alterius
profani sacramenti signum est θεὸς ἐκ πέτρας (XX, 1).

[3] Chap. xix, 1 (ed. Ziegler). M. J. Vermaseren thinks it probable that
"immediately after the initiation of the *Nymphus*, the Mithraeum was flooded
with a powerful light" (*Mithras, de geheimzinnige god* [Amsterdam and
Brussels, 1959], p. 117, Engl. trans., *Mithras, the Secret God* [London, 1963],
p. 39).

[4] Although, of course, Firmicus's understanding of νύμφος is not proof
positive that such was also its original significance in Mithraism, he nevertheless supplies valuable evidence for its meaning current in his own day.

in the two Roman inscriptions refers to a grade of initiation involving a ceremony of veiling and subsequent unveiling (as Cumont[1] and many other scholars[2] believe), or whether it involved the display of certain "hidden objects" (as Forcellini[3] and W. J. Phythian-Adams[4] maintain), or whether the word is to be derived from γρύψ, γρυπός (as Ernst Wüst[5] has argued, following a hint thrown out by Cumont[6]), or whether the snake was really the second Mithraic degree under the title of κρύφιος (as K. Benz[7] and G. W. Elderkin[8] independently conjectured), or whether, finally, the word refers to youths who, like the Spartan κρυπτοί, have not yet been received

---

[1] *Textes et Monuments*, I, p. 316 (Engl. trans., *The Mysteries of Mithra* [Chicago, 1903], p. 154). After Cumont had suggested this interpretation, an interesting relief from Arčar (Ratiaria) was published (Gawril Kazarow, "Die Kultdenkmäler der sog. thrakischen Reiter in Bulgarien," *Archiv für Religionswissenschaft*, XV (1912), pp. 156f. and plate I, fig. 4) showing a kneeling figure, who is wearing the "Phrygian" cap, partly hidden by a veil held before him by two other figures. Rostovtzeff explains this scene in terms of the Mithraic *ostenderunt cryfios* (*Predstavlenie o monarchitcheskoi vlasti v Skithii i na Bospore* [Petrograd, 1913], p. 53, quoted by H. Stuart Jones in Hastings' *Encyclopædia of Religion and Ethics*, VIII [1916], 756b, n. 1).

[2] This opinion, with variations, is held, e.g., by Sir Samuel Dill, *Roman Society from Nero to Marcus Aurelius* (2nd ed., London, 1905), pp. 611f.; Eduard Roese, *Über Mithrasdienst* (Stralsund, 1905), pp. 18f.; Jules Toutain, *Les Cultes païens dans l'Empire romain*, II (Paris, 1911), 141; L. Patterson, *Mithraism and Christianity; a Study in Comparative Religion* (Cambridge, 1921), p. 46; R. Pettazzoni, *I Misteri; saggio di una teoria storico-religiosa* (Bologna, 1924), p. 262; L. Deubner in Chantepie de la Saussaye, *Lehrbuch der Religionsgeschichte*, 4te Aufl., II (Tübingen, 1925), 498; and Cornelius I. M. I. van Beek, "Ostenderunt Cryfios," in *Pisciculi; Studien zur Religion und Kultur des Altertums* (F. J. Dölger's *Festschrift* [Münster in Westfalen, 1939]), p. 53. Whether the unveiling results in the nudity of the initiate is debatable; for examples of nude figures in Mithraic art, see Josephus Heckenbach, *De nuditate sacra sacrisque vinculis* (= *Religionsgeschichtliche Versuche und Vorarbeiten*, IX, 3; Giessen, 1911), p. 13.

[3] *Totius Latinitatis Lexicon, s. v.*

[4] *Journal of Roman Studies*, II (1912), 56-64, where he makes the suggestion that perhaps the "hidden objects" were statues of the curious leontocephalous god; in his later and much more popular treatment (*Mithraism* [London, 1915], p. 77) he does not commit himself as to the nature of these "hidden objects."

[5] Pauly-Wissowa, *Real-Enc.*, XV, col. 2142, and *Archiv für Religionswissenschaft*, XXXII (1935), 211-215. Before Wüst wrote (and apparently without his knowledge) W. Kroll also offered the suggestion that the second grade of Mithraic initiations was that of the griffin (in Gunkel, Schiele, and Zscharnack's *Religion in Geschichte und Gegenwart*, V [1913], 1051).

[6] *Textes et Monuments*, II, p. 93, note added to inscription no. 9.

[7] "Die Mithrasmysterien," *Historisches Jahrbuch*, XXXIX (1918-1919), 10ff.

[8] *Kantheros; Studies in Dionysiac and Kindred Cult* (Princeton, 1924), pp. 31f. and 39.

as official members into the clan or cult, and hence are "hidden ones" that have not yet appeared in the full light of the public eye (as W. Vollgraff has urged),[1] need not be explored at length here. It is sufficient to observe that objections more or less serious can be leveled against each proposal. With reference to the first, whereas five grades of initiation in the Roman inscriptions are distinguished by neuter adjectives, it is difficult to understand the masculine *cryfios* (*chryfios*) as a stage of initiation in the same sense; *cryfiaca* ought to have been used. Furthermore, although each of the other grades is the object of *tradere* (as is also *chryfios*), in inscription no. 751[a] *cryfios* is the object of *ostendere*. These two considerations suggest that *cryfios* is not in the same category with the other words that clearly designate grades or stages of initiation.

Regarding the second interpretation, that the word refers to "hidden objects" which are revealed to the devotees, one must acknowledge that the balance of probability is against the chance that a masculine noun should refer to objects. Again, this understanding of *cryfios* involves the lack of the name of the grade of initiation, which one would expect to find in connection with the citation of the other grades.

Against the third proposal, that the Latin word represents γρύψ, is the total absence of griffins both in Mithraic art and in all other Mithraic sources.[2]

The fourth interpretation, born no doubt of a desire to find a place in the hierarchy of initiations for the serpent which figures in almost every representation of the tauroctony, has no cogent evidence in its favor and must remain a mere conjecture.

Finally, though the last mentioned proposal attempts to restate the first interpretation without involving any ceremony, it must be recognized that, had such groups of, so-to-speak, Mithraic catechumens existed, it is altogether probable that more information would have been preserved about them in other sources.

If, however, there really was a grade of initiation involving *cryfios* (*chryfios*), the significance of which eludes us, how should it be related to St. Jerome's testimony? Is it possible that local congre-

---

[1] "Les cryfii des inscriptions mithriaïques," in *Hommages à Waldemar Deonna* (Brussels, 1957), pp. 517-530.

[2] Cf. Cumont, *Textes et Monuments*; Johannes Leipoldt, *Die Religion des Mithra* (= Hans Haas' *Bilderatlas zur Religionsgeschichte*, Lieferung xv [Leipzig, 1930]); and Fritz Saxl, *Mithras; typengeschichtliche Untersuchungen* (Berlin, 1931).

gations of Mithraists may have devised certain "heretical"[1] grades of initiation and that the *cryfii* belonged to such a grade? Scholars customarily refer to Porphyry, *De abstinentia*, iv, 16, for evidence as to the existence of local or provincial grades of initiation other than the seven mentioned by St. Jerome. This writer makes the surprising assertions not only that there were initiates called ἀετοί and ἱέρακες but also that there was a female grade in the cult whose initiates he names ὕαιναι.[2] It is, however, not at all clear that Porphyry's evidence can be trusted. In the first place, the immediate context is obviously corrupt, and Nauck, the editor of the Teubner text, prints the passage with an indication of a lacuna.[3] In the second place, there is really no other evidence, whether documentary, epigraphical, or monumental, which gives the slightest hint that women took any part in the Mithraic cultus.[4] Not only has no woman left her name in the numerous records of Mithraic communities, but even when one should expect to find such a reference it is lacking. For instance, in an inscription[5] which enumerates in

---

[1] Perhaps the word "heretical" is too strong and the adjective "divergent" should be used; in any case, however, there is ample evidence that in more than one respect the symbolism expressed in Mithraic artifacts discovered at Rome differs in significant details from that preserved elsewhere (see M. J. Vermaseren, *De Mithrasdienst in Rome*, Diss. [Nijmegen, 1951], pp. 111ff.; Engl. summary, pp. 150ff.). Unfortunately the mural paintings in the Mithraeum of S. Prisca in Rome, which depicts a procession of the seven grades, is very badly preserved at several places, including the representation of the grade of the *Nymphi*. Since each of the grades is mentioned in the plural, Vermaseren thinks that they may may be intended to be representative of all Mithraic grades in the Empire. He continues, "This is important as it may suggest that the Mithraeum on the Aventine with its side chapels was, in the third century, the capital *spelaeum* connected with the official state cult" (M. J. Vermaseren and C. C. van Essen, *The Excavations in the Mithraeum of the Church of Santa Prisca in Rome* [Leiden, 1965], p. 158).

[2] This word is usually emended to λέαιναι. Accepting the emendation as valid, M. Clermont-Ganneau thought that he had discovered some evidence in North Africa which substantiated Porphyry's (emended) statement that women were called "lionesses" in the Mithraic cultus (*Comptes rendus de l'Académie des inscriptions et belles-lettres*, 1903, pp. 357-363). On the tombs of a man and his wife at Guigariche in Tripoli are the picture of a lion and the inscription [qu]i leo iacet and the picture of a lioness and the inscription quae lea iacet. Since, however, there is nothing which connects either person with the Mithraic religion, it must be concluded that the inscription on the woman's tomb is not germane to the argument.

[3] The text of Nauck (254, 6-9) is: ... ὡς τοὺς μὲν μετέχοντας τῶν αὐτῶν ὀργίων μύστας λέοντας καλεῖν, τὰς δὲ γυναῖκας λεαίνας, τοὺς δὲ ὑπηρετοῦντας κόρακας, ἐπί τε τῶν πατέρων ... ἀετοὶ γὰρ καὶ ἱέρακες οὗτοι προσαγορεύονται.

[4] See note 2 above.

[5] *C.I.L.*, VI, 1779 (= Dessau, 1259).

parallel fashion the religious titles of a husband and wife, though
both are said to have been initiated into several religious cults, it
is only the man who is commemorated as a devotee of Mithra.[1]
Likewise, the fact that frequently a sanctuary of Cybele (Magna
Mater) was built near or contiguous to a Mithraeum seems to
suggest that women had no part or lot in the Persian cult.[2] Because,
therefore, it is exceedingly difficult to place any credence in Porphyry's statement that women were initiated in Mithraism, it is
correspondingly doubtful how much reliance can be placed on his
testimony concerning the existence of the grades of "eagles" and
"falcons."[3] It must be concluded, therefore, that no certain and

---

[1] He was *sacratus Libero et Eleusi*[*ni*]*s*; she was *sacrata Cereri et Eleusiniis*.
Both were *tauroboliati*, a ceremony attached to the rite of Cybele. He was a
hierophant, she a hierophantria (of the triple Hecate; see *C.I.L.*, VI, 1779,
line 28 [= Dessau, I, 1259, line 28]). He was *pater patrum*, the highest grade
in Mithraism, but she was not even *sacrata Mithrae*. The religious pedigree
of each is given more fully in two other inscriptions (*C.I.L.*, VI, 1778 and 1780
[the latter is reproduced in Dessau, 1260]), but there too the woman's list
makes no reference to Mithraism.

[2] Henri Graillot, *Le Culte de Cybèle, Mère des Dieux, à Rome et dans l'Empire romain* (Paris, 1912), pp. 192f., goes so far as to say that "in almost all
the localities where we find the Goddess, we find Mithra ... One complemented
the other." On the exclusion of women from the Mysteries of Mithra, see
Cumont, *Textes et Monuments*, I, 329f., and Theodor Wächter's comments in
his *Reinheitsvorschriften im griechischen Kult* (= *Religionsgeschichtliche Versuche und Vorarbeiten*, IX, 1; Giessen, 1911), p. 129, n. 2.

[3] No other evidence for the Mithraic grade of falcons is known. With
regard to the grade of eagles, several scholars, beginning with Erwin Rohde
in 1894 (*Psyche; Seelencult und Unsterblichkeitsglaube der Griechen*, 9te/10te
Aufl., II [Leipzig, 1925], 392, Anm. 1 [Eng. trans. from 8th Germ. ed. (London,
1925), p. 576, n. 153]), think that Porphyry's statement is corroborated by
an inscription found on a sarcophagus at Derbe in Lycaonia. The inscription,
published definitively in *Papers of the American School of Classical Studies
at Athens*, III, 26f. (only part of the inscription is provided in *B.C.H.*, X [1886],
510), is as follows: [Λ]ούκιος ἀνέστησε Τήλεφον καὶ Μάρκον καὶ Σέξτο[ν|καὶ]
ἑαυτὸν ἀετὸν καὶ "Αμμουκιν Βαβόου τὸν π[α|τέρα] ἀετὸν τειμῆς χάριν. At first
Cumont refused to accept Rohde's proposed interpretation of the inscription,
making a point of the total lack of Mithraic monuments and inscriptions in
Lycaonia (*Textes et Monuments*, II, 173). But Dieterich (*Bonner Jahrbücher*,
CVIII/CIX [1902], 37), with some degree of justice, sarcastically inquired how
the fact that there were no (other) Mithraic remains in Lycaonia could prove
that this inscription was non-Mithraic. Later the discovery of a Mithraic
bas-relief in Baris (Isbarta), Pisidia, seemed of sufficient significance to
Cumont to decide that Rohde's interpretation was "very probable" (*Revue
de l'histoire des religions*, LXII [1910], 146, n. 2; reprinted in Cumont's *Études
syriennes* [Paris, 1917], p. 57, n. 3). Still later Cumont returned to his former
opinion ("Mithra en Asie Mineure," in *Anatolian Studies Presented to William
Hepburn Buckler* [Manscheter, 1939], p. 71, n. 3). The plain fact is that
absolutely nothing in the inscription except the point in dispute gives any

unequivocal evidence points to the presence of variations from the norm in Mithraic initiations, and the suggestion that *cryfios (chryfios)* be interpreted as involving such a "heretical" divergence must remain no more than a mere suggestion.

The one assured conclusion of this investigation is that, although there may or may not have been a grade of Mithraic initiation designated *cryfios (chryfios)*, it will no longer be licit to emend St. Jerome's text to make him bear witness to its existence at the expense of eliminating from his text the grade *nymphus*.

---

warrant for regarding it as Mithraic, and Porphyry's statement, in a corrupt context, is still the only evidence for the Mithraic grade of eagles. The quotation that Franz Boll (*Archiv für Religionswissenschaft*, XIX [1916-19], 553f.) adduces with so much confidence from the second Teukros text (edited by him in *Sphaera* [Leipzig, 1903], p. 50, lines 15-18: ὁ ἀετὸς [δηλοῖ] μύστας, φανταζομένους πρόσωπα βασιλικά, ἢ περὶ βασιλεῖς ὄντας) does not prove that the eagle was a *Mithraic* grade of initiation. Nor again is Dieterich's emendation at the beginning of the so-called Mithraic liturgy germane to the problem (*Eine Mithrasliturgie*, 3te Aufl., 1923, p. 2: ὅπως ἐγὼ μόνος αἰητὸς [MS αιητης] οὐρανὸν βαίνω καὶ κατοπτεύω πάντα, cf. also pp. 54 and 220; other emendations equally appropriate—or inappropriate!—in the context are given by Karl Preisendanz, *Papyri graecae magicae*, 1 [Leipzig and Berlin, 1928], 89). On the paucity of Mithraic remains in Asia Minor, see Cumont, *Les Religions orientales dans le Paganisme romain*, 4ᵐᵉ éd. (Paris, 1929), pp. 132f. and 274, n. 23; *idem, Die Mysterien des Mithra*, deutsche Ausg. von G. Gehrich, 3te Aufl. besorgt von K. Latte (Leipzig and Berlin, 1923), p. 229; and Wüst, *op. cit.*, col. 2151.

CHAPTER THREE

A GREEK AND ARAMAIC INSCRIPTION
DISCOVERED AT ARMAZI IN GEORGIA

In the autumn of 1940 the Georgian archaeologist, the late I. Javakhishvili, excavated a tomb, dating from the second century A.D., in the region of Armazi,[1] the ancient capital of Iberia (Georgia). In the course of the excavation five inscriptions were discovered, three in Greek, one in Aramaic, and one in Greek and Aramaic. The three Greek inscriptions, which are brief and of much less interest and importance than the bilingual inscription, are as follows.[2]

(1) A gem with the portrait of a man bears the inscription Ἀσπαυροῦκις πιτιάξης, "Aspauroukis the pitiax." On the title, pitiax, see below.

(2) A gem with two portraits, one of a woman and the other of a man, bears the inscription Κάρπακ Ζευάχης ζοή [i.e., ζωή] μου. On the man's name, see below where it reappears under the form Ζηουάχης.

(3) A silver cup carries around its circumference the words Ἐγὼ

---

[1] The ruins of Armazi are two km. northwest of Mtzkheta (Mcḫeta) and 22 km. north of Tiflis, the present capital of Georgia. The ancient geographers (e.g., Strabo xi. 501) spelled the name Ἁρμοζική; see also Tomaschek in Pauly-Wissowa, *Real-Encyclopädie*, II, col. 1177.

[2] The three short Greek inscriptions were edited in Georgian, with a summary in Russian, by S. G. Qaukhchishvili in *Soobschcheniya akademii nauk gruzinskoĭ SSR*, II (1941), 169-76. This publication has not been available to me, and for knowledge of its contents I have depended on H. S. Nyberg, "Quelques inscriptions antiques découvertes récemment en Géorgie," *Eranos, acta philologica suecana*, XLIV (1946), 228-43, and on G. V. Tseret'eli, "Epigraficheskie nakhodki v Mtzheta—drevneĭ stolitze Gruzii," *Vestnik drevneĭ istorii*, II [XXIV] (1948), 49-57.

According to Nyberg, *op. cit.*, p. 232, Qaukhchishvili explains Δάδης in the third Greek inscription as a Georgian name, *Dadi*. It ought to be added to Nyberg's discussion that what is fundamentally the same name, Δάδα (genitive case; compare one other instance of this name in F. Preisigke, *Namenbuch* [Heidelberg, 1922]), occurs in a hitherto neglected Greek inscription from the early second century of the Christian era which is now in the Museum at Temruk; see N. I. Novosadskiĭ, "Neizdannaya nadpis Temryukaskogo muzeya," *Doklady akademii nauk SSR*, B, 1930, pp. 224-27 (line 9 of the inscription).

βασιλεὺς Φλ[αύιος] Δάδης ἐχαρισάμην Βερσοῦμα πιτιάξῃ, "I, King Flavius Dades, have given [this cup] to Bersouma the pitiax." Bersouma is undoubtedly the well-known Syriac name, Bar-ṣaumā. It has been established from various historical sources that during the first half of the first millennium of the Christian era a colony of Syrians lived in central Georgia.[1]

(4) The Aramaic inscription has most recently been discussed by Altheim and Stiehl.[2]

(5) The bilingual inscription, which forms the basis of this study, is a Greek and Aramaic epitaph of exceptional interest and importance. It was published in 1941 by G. V. Tseret'eli with an extensive discussion in Russian dealing with epigraphical, linguistic, and historical considerations;[3] in the following year, Tseret'eli republished his study in Georgian, supplying at the same time an abbreviated account in English.[4]

From Tseret'eli's description and photographs of the tombstone of the following description has been compiled.

---

[1] Cf. Harnack in *Sitzungsberichte der königlich preussischen Akademie der Wissenschaften zu Berlin*, 1901, p. 882, Anm. 5, and, more recently, N. Pigulevskaja's thorough study of the Syriac sources for the history of the peoples of Russia (*Sirisǐkie istochniki po istorii narodov SSSR* [Leningrad, 1941]).

[2] A preliminary transcription of the first three lines of the inscription, with a tentative translation in Russian, is supplied by Tseret'eli on p. 62 of the volume described in the following footnote. The entire inscription, with a plate, is available in Franz Altheim and Ruth Stiehl, "Die Zweite (aramäische) Inschrift von Mcḥet'a," *Forschungen und Fortschritte*, XXXV (1961), 172-178; reprinted in their volume *Die aramäische Sprache unter den Achaimeniden*, I, *Geschichtliche Untersuchungen* (Frankfurt am Main, 1963), pp. 243-261.

[3] The volume has title pages in Russian, English, and Georgian. The first two title pages are as follows: G. V. Tsereteli, *Armazskaya bilingva, dvujazychnaja nadpis; naïdennaja pri arkheologicheskikh raskopkakh v Mtzkheta-Armazi* (Akademija nauk gruzinskoĭ SSR, Institut istorii). Tbilisi: Izdatelstov akademii nauk gruzinskoĭ SSR, 1941.

George Tsereteli, *A Bilingual Inscription from Armazi near Mthskheta in Georgia* (The Academy of Sciences of the Georgian SSR. The Institute of History). Tbilisi: Publishing House of the Academy of Sciences of the Georgian SSR, 1941.

[4] Tseret'eli's study is Vol. XIII of *The Bulletin of the Marr Institute of Languages, History and Material Culture*. Bibliographical details of the single title page are as follows: Giorgi Tseret'eli, *Armazis bilingva. A Bilingual Inscription from Armazi near Mcḥeta in Georgia*, by George Tseretheli. Tiflis: Sakartvelos SSR mecnierebata Ak'ademia—The Academy of Sciences of the Georgian SSR, 1942. Georgian text, pp. 1-48, English text, pp. 49-83, 4 plates. The Georgian form of the monograph has several footnotes not present in the Russian form.

A slab of basalt (see Plate I A), roughly rounded at the top and measuring 1.92 m. high and 64-66 cm. broad, contains two similar but slightly divergent forms of a funerary inscription. At the top of the stela the Greek epitaph of ten lines occupies an area of 31 × 62 cm.; underneath this the Aramaic inscription of eleven lines occupies an area of 63 × 61.5 cm. The Aramaic portion supplies examples of all twenty-two letters of the alphabet,[1] as well as signs indicating the numeral 21. Tseret'eli proposes to call this script, which in some respects is a new variety of Aramaic, Armazian Aramaic. On the basis of various considerations he inclines to date the stela in the second century of the Christian era. The inscription possesses therefore considerable significance for the epigrapher in tracing the development of writing in Georgia as well as for the historian in studying the cultural and social life of ancient Georgia.

In the following transcription the Greek majuscules of the epitaph are represented by lower case letters, and accent and breathing marks (lacking in the inscription) have been supplied. The Armazian Aramaic script is represented here by means of the conventional square Hebrew characters. The *scriptio continua* of both portions of the inscription has been divided into words.

TEXT

Σηραπεῖτις Ζηουάχου
τοῦ νεωτέρου πιτιάξου
θυγάτηρ, Πουπλικίου Ἀγρίππα πιτι-
άξου υἱοῦ Ἰωδμανγάνου γυνὴ
5 τοῦ πολλὰς νείκας ποιήσαντος,

---

[1] A small-sized reproduction of the Aramaic portion of the inscription may be seen in David Diringer, *The Alphabet, a Key to the History of Mankind*, 2nd ed. (New York, 1953), p. 268. For a comparative tabulation of eight alphabets having an Aramaic base, including the alphabets used in the Armazian inscription as well as in a still more recently discovered group of more than one thousand ostraca (dating from the first century B.C.) from the ruins of ancient Nisa in Parthia, see I. M. Djakonov, M. M. Djakonov, and W. A. Livshits, "Parfyanskij arkhiv iz drevnej Nisy," *Vestnik drevneĭ istorii*, IV (1953), 114-30 (German translation, "Das parthische Archiv aus dem antiken Nisā," *Sowjetwissenschaft, Gesellschaftswissenschaftliche Abteilung*, 1954, pp. 557-77); for further studies of this important find, see the articles by I. N. Vinnikov in *Vestnik drevneĭ istorii*, II (1954), 114ff., and M. M. Djakonov, *ibid.*, IV (1954), 169-73. Sixteen of the Nisa texts have been edited by M. Sznycer, "Ostraca d'époque parthe trouvés à Nisa (U.R.S.S.)," *Semitica*, V (1955), 67-98.

ἐπιτρόπου βασιλέως Ἰβήρων
μεγάλου Ξηφαρνούγου, ἀπέ-
θανε νεωτέρα ἐτῶν κ̄ᾱ,
ἥτις τὸ κάλλος ἀμείμητον
10 εἶχε.

אנה סערפיט ברתי זי
זיוח קליל בטחש זי פרסמן
מלך אנתת זי יודמנגן ונציח
וכביר ארוסת עבידא רב
15 תרבץ זי חסיפרנוג מלך ברי
זי אגריף רב תרבץ זי
פרסמן מלך חבל חבליך מא
זי פרנוש לא גמיר והכין
טב ושפיר יהוה היך זי בר
20 איניש לא דמע יהוה מן
טבות ומאיתין בשנת כא·

TRANSLATION[1]

"Serapitis, daughter of Zewaḥ the younger, pitiax, wife of the
son of pitiax Publicius Agrippa, Yodmangan, (5) he who has gained
many victories as steward of the great king of the Iberians, Xepharnūg—she died too young, [being] twenty-one years [of age], she
who had inimitable beauty.

(11) "I am Serapit, daughter of Zewaḥ the younger, bitaḫš of
Parsman the king, wife of Yodmangan—both victorious and having
wrought many victories [as] chief (15) of the court of Ḥsepharnug
the king—son of Agrippa, chief of the court of Parsman the king.
Woe, woe [for her] who did not reach full age, incomplete, and so
good and beautiful that (20) no one was like her in goodness—she
died in [her] twenty-first year."

COMMENTS

The Greek text involves three instances of itacism where ει is
written in the place of ι: Σηραπεῖτις (line 1), νεῖκας (line 5), and
ἀμείμητον (line 9). Palaeographically the Greek letters are without
any special or distinguishing traits.

---

[1] At several points the translation of the Aramaic portion of the inscription
is tentative, being one of several possible renderings. See the linguistic
comments for alternative renderings.

In several points the Aramaic, *qua* Aramaic, is ungrammatical;[1] e.g., the feminine gender of Serapit is totally neglected in the phrase which describes her beauty (line 19), and the form מאיתין (line 21), which is the masculine plural, expresses the idea "she died," ἀπέθανε. Furthermore, in more than one instance Pahlavi elements are present; e.g., the third singular pronominal suffix, -š, appears in line 18.

The presence of such anomalous forms has led several scholars to raise the question whether the inscription was intended to be read in Aramaic. Nyberg, who reconstructed an Arsacid text of the inscription, contended that the text should be read in Iranian.[2] Frye, following a suggestion made by Freiman,[3] has argued that the Armazian inscription by heterography represents a form of ancient Georgian written in Aramaic. Altheim and Stiehl pointed out, however, that such a hypothesis "ist eine Möglichkeit, die sich vornherein weder bejahen noch verneinen lässt."[4] Subsequently Frye, reiterating his view that it is not to be read as Aramaic, suggested that "the inscription might be read in MP [Middle Persian]."[5]

---

[1] The irregularities remind one of somewhat similar features in the Aramaic words of Sassanian inscriptions; see W. B. Henning, "The Monuments and Inscriptions of Tang-i Sarvak," *Asia Major*, N.S. II (1952), 151-78; Altheim and Stiehl, "Pahlawīk and Pārsīk," *Parola del passato, rivista di studi classica*, fasc. XXXI (1953), 307-17; the articles by Djakonov, *et al.*, referred to above, p. 36, note 1; and Altheim and Stiehl, "Das Pahlawīk-Pergament von Āwromān," in the journal published at Osaka by the Paleological Association of Japan, entitled *Palaeologia*, III (1954), 45-51.

[2] Nyberg, *op. cit.*, pp. 234f.

[3] Frye, *op. cit.*, p. 96, refers to A. A. Freiman, "Neskol'ko zamečanij k Armazskoj bilingve G. V. Cereteli," *Izvestija akademii nauk*, otdelenie literatury i jazyka, V (1946), 156ff.

[4] Altheim and Stiehl, *Das erste Auftreten der Hunnen ...*, p. 59.

[5] *Bibliotheca orientalis*, XI, No. 3/4 (Mai-Juli, 1954), 134, to which Altheim and Stiehl make reply in their *Ein asiatischer Staat, Feudalismus unter den Sassaniden und ihren Nachbarn*, I (Wiesbaden, 1954), 293-94. Compare also Frye's contribution, "Pahlevi Heterography in Ancient Georgia?" to *Archaeologica orientalia in memoriam Ernst Herzfeld* (Locust Valley, N.Y., 1952), pp. 89-101. More recently Frye expressed himself somewhat more guardedly: "The question whether the Armazi inscriptions are written in ungrammatical Aramaic or in heterographic ancient Georgian or in an Iranian tongue is not resolved" (*The Heritage of Persia* [Cleveland and New York, 1963], p. 267 note 37). A somewhat similar situation is reflected in the important Greek and Aramaic inscription of Aśoka discovered in Afghanistan; cf. *A Bilingual Graeco-Aramiac Edict by Aśoka; The First Greek Inscription Discovered in Afghanistan*, Text, Translation and Notes by G. Pugliese Carratelli and G. Garbini, Foreword by G. Tucci, Introduction by U. Scerrato (Rome, 1964). For an interesting map showing the several scores of places at which Aramaic inscriptions have been found in the Near and Middle East, see J. T. Koopmans, *Aramäische Chrestomathie. Ausgewählte Texte (Inschriften, Ostraka und*

Impressed by the circumstance that almost all of the approximately fifty words in the second part of the inscription (with the exception of the proper names) are *prima facie* Aramaic, the present writer will refer to this portion as Aramaic without prejudging the question whether it is a corrupt form of Aramaic or whether by heterography it was intended to be read as something else.

Differences between the two parts of the inscription include the following. (*a*) The Aramaic has nothing corresponding to Πουπλικίου 'Αγρίππα (line 3) and 'Ιβήρων μεγάλου (lines 6 and 7). (*b*) On the other hand, the Greek lacks several features of the Aramaic: the opening word אנה; the phrase פרסמן מלך which follows the title given to Zewaḥ (lines 12 and 13) and to Agrippa (line 17); and the exclamation חבל חבליך (line 17). (*c*) The same Aramaic phrase רב תרבץ (lines 14, 15, and 16) corresponds to both πιτιάξης (line 3) and ἐπίτροπος (line 6). (*d*) The order followed is not quite the same. This is especially noticeable in the last lines of each part.

Line 1. The name Zewaḥ occurs on the gem described above (where it is spelled Ζευάχης). Justi, who lists a certain Ζευάκος, compares the Avestan *zaoya* (accus. *zewīm*) meaning "strong, mighty."[1]

Line 2. The office of pitiax was one of the highest in the provincial administration of the Parthian Empire. The word appears in a variety of spellings. The remarkable trilingual inscription (in Pahlavi, Parsic, and Greek), discovered in the so-called Kaʿaba of Zoroaster near Persepolis, contains two Greek forms of the word, πιτιάξ[ης] (as here in the Armazi inscription) and βιδιξ.[2] In Pahlavi texts the title appears as *bitaχš*[3] (compare בטחש in line 12), which was borrowed by the Armenians under the form *bdeašχ*.[4] Whether the fact that occasionally Agathangelos and Faustos of

Papyri) *bis zum 3. Jahrhundert n. Chr.*, I. Teil, *Einleitungen, Literatur und Kommentare* (Leiden, 1962), facing p. 1.

[1] Ferdinand Justi, *Iranisches Namenbuch* (Marburg, 1895), p. 385.

[2] Edited in a rather unsatisfactory and incomplete manner by Martin Sprengling, *American Journal of Semitic Languages and Literatures*, LVII (1940), 341-420; see especially pp. 410 and 412; and re-edited in part by G. P. Carratelli, *Parola del passato*, fasc. IV (1947), 209-39, 356-62, see especially p. 237.

[3] Ernst Herzfeld, *Paikuli*, I (Berlin, 1924), pp. 155f.; and Antonio Pagliaro, "Il testo pahlavico Ayātkār-i-Zarērān," *Rendiconti della R. accademia nazionale dei Lincei*, Classe di scienze, morali, storiche e filologiche, VI ser., I (1925), 569.

[4] H. Hübschmann, *Armenische Grammatik*, I. Theil, *Armenische Etymologie* (Leipzig, 1897), pp. 119f.

Byzantium refer to the *bdeašχ* of Ałdznik as "the great *bdeašχ*"[1] implies a gradation of authority among those of this rank is not clear.[2] The corresponding Georgian form, *pit'iaχši* (*pat'iaχši*), is represented in Greek on a sardonyx from the fifth century belonging to a certain notable named Ašuša, who is characterized as [AC]-ΟΥϹΑϹ ΠΙΤΙΑΞΗϹ ΙΒΗΡΩΝ ΚΑΡΧΗΔΩΝ.[3] The sixth-century Acts of the Martyrdom of Saint Eustatius of Mtzkheta (near which this bilingual inscription was found) refers to a *pit'iaχši* named Arbuba (or Arschuscha).[4] In Syriac two forms of the title have been preserved. The so-called *Ecclesiastical History* by Zacharias Rhetor (of Mitylene) speaks of the ܒܝܛܝܐܫ,[5] and in the Syriac narratives of the Persian Martyrs it is spelled ܒܝܛܝܐ.[6] In the Talmud one finds ברקשא (Sab. 110*a*) which, according to Siegmund Fraenkel, must be read בדקשא.[7] In Latin Ammianus Marcellinus of the fourth century refers to the *vitaxae* (the initial *v* of course represents *b*) as leaders in the Persian provinces.[8] Probably βατησα, found in a con-

---

[1] Agathangelos, 596, and Faustos of Byzantium, 21 and 211. In the Arabic translation of Agathangelos the title appears as بطشق (so N. Marr, *Kreščenie armyan, gruzin, abkhazov i alanov svyatym Grigoriem*, p. 114).

[2] See J. Marquart's excursus, "Die armenischen Markgrafen (bdeašxkʻ)," in his *Eranšahr nach der Geographie des Ps. Moses Xorenacʻi* (Berlin, 1901), pp. 165ff. (= *Abhandlungen der könig. Gesell. d. Wiss. zu Göttingen*, Phil.-hist. Kl., N.F., III, No. 2).

[3] First published by V. Langlois in *Revue archéologique*, VIII (1852), 530-32, and most recently by Herzfeld, *op. cit.*, p. 78, no. 3. Curiously, the line drawings of the gem in the two publications differ as to the spelling of the title; according to Langlois it is clearly πητιάξης and according to Herzfeld it is just as clearly πιτιάξης!

[4] Prince Dschawachoff and Ad. von Harnack, "Das Martryium des heiligen Eustatius von Mzchetha, aus dem Georgischen übersetzt," *Sitzungsb. d. könig. preuss. Akad. d. Wiss. zu Berlin*, 1901, p. 880, Anm. 4. Tseretʻeli supplies several other examples of the occurrence of the word in ancient Georgian literature.

[5] Ed. by J. P. N. Land, *Anecdota syriaca*, III (Leiden, 1870), p. 253, line 10; p. 259, line 1, 13, 25; p. 260, line 1ff.; and by E. W. Brooks, *CSCO*, LXXXIV, *Scriptores syri*, XXXIX (Ser. III, tom. vi; Paris, 1921), p. 88, line 18; p. 96, lines 2, 17; p. 97, lines 5, 9ff.).

[6] Paul Bedjan, ed., *Acta martyrum et sanctorum*, III, 497, line 17, and IV, 221, line 17, and n. 1; see Mrs. J. P. Margoliouth's *Supplement to the Thesaurus Syriacus* (Oxford, 1927), p. 262, *s. v.*

[7] So Fraenkel in a communication to Nöldeke, published in *Zeitschrift der deutschen morgenländischen Gesellschaft*, XLIV (1890), 532; cf. Nöldeke, *ibid.*, XXXIII (1879), 159, Anm. 2.

[8] Ammianus Marc. xxiii. 6, 14, Sunt autem in omni Perside, hae regiones maximae, quas vitaxae (id est magistri equitum) curant, et reges et satrapae —nam minores plurimas recensere difficile est et superfluum—Assyria, Susiana, Media, Persis, Parthia, etc.

tract preserved at Dura-Europos, also represents the Iranian title.[1] At the beginning of the eighth century in the *Chronology* of Theophanes we meet a leader of the Alanen with the title Ἰτάξης.[2]

It may be, as Pagliaro attempted to show in an important article[3] (of which unfortunately Tseret'eli made no use), that the functions exercised by the official who is often referred to as "The Eye of the King"[4] during the Achaemenid era were taken over during the Sassanian era by the *bitaχš*.[5]

Tseret'eli argues that τοῦ νεωτέρου πιτιάξου, in view of the Aramaic קליל בטחש, must mean "young, or junior pitiax," and that therefore this inscription discloses a hitherto unattested feature[6] of ancient Iberian state-organization, involving various ranks within the broad category of pitiax. On the contrary, however, the overwhelming usage of the Greek epithet νεώτερος elsewhere, as Tod points out,[7] suggests that the word here is to be construed with the preceding proper name, "Zewaḥ the younger." See also line 12.

Line 3. Πουπλικίου, i.e., Publicius.

Line 4. The first part of the name Ἰωδμαγάνου (see also line 13) is found in the name Yōδmart in the inscription on the Ka'aba and in the Soghdian Yōδarazmak (ywδrzmk).[8]

Line 7. Qaukhchishvili, according to Tseret'eli, takes μεγάλου with what follows (i.e., "the king of the Iberians, great Xepharnūg"), but this is far less natural than the construction adopted in the

---

[1] Edited by M. I. Rostovtzeff and C. Bradford Welles, *Yale Classical Studies*, II (1931), 51; cf. Paul Koschaker, *Abhandlungen der sächsischen Akad. d. Wiss.*, Phil.-hist. Kl., XLII, 1 (1931), 5.

[2] Theophanes, *Chronographia*, ed. de Boor, 1 (Leipzig, 1883), 392, 27 (A.M. 6209 = A.D. 717); see also J. Marquart, *Osteuropäische und ostasiatische Streifzüge* (Leipzig, 1903), p. 168.

[3] A. Pagliaro, "Mediopersiano *bitaχš*, armeno *bdeaš̌χ*: ὁ ὀφθαλμὸς τοῦ βασιλέως," *Rivista degli studi orientali*, XII (1929/30), 160-68.

[4] E.g., Xenophon, *Cyr.*, viii. 6, 16; cf. Suidas, *s. v.* ὀφθαλμὸς βασιλέως.

[5] For other discussions of the etymology and meaning of πιτιάξης see Paul de Lagarde, *Gesammelte Abhandlungen* (Leipzig, 1866), pp. 187f.; R. von Stackelberg, "Beiträge zur persischen Lexikographie," *Wiener Zeitschrift für die Kunde des Morgenlandes*, XVII (1903), 52f.; N. C. Debevoise, *A Political History of Parthia* (Chicago, 1938), p. 241, n. 5; and Arthur Christensen, *L'Iran sous les Sassanides*, 2e éd. (Copenhagen, 1944), pp. 22f. and 102.

[6] Unless the occasional reference to the *bdeaš̌χ* of Ałdznik as "the great *bdeaš̌χ*" (see above, p. 40) can be construed as evidence for such differentiation in rank.

[7] M. N. Tod, *Journal of Roman Studies*, XXXIII (1943), 84.

[8] Hans Reichelt, *Die soghdischen Handschriftenreste des Britischen Museums*, II (Heidelberg, 1931), glos.

translation given above. The name Ξηφάρνουγος is apparently unknown outside this bilingual inscription; perhaps Ξιφάρης is a variation.[1] Nyberg[2] points out that the first part of the word is obviously related to the Iranian root *hšāy-* "to rule."

Line 8. The words ἀπέθανε νεωτέρα ἐτῶν κα̅ may be construed in three different ways: (*a*) "she died young, in [her] twenty-first year" (so Tseret'eli); (*b*) "she died [being] younger than twenty-one years" (so Tod); (*c*) "she died too young, [being] twenty-one years [of age]" (suggested to me by Professor A. E. Raubitschek, formerly of Princeton University and The Institute for Advanced Study, now of Stanford University). Plausible reasons can be found supporting each of these translations: (*a*) Hesychius observed that νεώτερον οὐ μόνον συγκριτικῶς, ἀλλὰ καὶ νέον 'Αττικοί (cf., in addition to the examples which Liddell and Scott cite for this usage, the Septuagint Judg. 8.20, Ps. 36.25 (26), and 148.12); (*b*) more than one inscription can be found which contains the genitive of comparison after νεώτερος;[3] (*c*) the elative use of the comparative[4] agrees with the sense of the corresponding part of the Aramaic text.

Line 11. The use of the first person at the beginning of the Aramaic inscription reminds one of the so-called "I-style" which not infrequently is found in certain ancient religious and quasi-religious texts.[5] The spelling אנה, which Frye strangely thinks is erroneous,[6] has parallels in the Aramaic of other places and times.[7]

---

[1] Justi, *op. cit.*, p. 176.

[2] *Op. cit.*, p. 239.

[3] Tod cites the following examples, *IG*, v (1), 1390, 123; xii (7), 54, 14; xii (9), 194, 6.

[4] An example frequently cited by grammarians (e.g., Eduard Schwyzer, *Griechische Grammatik*, ii [München, 1950], 184) is *Odyssey* 21.132, νεώτερός εἰμι, "I am too young."

[5] See Eduard Norden, *Agnostos Theos* (Leipzig, 1913), pp. 189ff.; Eduard Schweizer, 'Εγώ εἰμι ... *Die religionsgeschichtliche Herkunft und theologische Bedeutung der johanneischen Bildrenen* ... (Göttingen, 1939), pp. 38f. and Franz Altheim, *Literatur und Gesellschaft im ausgehenden Altertum*, i (Halle/Salle, 1948), 243ff. For further examples, preserved in Coptic, see A. M. Kropp, *Ausgewählte koptische Zaubertexte* (Bruxelles, 1931), nos. ii, v, and vi. Cf. also the survey by the Latvian scholar, Karlis Kundzinš, "Zur Diskussion über die Ego-Emi-Sprüche des Johannesevangeliums," in *Charisteria Iohanni Kôpp octogenario oblata* (Stockholm, 1954), pp. 95-107.

[6] Frye in *Herzfeld Festschrift*, p. 94 (see above, p. 38, note 5).

[7] On the spelling אנה see Hans Reichelt, "Aramäische Inschriften aus Kappadocien," *Wiener Zeitschrift für die Kunde des Morgenlandes*, xv (1901), 51-56, and M. Lidzbarski, *Ephemeris für semitische Epigraphik*, i (1902), 321. Cf. Uto Melzer, "Zur Aussprache der aramäischen Wörter im Mittelpersischen," *Zeitschrift für Semitistik und verwandte Gebiete*, v (1927), 312-38,

The relative זי (which appears eight times in this inscription) is generally considered to be typical of Old Aramaic.[1]

Line 12. The meaning and reference of קליל are disputed. Tseret'eli is convinced that it means "junior" and that it goes with the following title, *bitaḫš* (see above on νεωτέρου, line 2). It must be noted, however, that in general Aramaic prefers to place the adjective after the noun it qualifies, and that probably the sense of the Greek (which is almost certainly "Zewaḫ the younger") should be allowed to influence one's understanding of the corresponding Aramaic.

The name פרטמן appears in Armenian as *Pʿarsman*, in Greek as Φαρασμάνης or Φαρισμάνης, and in Latin as *Pharasmanes*. History knows of five kings of Georgia bearing this name, from the first century to the middle of the sixth century.[2]

Line 14. The word ארוסת, which Tseret'eli could not identify, is, according to Bailey[3] and Nyberg,[4] the Old Persian *aruvasta-*, a word of disputed meaning but which here, being parallel to the Greek νείκας, may signify something like "victorious."[5]

Line 15. To the examples of תרבץ (also in line 16) previously noted in the lexica, add its occurrence in G. R. Driver's edition of *Aramaic Documents of the Fifth Century B.C.* (Oxford, 1954).[6]

On the name Ḥsepharnug, see above on line 7.

Line 17. Nyberg thinks that חבל חבליך represents the indigenous name of the Georgians, but confesses that "j'ignore comment il faut le lire et l'expliquer."[7] In the Palmyrene grave-inscriptions, however, the word חבל occurs frequently as an exclamation of grief ("alas!").[8] The chief problem here involves the termination ־יך

---

especially p. 323. Besides appearing consistently in biblical Aramaic, the form also is frequently found in texts included in *The Brooklyn Museum Aramaic Papyri*, ed. Emil G. Kraeling (New Haven, 1953).

[1] To the examples cited in the lexica (e.g., Charles-F. Jean, *Dictionnaire des inscriptions sémitiques de l'ouest*, fasc. 1 [Leiden, 1954], s. v.), add those in Kraeling, *op. cit.*, and in *Aramaic Documents of the Fifth Century B.C.*, ed. G. R. Driver (Oxford, 1954).

[2] Justi, *op. cit.*, p. 91.

[3] *Op. cit.*, pp. 2f.

[4] *Op. cit.*, p. 239.

[5] Pierre Grelot, however, thinks that "victorieux" is too precise a translation and prefers "habiléte"; see his "Remarques sur le bilingue grec-araméen d'Armazi," *Semitica*, VIII (1958), pp. 14f.

[6] See especially Driver's note, *op. cit.*, p. 25.

[7] *Op. cit.*, p. 239.

[8] Many examples are conveniently found in J. Cantineau, *Inventaire des*

added to the second occurrence of the word. Tseret'eli points out
that it may be considered as the Pahlavi suffix -*ik* or the Aramaic
second person singular suffix. Altheim and Stiehl propose the emendation of a final *n* for the final *k* (i.e. "Verderbnis der Verderbnisse"),
remarking, "Den Aberglauben, dass konjekturen allein in Handschriften erlaubt, in Inschriften unzulässig seien, haben wir nie ge-
teilt."[1] On the contrary, however, the present writer must confess
a certain sympathy with the point of view expressed by Frye in
his rejection of this conjectural emendation ("To hammer the inscription into correct Aramaic by reading what is not there is
unacceptable").[2]

Line 18. Bailey interprets the word פרנוש, which Tseret'eli did
not recognize, as "probably a modification defectively written of an
Old Iran. **aprnāyuš* 'not of full age.' "[3]

Lines 19-20. The word בראינש, which strangely enough Nyberg
finds difficult,[4] is without doubt the common Aramaic expression
for "someone" (literally "son of man; a man"), cf. biblical Aramaic
בַּר אֲנָשׁ, Syriac ܒܰܪ ܢܳܫܳܐ.

Line 21. The formation of the numeral representing 20 is curious.
It consists of two angles, placed one above the other, facing left.
As Tseret'eli suggests, the numeral gives the impression that it
consists of two signs, each of which has the value of 10. One might
compare the formation in Greek of the *digamma*, which resembles
two capital gammas, one on top of the other (3 + 3 = 6). The
numeral representing 1 is not simply a vertical line (as in most
other Semitic inscriptions), but is strongly reminiscent of the letter
ז in the Armazian script.

---

inscriptions de Palmyre, IV (Beyrouth, 1930), 25; VII, 24; VIII, *passim*. Cf.
also Cantineau, *Grammaire du palmyrénien épigraphique* (Cairo, 1935), p. 140,
and Franz Rosenthal, *Die Sprache der palmyrenischen Inschriften und ihre
Stellung innerhalb des Aramäischen* (= *Mitteilungen der vorderasiatisch-aegyp-
tischen Gesellschaft*, XLI, 1 [Leipzig, 1936]), p. 83. The geminated form (חבאל
חבאל) appears in Mandaic (Ginza R., 82 *ult.* and 84.11). See also I. N.
Vinnikov's Dictionary of Aramaic Inscriptions in *Palestinskii sbornik*, VII
(70, 1962), 192-237.
    [1] *Das erste Auftreten der Hunnen* ..., p. 57; repeated in Altheim and Stiehl,
Supplementum Aramaicum, Aramäisches aus Iran (Baden-Baden, 1957),
pp. 80f. Grelot (*op. cit.*, p. 18) also prefers to emend the text, and renders
the phrase "Malheur de malheurs!"
    [2] Frye in *Bibliotheca orientalis*, XI, No. 3/4 (Mai-Juli, 1954), 134.
    [3] *Op. cit.*, p. 3.
    [4] *Op. cit.*, pp. 240f.

SUMMARY

Six people are mentioned in the inscription, two kings (Pharsman, Xepharnūg, three dignitaries (Publicius Agrippa, his son Yodmangan, and Zewaḥ), and the deceased young woman (Serapitis, daughter of Zewaḥ and wife of Yodmangan). The relations may be expressed diagrammatically as follows:

KINGS	DIGNITARIES	
Pharsman	Publicius Agrippa	Zewaḥ
Xepharnūg	his son Yodmangan *married*	his daughter Serapitis

Since two successive generations are represented by the officials, it is well within the range of probability that Pharsman was succeeded immediately by Xepharnūg, who is otherwise unknown to history.

The date of the inscription can be fixed within relatively narrow limits, although perhaps not quite so narrow as Tseret'eli attempts to prove. The *terminus a quo*, so the editor argues, must fall sometime within the reign of Hadrian (A.D. 117-138). Tseret'eli bases his argument on the reference to Yodmangan as "ἐπίτροπος of the great king of the Iberians" (line 6), and refers to Hirschfeld's dictum[1] that before the time of Hadrian the word ἐπίτροπος was used to designate a private administrator and from A.D. 142 onwards it comes to be used also of the representative of the Roman Emperor in a province or administrator of the imperial domains. Tseret'eli, however, as well as Hirschfeld, overlooked the evidence of a bilingual inscription from the first century which equates *procurator* with ἐπίτροπος (in Bithynia, A.D. 58).[2]

The *terminus ad quem* of the inscription is even more difficult to determine. Nyberg is impressed by the presence of two Latin names (Flavius, in the third Greek inscription mentioned above, and Publicius in the bilingual inscription) and argues that these suggest that the Roman influence was still very strong.[3]

---

[1] Otto Hirschfeld, *Die kaiserlichen Verwaltungsbeamten bis auf Diocletian*, 2te Aufl. (Berlin, 1905), p. 356.

[2] See *CIG*, 3743 = *CIL*, III, 346; cf. David Magie, *De Romanorum iuris publici sacrique vocabulis sollemnibus in Graecum sermonem conversis* (Leipzig, 1905), pp. 111f. and Ludwig Hahn, *Rom und Romanismus im griechisch-römischen Osten* ... (Leipzig, 1906), p. 224, n. 2, and p. 227, n. 5.

[3] *Op. cit.*, p. 243.

If one seeks to identify the Pharsman mentioned in the inscription (line 12) with one of the five kings of Georgia known to have borne this name, the most likely candidate is Pharsman III. According to Latin sources (where he is called Pharasmanes),[1] he was on the Iberian throne during the reigns of Hadrian and Antoninus Pius.[2]

This relatively brief inscription raises many interesting and perplexing questions. How far should the bilingualism of the stela be regarded as typical of Armazian culture? According to early traditions the invention of the Georgian alphabet is attributed to the great Armenian missionary St. Mesrop, whose work assisted in fusing the several language-groups and dialects within ancient Georgia into one language.[3] How widespread were Greek and Aramaic among these languages? The earliest monuments in the Georgian language come from the fifth century[4] and date from a period subsequent to the Christianization of the Iberians.[5] From then onwards it is possible to trace the development of Georgian palaeography.[6] How long did different languages and scripts, such

---

[1] Dio Cassius, lxix. 15, 1; lxix. 15, 1f., and Aelius Spartianus, *de vita Hadriani*, xiii. 9, xvii. 11-12, and xx. 9. For the genealogy of this Pharsmanes, see *Prosopographia Imperii Romani*, III, 32, No. 250; cf. Alexandre Manvelichvili, *Histoire de Géorgie* (Paris, 1951), p. 88.

[2] Tod (*op. cit.*, p. 86) follows Tseret'eli in adopting this identification.

[3] Koriun, *Life and Death of St. Mesrop*, Chap. 12 (ed. Simon Weber, *Ausgewählte Schriften der armenischen Kirchenväter*, I [München, 1927], 213f.).

[4] Edited and studied by Michel Tarchnisvili, "Les récentes découvertes épigraphiques et littéraires en Géorgien," *Muséon*, LXIII (1950), 249-60.

[5] On the divergent traditions in Armenian and Georgian sources regarding the Christianization of Georgia, reference may be made to Kornelios Kekelidze, *Die Bekehrung Georgiens zum Christentum* (*Morgenland, Darstellungen aus Geschichte und Kultur des Ostens*, Heft 18 [Leipzig, 1928]); Josef Markwart, "Die Bekehrung Iberiens und die beiden ältesten Dokumente der iberischen Kirche," *Caucasica; Zeitschrift für die Erforschung der Sprachen und Kulturen des Kaukasus und Armeniens*, VII (1931), 111-67; Gregor Peradze, "Die Probleme der ältesten Kirchengeschichte Georgiens," *Oriens christianus*, 3te Ser., VII (1932), 153-74; and Arthur Vööbus, *Early Versions of the New Testament* (Stockholm, 1954), pp. 173-84.

In spite of Lemm's correct interpretation of ⲧⲣⲃⲏⲣⲓⲁ as "the Iberian" (instead of "Tiberian" [i.e., one from the city Tiberias], as proposed by Zoega and Guidi), which occurs in a key position in several Coptic fragments of the *Historia Lausiaca* (Oscar von Lemm, *Kleine koptische Studien*, I [St. Petersburg, 1899], 14-32), E. Amélineau shows beyond any doubt the legendary character of these Coptic materials as regards the details of the conversion of the Iberians ("Les Coptes et la conversion des Ibères au Christianisme," *Revue de l'histoire des religions*, LXIX [1914], 142-82, 289-322).

[6] Monographs on Georgian paleography, with specimens of scripts, include I. Javakhishvili, *Kharthuli paleographia* (Tiflis, 1926); I. Abuladze, *Kharthuli*

as Greek and Aramaic, continue to maintain themselves among
Christianized Georgians? Questions such as these are easier to ask
than to answer, but it is owing in part to this bilingual inscription
from Armazi that they can be formulated at all.[1]

'tseris nimushebi, paleographiuli albomi (Tiflis, 1949); and I. Javakhishvili,
Kharthuli dam-'tserlobathamtzodneoba anu paleographia, meore gamotzema
(Tiflis, 1949). For recent discussions concerning the age of Georgian writing,
see Gerhard Deeters, "Das Alter der georgischen Schrift," *Oriens Christianus*,
XXXIX (1955), 56-65; George Tseret'eli, "The Most Ancient Georgian In-
scriptions in Palestine," *Bedi Karthlisa*, XI-XII, No. 36-37 (1961), 111-130;
and K. Salia, "Note sur l'origine et l'âge de l'alphabet géorgien," *ibid.*,
XV-XVI, No. 43-44 (1963), 5-18, who concludes that "the existence of a
Georgian script before the fifth century seems at present altogether possible"
(p. 18).

[1] For a discussion of other archeological evidence relating to the culture
of ancient Georgia, see B. A. Kuftin, "K voprosu o drevneĭshikh kornyakh
gruzinskoĭ kul'tury na kavkaze po dannym arkheologii," *Bulletin du Musée
de Géorgie*, XII-B (1944), 291-439, and especially *Mtskheta*; *Itogi arkeologi-
scheskikh issledovaniĭ*, I: A. M. Apakidze, G. F. Gobedzhishvili, A. N.
Kalandadze, and A. A. Lomtatidze, *Arkeologischikie pamyatniki Armazis-
Khevi 1937-1946* (Tiflis, 1958), with an English summary entitled "Archaeological Excavations at Armasis-Khevi near Makhetha in 1937-1946," pp.
275-[282].

CHAPTER FOUR

THE "LOST" SECTION OF II ESDRAS (= IV EZRA)

It is generally known that II Esdras in the English Revised Version of the Apocrypha (finished in 1894 and published in 1895) contains a section embracing some seventy verses not present in the King James or so-called Authorized Version.[1] Through the fortunate discovery of a ninth century Latin manuscript in the public Library of Amiens containing the passage, Professor Robert L. Bensly of the University of Cambridge was enabled to publish a noteworthy edition entitled *The Missing Fragment of the Latin Translation of the Fourth Book of Ezra* (Cambridge, 1875).[2] Bensly's research on the Latin text of the entire book[3] formed the textual basis for the work of the English revisers.

What is not generally known is that, a century and a half before the publication of the English Revised Version, Bibles had been published on both sides of the Atlantic which contained the "missing" fragment. Valuable as Bensly's work proved to be, it is not correct to refer to his discovery as though no one had previously known of the passage as part of II Esdras.[4] The following editions of the Bible include the "missing" section.

---

[1] These verses follow II Esd. 7.35. In 1856 Johannes Gildermeister discovered a Latin Vulgate manuscript dated A.D. 822, which is now at Bibliothèque Nationale (*Fonds latins*, 11505), from which a leaf (that had originally contained the missing fragment) had been cut out in early times. It is probable that dogmatic motives lay behind the mutilation, for the passage contains an emphatic denial of the value of prayers for the dead (verse 105).

[2] Curiously enough, Bensly had been anticipated in his discovery by Professor John Palmer of St. John's college, Cambridge, who, in 1826, found a ninth or tenth century Latin manuscript in Spain (formerly in the Library of the University of Alcalá de Heñares and now the Library of the Central University of Madrid) which contains the "missing" section. The transcription which he made of the portion was published a generation after his death by J. S. Wood in an article, "The Missing Fragment of the Fourth Book of Esdras," *Journal of Philology*, VII (1877), 264-78.

[3] *The Fourth Book of Ezra, the Latin Version edited from the MSS*, by the late Robert L. Bensly, with an Introduction by Montague Rhodes James (= *Text and Studies*, ed. J. Armitage Robinson, Vol. III, No. 2 [Cambridge, 1895]). Bensly made this material available to the Revisers prior to the publication of the Apocrypha in the English Revised Version.

[4] M. R. James, e.g., writes of Bensly's work as follows: "His unique

In the first quarter of the eighteenth century a German mystic, Johann Heinrich Haug, organized in western Germany numerous conventicles of those who called themselves Philadelphians (a sect which was founded by Jane Lead of England). Having been expelled from Strassburg by ecclesiastical authorities for his participation in this group, Haug found refuge in the castle of Count Casimir at Berleburg in Westphalia. In the interest of furthering mysticism he made a revision of Luther's version of the Bible, to which he appended numerous annotations and comments.[1] In this edition, which appeared at Berleburg between 1726 and 1742 in eight large folio volumes, Haug helped to prepare the way for historical criticism by including an appendix containing both Old Testament and New Testament apocrypha, pseudepigrapha, and several post-apostolic books. At the appropriate place in II Esdras, Haug supplied the missing portion. It is prefaced with the caption, "Hier hat nun eine gewisse arabische Übersetzung, die nur schriftlich in Engeland gefunden wird, noch ein grosses Stück, das in andern nicht gefunden wird; das lautet also:," followed by a German translation of the passage.[2] What is this Arabic version to which Haug refers, and through what channel did he learn of it?

It was probably that polymathic scholar, John Gregory of Christ Church, Oxford, who was the first to draw attention to an Arabic manuscript in the Bodleian Library which contains the Second Book of Esdras.[3] In any case, at the beginning of the eighteenth century, at the request of the learned and eccentric William Whiston, Simon Ockley, the noted Arabist at Oxford, prepared an English trans-

---

achievement—the discovery of a lost chapter of the Bible, in the shape of a long passage in the seventh chapter of this book [II Esdras]—is familiar to many who are not professed students of apocryphal literature," op. cit., p. xi.

[1] For the theology of Haug's exegetical notes, see Martin Hofmann, Theologie und Exegese der Berleburger Bibel (1726-42) (= Beiträge zur Förderung christlicher Theologie, XXXIX; Gütersloh, 1937).

[2] Der Berlenburgischen Bibel, achter und letzter Theil, bestehend in einem Zusatz von apocryphischen Schriften des Alten und Neuen Testaments ... (Berlenburg, 1742), pp. 105f.

[3] Gregory had a very high opinion of this manuscript. He writes, "I have cause to beleive [sic!] that it is the most authenticke remaine of this Booke [IV Ezra]," Notes and Observations upon Some Passages of Scripture (London, 1646), p. 76. The manuscript, known today as Oxford Bodl. Or. Ms. 251, was written A.D. 1354. It was first edited by Heinrich Ewald in his "Das vierte Esdrasbuch nach seinem Zeitalter, seinen arabischen Übersetzungen und einer neuen Wiederherstellung," Abhandlungen der kgl. Gesellschaft der Wissenschaften zu Göttingen, XI (1863).

lation of this version of II (= IV) Esdras for inclusion in the former's curious work entitled *Primitive Christianity Reviv'd* (London, 1711).[1] The Arabic version attained still wider circulation, particularly on the Continent, through a Latin translation which Fabricius made of Ockley's rendering.[2] Whether Haug consulted Whiston or Fabricius for his information of the contents of this Arabic manuscript of Esdras is not known, but probably it was the latter.

Another Bible in which the "missing" portion of II Esdras also appeared happens to be the first Bible in a European language[3] to be printed in America. It was issued by the industrious and philanthropic printer of Germantown, Pennsylvania, Christoph Sauer.[4] Because the volumes of the Berleburg Bible were expensive and out of reach of the poor, and because many of the current editions of Luther's Bibles were set in painfully small type, Sauer advocated the printing of Bibles in America in a type large enough for the aged to read them. Through the munificence of Dr. H. E. Luther, a type-founder of Frankfort-on-the-Main, Sauer received as a gift a font of type suitable for Bible printing. Despite many obstacles,[5] in 1743 Sauer issued an edition of 1200 copies of the German Bible, based on the 34th edition of Luther's Bible, published at Halle. Since, however, Luther's Bible lacked I and II Esdras (which Luther had never translated, declaring them to "contain

---

[1] Whiston acknowledges his indebtedness to Ockley in Vol. I, p. v. The English translation appears in what can be called the second appendix to Vol. IV (separately paginated), pp. 1-140. It is an interesting side-light that though Ockley had obliged Whiston by making this rendering, in 1712 he wrote to Mr. Styan Thirlby as follows: "You shall have my Esdras in a little time; Two Hundred of which I reserv'd when he [Whiston] printed his, purely upon this Account; because I was loath that any thing with my Name to it, should be extant only in his Heretical Volumes" (Simon Ockley, *An Account of the Authority of the Arabick Manuscripts in the Bodleian Library, Controverted between Dr. Grabe and Mr. Whiston. In a Letter to Mr. Thirlby* [London, 1712]). Bruno Violet is in error in calling Ockley "Rabbi" (*Die Esra-Apokalypse* [Leipzig, 1910], p. xxxi); Ockley was vicar of Swavesey, Cambridgeshire (so the *Dictionary of National Biography, s. n.*).

[2] J. A. Fabricius, *Codicis pseudepigraphi Veteris Testamenti*, II (Hamburg, 1723), 173-307.

[3] As is commonly known, the first Bible printed in America was John Eliot's translation into Massachusetts or the Algonquin Indian language; the New Testament was published at Cambridge, Massachusetts, in 1661; the Old Testament in 1663 (see Eric M. North, *The Book of a Thousand Tongues* [New York, 1938], pp. 231f.).

[4] Also spelled Saur and Sower.

[5] For an account of some of these obstacles, see P. Marion Simms, *The Bible in America* (New York, 1936), pp. 121ff.

absolutely nothing which one could not more easily find in Aesop or in even more trival books"),[1] it was from the Berleburg Bible that Sauer printed sheets containing these two books (called III and IV Esdras) as well as III Maccabees, which he offered to bind in as an appendix for those who desired them. What is of interest here is that Sauer reprinted the "missing" portion of Esdras, with the same prefatory caption as that found in Haug's edition.

Thus, one hundred fifty years before the English-speaking world recognized the right of these verses to appear in II Esdras, editions of the Bible in German had appeared on both sides of the Atlantic containing the "missing" portion.[2]

---

[1] So Luther's Preface to the Book of Baruch. Later editions of Luther's Bible contain Daniel Cramer's rendering of I and II Esdras.

In this connection it will be recollected that the Council of Trent (1546), pronouncing an anathema upon all who do not receive Jerome's Vulgate as the authentic text, did not include I and II Esdras, and the Prayer of Manasseh, among the canonical books of Scripture. Nevertheless, official copies of the Clementine Vulgate Bible print these three books as an appendix after the New Testament, "lest they should utterly perish" (*ne prorsus interirent*) from neglect. The Rheims-Douay English version, finished in 1609-10, included them at the close of the Old Testament. At the head of this section the following caption appears: "The Prayer of Manasses, with the second & third books of Esdras, extant in most Latin and vulgare Bibles, are here placed after the Canonical bookes, of the old Testament: because they are not receiued into the Canon of Diuine Scriptures by the Catholique Church" (p. [1001]; through a printer's error it is the second page assigned the number 1001). Here II and III Esdras refer to what are called I and II Esdras in Protestant Bibles. Curiously the actual titles and the running titles of the pages in this edition are "Third Booke of Esdras" and "Fourth Booke of Esdras."

[2] Bensly (*op. cit.*, pp. 2f.) implies that the handsome *editio princeps* of the Armenian Bible (edited by Uscan and published at Amsterdam in 1661) contains the "lost" section. This is not true, and it is strange that Bensly could have fallen into such an error had he consulted the 1661 edition itself, instead of relying on statements about the edition made by Masch, Bredenkamp, Scholz, and others—although a careful reading of the statements made by these scholars discloses nothing relative to the addition in chap. 7. On the other hand, Bensly makes no mention of the fact that John Zohrab's critical edition, published at Venice in 1805, was the first Armenian Bible to incorporate the "lost" section in its proper place in III (i.e. IV) Ezra (printed in the Appendix of vol. IV, pp. 54-57).

According to information received (July 21, 1967) from Prof. Michael E. Stone of the Hebrew University of Jerusalem, all three manuscripts (dating from the seventeenth century) that Zohrab used for IV Ezra contain the section under discussion. Likewise, of the fifteen additional manuscripts (the oldest dating from the end of the thirteenth century) that Stone has collated for a critical edition of the Armenian version of IV Ezra, all contain the passage. See Stone's forthcoming article on the subject in *Textus; Annual of the Jerusalem Bible Project*.

CHAPTER FIVE

THE FORMULAS INTRODUCING QUOTATIONS
OF SCRIPTURE IN
THE NEW TESTAMENT AND THE MISHNAH

A comparison of the formulas introducing quotations of Scripture
in the New Testament and in the Mishnah is both practicable and
desirable. It is practicable because much of both the New Testament
and the Mishnah reflects the methods of argumentation employed
by those who had been reared and trained in orthodox Judaism of
the first century.[1] Such an investigation is also desirable insofar as
it may afford an additional means of comparing and contrasting the
habits of thought and religious presuppositions entertained by the
authors of both corpora of literature. To the extent that such an
investigation appears to be both practicable and desirable, to that
degree it is surprising that no satisfactory treatment of the subject
is available. True enough, there is no lack of articles and books on
the subject of the quotations from the Old Testament in the New
Testament,[2] several of which deal with formulas of quotation.[3]

---

[1] Although the sixty-three tractates of the Mishnah were not finally
reduced to writing until about the close of the second century, by the
Patriarch Judah (died *c.* 219), it is commonly allowed that their contents
faithfully reproduce the oral teaching of the generations of the Tannaim,
who date from about the beginning of the Christian era; cf. George Foot
Moore, *Judaism in the First Centuries of the Christian Era, the Age of the
Tannaim*, I (Cambridge, 1932), 3-4.

[2] For an extensive catalogue of titles of such works (from 1600 to 1943),
reference may be made to the bibliographical appendix in Elwyn E. Tilden's
unpublished Th.D. dissertation, *The Function of the Old Testament in the
Sayings of Jesus as Recorded in the Synoptic Gospels* (1945), pp. 296-306,
which is on deposit in the Library of Princeton Theological Seminary.

[3] Notably David McCalman Turpie, *The New Testament View of the Old,
A Contribution to Biblical Introduction and Exegesis* (London, 1872), Eugen
Hühn, *Die altestamentlichen Citate und Reminiscenzen im Neuen Testamente*
(= *Die messianischen Weissagungen des israelitisch-jüdischen Volkes bis zu den
Targumim*, II. Teil; Tübingen, 1900), pp. 272-277; Otto Michel, *Paul und
seine Bibel* (= *Beiträge zur Förderung christlicher Theologie*, II. Reihe, 18.
Band; Gütersloh, 1929), p. 72; L. Venard, "Citations de l'Ancien Testament
dans le Nouveau Testament," *Dictionnaire de la Bible, Supplément*, II (Paris,
1934), cols. 23-51, especiallly 30-31; and E. Earle Ellis, *Paul's Use of the
Old Testament* (Grand Rapids, 1957), especially pp. 22-25 and 48-49.

There is, furthermore, at least one definitive treatment of the terminology employed by the Tannaim in their Scriptural exegesis, the well-known work by Wilhelm Bacher.[1] But apparently no scholar, interested in both the New Testament and the Mishnah, has heretofore undertaken a comprehensive and scientific comparison of the formulas of Scriptural quotations in both the New Testament and the Mishnah.[2] By way of making a beginning of such a comparison, it is the purpose of the present study (I) to list all of the separate formulas which introduce quotations of Scripture in the New Testament and in the Mishnah,[3] and (II) to discuss the significance of similarities and differences between the usages of the two corpora.

---

[1] *Die älteste Terminologie der jüdischen Schriftauslegung, ein Wörterbuch der bibelexegetischen Kunstsprache der Tannaiten* (= *Die exegetische Terminologie der jüdischen Traditionsliteratur*, I. Teil; Leipzig, 1899). A brief treatment of several of the formulas of citation may be found in Georg Aicher, *Das Alte Testament in der Mischna* (= *Biblische Studien*, ed. Otto Bardenhewer, XI. Band, 4. Heft; Freiburg im B., 1906), pp. 41-44. Unfortunately Samuel Rosenblatt pays scant attention to this subject in his *Interpretation of the Bible in the Mishnah* (Baltimore, 1935), pp. 24 and 35. None of these (or any other, so far as the present writer is aware) includes a comprehensive list of the formulas of quotation in the Mishnah.

[2] There is, of course, a multitude of scattered comments on individual formulas in every scientific commentary on the New Testament and on the Mishnah, notably in [Hermann L. Strack and] Paul Billerbeck, *Kommentar zum Neuen Testament aus Talmud und Midrasch* (München, 1922-28) and in G. Beer and O. Holtzmann, *Die Mischna; Text, Übersetzung und ausführliche Erklärung* (Giessen, 1912-00). Schrenk and Kittel touch upon the subject in their respective articles on γράφω and λέγω in Kittel's *Theologisches Wörterbuch*, I, 747f. and IV, 110f. The statement in the text above is not contradicted by the existence of the volume entitled ספר המשוה *sive* ΒΙΒΛΟΣ ΚΑΤΑΛΛΑΓΗΣ *in quo secundum veterum theologorum hebraeorum formulas allegandi, & modos interpretandi conciliantur loca ex V. in N. T. allegata*, auctore Guilielmo Surenhusio (Amstelaedami, 1713), for Surenhusius's method and purpose prevented his making a completely satisfactory examination of the evidence. His method, it may be remarked, was an eclectic one ranging over every area and date of rabbinical writings, and his purpose was to defend the interpretation of the apostles against the Jews of his own time, so that if blame be attached to the New Testament writers for their modes of quotation, it must equally belong to the Talmudical doctors. For other criticisms of Surenhusius, reference may be made to Thomas H. Horne, *An Introduction to the Critical Study and Knowledge of the Holy Scriptures*, 13th ed., II (London, 1872), 186-187, and Crawford H. Toy, *Quotations in the New Testament* (New York, 1884), pp. xxx-xxxi.

[3] It has not been the purpose of the author to supply an exhaustive list of all the passages where the formulas occur; this information can be secured from concordances of the Greek New Testament (e.g. that by Moulton and Geden) and of the Mishnah (e.g. that by Kasovsky). Consequently only a few passages will be cited as examples of any one formula.

I

For convenience of listing, the formulas of quotation of Scripture will be grouped according as they are (A) quite general, (B) more precise, or (C) specific as to author or section cited.

(A)

By far the majority of quotations in the Mishnah are introduced by the verb אָמַר. It appears in the *qal* participle active, אוֹמֵר with the Scriptures implied as its subject (Pe'ah 8.9; Sheqalim 6.6; Aboth 6.7) or with God implied as its subject (Sanhedrin 10.3; Makkoth 3.15, see also Samuel Krauss's note in the Giessen edition). The verb is occasionally preceded by הוּא (Yebamoth 6.6; Sanhedrin 10.3) or by וְכֵן הוּא ("And likewise it [or he] says," Ta'anith 4.8; Nedarim 9.10; Qiddushin 4.14), or yet again by הֲרֵי הוּא ("Lo, it says," Makkoth 3.15). Sometimes an adversative expression is used, as אֵינוֹ אוֹמֵר... אֶלָּא... ("It does not say ..., but ...," Sanhedrin 4.4). The introductory word may be an interrogative, מַהוּ אוֹמֵר ("What does it say?" Qiddushin 4.14 *bis*). By far the largest number of instances of formulas containing אָמַר involve the *niph'al* form, נֶאֱמַר (Nazir 9.5; Sanhedrin 6.4; Ḥullin 8.4, etc., etc.), translated by Herbert Danby in his Oxford edition of the Mishnah, "It is written." Most frequent of all is the expression שֶׁנֶּאֱמַר (Makkoth 3.13; Shabbath 9.1, 2, 3, 4, 6; Yoma 1.1, and more than 300 other examples), rendered variously by Danby, "as it is written," "for it is written," and the like. As with the active form, the subject may be either the Scriptures or God. Like the active form, it is also elaborated adversatively, ... לֹא נֶאֱמַר ... אֶלָּא ... ("It is not said ..., but ...," Shebi'ith 9.2; Ta'anith 2.1), or in other ways which make the reference more pointed, as עַל זֶה נֶאֱמַר ("of such it is said," Pe'ah 8.9; Sukkah 2.6; Sanhedrin 3.7), עַל־זוּ נֶאֱמַר (Yebamoth 9.6), or מִשּׁוּם שֶׁנֶּאֱמַר ("because it is said," Bikkurim 1.2 *bis*), or מִמַּשְׁמַע שֶׁנֶּאֱמַר ("by inference from what is said," Sanhedrin 1.6). The interrogative formula appears in two forms, לָמָּה נֶאֱמַר ("Why is it said ...?" Sanhedrin 1.6) and אִם כֵּן לָמָּה נֶאֱמַר ("If so, why is it said ...?" Pesaḥim 9.1; Makkoth 1.6).

In a chain of quotations, frequently the passive form appears first followed by the active form linked by the simple connective, שֶׁנֶּאֱמַר ... וְאוֹמֵר ... (Sanhedrin 1.4; Aboth 6.7).

Occasionally the Mishnah employs the word דָּבָר to introduce a quotation, as לַדָּבָר (Shabbath 8.7) and דָּבָר אַחֵר ("another saying is," Sanhedrin 4.4; Makkoth 1.9).[1]

The introductory formulas in the New Testament which involve a verb of saying are more varied than those in the Mishnah, no doubt because the Greek language is correspondingly richer in verbs of saying than is Hebrew; thus φησίν (I Cor. 6.16, with ὁ θεός understood as the subject), λέγει (Rom. 15.10), ἐρρέθη (Matt. 5.27), εἴρηται (Luke 4.12), ἐν τῷ λέγεσθαι (Heb. 3.15), and κατὰ τὸ εἰρημένον (Rom. 4.18). As דָּבָר is used in the Mishnah, so ὁ λόγος (John 4.37), ὁ λόγος οὗτος (Rom. 9.9), and ὁ λόγος ὁ γεγραμμένος (I Cor. 15.54) appear in the New Testament. The one speaking is identified as God, καθὼς εἶπεν ὁ θεός (II Cor. 6.16), οὐκ ἀνέγνωτε τὸ ῥηθὲν ὑμῖν ὑπὸ τοῦ θεοῦ λέγοντος as a question (Matt. 22.31), and the Holy Spirit, καθὼς λέγει τὸ πνεῦμα τὸ ἅγιον (Heb. 3.7). With the last may be compared רוּחַ הַקֹּדֶשׁ מְבַשַּׂרְתָּן ("The Holy Spirit proclaims to them," Sotah 9.6).

Once Paul refers to the Scriptures as though to a book of oracles, τί λέγει ὁ χρηματισμός; (Rom. 11.4). In addition to a prefixed formula of quotation, Paul occasionally adds within or at the end of the quotation the words λέγει κύριος (Rom. 13.19; I Cor. 14.21; II Cor. 6.17).

The Mishnah employs the root כתב in both nominal and verbal forms in referring to the Scriptures. Thus הַכָּתוּב אוֹמֵר ("The Scripture says," Yebamoth 4.4 tris), ··· כָּתוּב אֶחָד אוֹמֵר ··· כָּתוּב אֶחָד אוֹמֵר ("One verse of Scripture says ... and another ...," Danby's rendering of 'Arakin 8.7) and דִּכְתִיב ("that which is written," Aboth 6.10, four times). Unmistakably personalized is מַעֲלֶה עָלָיו הַכָּתוּב ("The Scripture reckons it unto him," Aboth 3.2). The New Testament authors allow themselves more freedom in attributing personality to the Scriptures than do the Tannaim. Not only are verbs of speaking used, as in the Mishnah, such as ἡ γραφὴ λέγει (Jas. 4.5, 6) and λέγει ἡ γραφή (Rom. 10.11), τί ἡ γραφὴ λέγει; (Rom. 4.3) and τί λέγει ἡ γραφή; (Gal. 4.30), καθὼς εἶπεν ἡ γραφή (John 7.38), οὐχ ἡ γραφὴ εἶπεν as a question (John 7.42), ἑτέρα γραφὴ λέγει (John 19.37), but the power of foreseeing the future is also attributed to the Old Testament, as προϊδοῦσα ἡ γραφὴ ... προευηγγελίσατο (Gal. 3.8). Perhaps there should also be added here the personification of a scriptural word as "Consolation" or "Exhortation," ἐκλέλησθε τῆς παρακλήσεως, ἥτις ὑμῖν ... διαλέγεται (Heb. 12.5), as well as the

---

[1] Though not a formula introducing a quotation, the following comment in Baba Qamma 5.7 is also apposite, אֶלָּא שֶׁדִּבֶּר הַכָּתוּב בְּהוֹוֶה.

placing of Mosaic words into the mouth of "Righteousness-which-is-by-faith," ἡ δὲ ἐκ πίστεως δικαιοσύνη οὕτως λέγει (Rom. 10.6).

A type of formula that appears not infrequently in the New Testament is one that involves the perfect tense of γράφω. Often γέγραπται stands alone (Matt. 4.4; Rom. 12.19; I Pet. 1.16), or is preceded by οὕτως (Luke 24.46, I Cor. 15.45), by καθώς (Acts 15.15; Rom. 1.17), by καθάπερ (Rom. 3.4; 10.15), by ὥστε (I Cor. 10.7), by περὶ οὗ (Matt. 11.10; Luke 7.17), and, as a question, by οὐ (Mark 11.17).

The perfect passive participle appears in such combinations as ἦν γεγραμμένον (Luke 4.17), τὸ γεγραμμένον τοῦτο (Luke 20.17), κατὰ τὸ γεγραμμένον (II Cor. 4.13), and ὁ λόγος ὁ γεγραμμένος (I Cor. 15.53).

Likewise the noun γραφή is used in the following combinations not hitherto listed: κατὰ τὴν γραφήν (Jas. 2.8), περιέχει ἐν γραφῇ (I Pet. 2.6), ἵνα ἡ γραφὴ πληρωθῇ (John 13.18; 17.12), ἵνα τελειωθῇ ἡ γραφή (John 19.38), and, as questions, οὐδὲ τὴν γραφὴν ταύτην ἀνέγνωτε (Mark 12.10), οὐδέποτε ἀνέγνωτε ἐν ταῖς γραφαῖς (Matt. 21.42), and οὐκ [οὐδέποτε] ἀνέγνωτε (Matt. 19.4; 21.16).

Very rarely the *pi'el* of the verb קוּם, "to establish, fulfill," introduces a quotation, as שְׁנֵי כְתוּבִים קַיָּמִים ("both Scriptures are fulfilled," Sheqalim 6.6) and קִיַּמְתָּ ("thou hast fulfilled," Baba Qamma 3.9 *bis*).

Two indefinite expressions which occur infrequently in the Mishnah are וַהֲלֹא כְּבָר נֶאֱמַר ("But was it not once said ...?" Nazir 9.5) and וּלְהַלָּן הוּא אוֹמֵר ("and elsewhere it says," Soṭah 6.3). The only book in the New Testament that contains examples of this quite indefinite type of formula is Hebrews. In this document the place of origin of quotations is twice indicated by the indefinite word "somewhere": διεμαρτύρατο δὲ πού τις λέγων (Heb. 2.6, where the subject is un-identified) and εἴρηκεν γάρ που (Heb. 4.4, where the subject is God).[1]

The prepositions -בְּ (Sukkah 13.9), -לְ (Pesaḥim 5.7), -מִן (Bik-kurim 3.6), and עַד (Pesaḥim 10.6), are used to introduce a quotation. The conjunction וְ connects quotations. Somewhat similar in brevity

---

[1] This formula (with που) appears also in Philo, *De Ebrietate*, § 14, *Quod Deus immutab.*, § 16, *De Profugis*, § 36, *De Congressu er. gr.*, § 31, and in Clement of Rome, [*I*] *Epist.* 15.2, 21.2, 26.2, 28.2, 42.5, and is generally taken as an Alexandrianism; yet see William Leonard, *The Authorship of the Epistle to the Hebrews* (London, [1939]), "Mode of Scriptural Citation," pp. 265-287, especially pp. 275 and 283. Olof Linton cites no example of this indefinite formula in Clement of Alexandria; cf. Linton, "Fornkristna evangeliecitat i traditionshistorisk belysning," *Svensk exegetisk årsbok*, II (1937), 107-136, especially 131-134.

of formula is the New Testament usage of τό (Matt. 19.18; Rom. 13.9) to introduce a quotation in the New Testament, and of πάλιν to link a subsequent quotation to an earlier one (Rom. 15.10-12). The conjunction γάρ (Rom. 2.24) or τὸ γάρ (Rom. 13.9), as well as μενοῦνγε (Rom. 10.18) and καθώς (Gal. 3.6), occur in Paul's writings.

The question πῶς ἀναγινώσκεις (Luke 10.26) finds a verbal parallel in הֵיאַךְ אַתָּה קוֹרֵא ('Abodah Zarah 2.5).

Several other conventionalized formulas, referring to an unnamed passage or division, appear in both the New Testament and the Mishnah. Thus καὶ ἐν ἑτέρῳ λέγει (where τόπῳ is probably to be understood, Heb. 5.6) finds a parallel in וּמִקְרָא אֶחָד אוֹמֵר ("and another passage says," Soṭah 5.3). The Mishnah also uses חֲבֵרוֹ מְלַמֵּד ("its fellow[-verse] teaches," 'Abodah Zarah 2.5), בַּפָּרְשָׁה ("in the section," Soṭah 5.1), בַּל ("a prohibitive law," Bikkurim 4.2; Qiddushin 1.7), and הַפָּרָשָׁה ("the parashah," Bikkurim 3.6).

The expression תַּלְמוּד לוֹמַר occurs not infrequently (Soṭah 6.3; Aboth 3.8; Ḥullin 8.4; 9.5; 10.1; Temurah 6.4; etc.).[1] This formula is variously interpreted. Marti and Beer in the Giessen edition of Aboth translate, "Aber die Schrift lehrt" (p. 73), dropping a footnote indicating that literally it is, "Belehrung ist zu sagen." In his *Wörterbuch* Levy (*s. v.* תַּלְמוּד) gives the sense with "Daher steht in der Schrift." Bacher interprets it, "Es liegt eine Lehre (eine Belehrung) der Schrift in dem, was sie sagt" (*op. cit.*, p. 200). Jastrow explains it in his *Dictionary* (*s. v.* תַּלְמוּד), "There is a teaching in the Scriptural text to intimate, the text reads (may be read)." Danby usually translates the phrase by "Scripture says." The New Testament has no verbal analogy to this formula. Perhaps the nearest in sense are λέγει γὰρ ἡ γραφή (Rom. 9.17) and ἀλλὰ τί λέγει ἡ γραφή; (Gal. 4.30).

(B)

Formulas which refer more precisely to some one part of the Scriptures are the following. Although the Mishnah refers to the Scriptures as a whole by the word תּוֹרָה (Aboth 6.7, where all six quotations thus introduced are from Proverbs), usually the word is used in its more precise meaning, as אָמְרָה תוֹרָה ("The Law has said," Ḥullin 12.5). The root כתב frequently appears with the word

---

[1] The form לוֹמַר is the *qal* infinitive of אמר with ל and is equivalent to לֵאמֹר; see A. Geiger, *Lehr- und Lesebuch zur Sprache der Mischnah* (Breslau, 1845), § 17, 4, and C. Siegfried and H. Strack, *Lehrbuch der neuhebräischen Sprache* (Berlin, 1884), § 98b.

"Law," as מַה־שֶּׁכָּתוּב בַּתּוֹרָה ("that which is written in the Law,"
Pesaḥim 6.2) and מִפְּנֵי הַכָּתוּב שֶׁבַּתּוֹרָה ("because of what is written in
the Law," Hallah 4.10; Bikkurim 1.3). Likewise in the New Testament the word νόμος refers occasionally to the Scriptures as a whole,
as ἐν τῷ νόμῳ γέγραπται (I Cor. 14.21, referring to Isaiah 28.11),
οὐκ ἔστιν γεγραμμένον ἐν τῷ νόμῳ ὑμῶν (John 10.34, quoting Psalm
82.6), and ἵνα πληρωθῇ ὁ λόγος ὁ ἐν τῷ νόμῳ αὐτῶν γεγραμμένος (John
15.25, quoting Psalm 35.19). But more frequently νόμος in the
following formulas precedes a quotation from the Pentateuch: ὁ
νόμος ἔλεγεν (Rom. 7.7), ἐν τῷ νόμῳ τῷ ὑμετέρῳ γέγραπται (John
8.17), καθὼς γέγραπται ἐν νόμῳ κυρίου (Luke 2.23), and κατὰ τὸ
εἰρημένον ἐν τῷ νόμῳ κυρίου (Luke 2.24). The New Testament also
refers anonymously to the Prophet(s), ὁ προφήτης λέγει (Acts 7.48),
οὕτως γέγραπται διὰ τοῦ προφήτου (Matt. 2.5), ἔστιν γεγραμμένον ἐν
τοῖς προφήταις (John 6.45), τὸ εἰρημένον ἐν τοῖς προφήταις (Acts 13.40),
and καθὼς γέγραπται ἐν βίβλῳ τῶν προφητῶν (Acts 7.42).

Among the more precise formulas are those which involve the
name of a Biblical character or section of Scripture. In the Mishnah
Moses, Joshua, David, and Ezekiel are referred to in introductory
formulas; thus, כַּכָּתוּב בְּתוֹרַת מֹשֶׁה עַבְדְּךָ לֵאמֹר ("as it is written in the
Law of thy servant Moses, saying," Yoma 3.8; 6.2; see also 4.2),
שֶׁאָמַר לוֹ יְהוֹשֻׁעַ ("for Joshua said to him [Achan]," Sanhedrin 6.12),
וְכֵן כָּתוּב בְּסֵפֶר תְּהִלִּים עַל יְדֵי דָוִד מֶלֶךְ יִשְׂרָאֵל ("and thus it is written in
the book of Psalms by the hands of David, King of Israel," Aboth
6.9, according to the *textus receptus*; MS Monacensis 95, ed. Strack,
reads וְעָלָיו הוּא מְפָרֵשׁ עַל־יְדֵי יְחֶזְקֵאל (שֶׁנֶּאֱמַר שָׁכֵן מָצִינוּ בְּדָוִד מֶלֶךְ יִשְׂרָאֵל), and
שֶׁנֶּאֱמַר ("whereof he speaks expressly through Ezekiel, where it is
said," Tamid 3.7; see also Middoth 4.2). In the New Testament
Μωϋσῆς occurs with λέγει (Rom. 10.19), εἶπεν (Matt. 22.24; Acts
3.22), γράφει (Rom. 10.5), and ἔγραψεν (Mark 12.19; Luke 20.28).
More precise is ἐν τῷ Μωϋσέως νόμῳ γέγραπται (I Cor. 9.9). Similarly
Isaiah, Jeremiah, Hosea, Joel, Daniel, and Enoch are quoted by
name in the following varieties of formulas: Ἡσαΐας λέγει (Rom.
10.16), Ἡσαΐας ἀποτολμᾷ καὶ λέγει (Rom. 10.20), εἶπεν Ἡσαΐας (John
12.39), Ἡσαΐας κράζει ὑπὲρ τοῦ Ἰσραήλ (Rom. 9.27), καθὼς προείρηκεν
Ἡσαΐας (Rom. 9.29), καθὼς εἶπεν Ἡσαΐας ὁ προφήτης (John 1.23),
ἐπροφήτευσεν Ἡσαΐας ... ὡς γέγραπται (Mark 7.6), ἐπροφήτευσεν περὶ
ὑμῶν Ἡσαΐας λέγων (Matt. 15.7), ἀναπληροῦται αὐτοῖς ἡ προφητεία
Ἡσαΐου ἡ λέγουσα (Matt. 13.14), ὡς γέγραπται ἐν βίβλῳ λόγων
Ἡσαΐου τοῦ προφήτου (Luke 3.4), καθὼς γέγραπται ἐν τῷ Ἡσαΐου τῷ

προφήτη (Mark 1.2), ἵνα ὁ λόγος Ἠσαΐου τοῦ προφήτου πληρωθῇ ὃν εἶπεν (John 12.38), ἵνα (or ὅπως) πληρωθῇ τὸ ῥηθὲν διὰ Ἠσαΐου τοῦ προφήτου λέγοντος (Matt. 4.14; 8.17; 12.17), οὗτός ἐστιν ὁ ῥηθεὶς διὰ Ἠσαΐου τοῦ προφήτου λέγοντος (Matt. 3.3), τὸ πνεῦμα τὸ ἅγιον ἐλάλησεν διὰ Ἠσαΐου τοῦ προφήτου ... λέγων (Acts 28.25), ἐπληρώθη τὸ ῥηθὲν διὰ Ἰερεμίου τοῦ προφήτου λέγοντος (Matt. 2.17; 27.9, although in this last passage it is really Zechariah who is quoted), ὡς ἐν τῷ Ὡσηὲ λέγει (Rom. 9.25), τοῦτό ἐστι τὸ εἰρημένον διὰ τοῦ προφήτου Ἰωήλ (Acts 2.16), τὸ ῥηθὲν διὰ Δανιὴλ τοῦ προφήτου (Matt. 24.15), ἐπροφήτευσεν δὲ καὶ τούτοις ἕβδομος ἀπὸ Ἀδὰμ Ἐνὼχ λέγων (Jude 14).

The Psalter is referred to as follows: γέγραπται ἐν βίβλῳ ψαλμῶν (Acts 1.20), Δαυὶδ λέγει ἐν βίβλῳ ψαλμῶν (Luke 20.42), Δαυὶδ λέγει (Rom. 11.9; compare Acts 2.34), Δαυὶδ εἶπεν ἐν τῷ πνεύματι τῷ ἁγίῳ (Mark 12.36), ἔδει πληρωθῆναι τὴν γραφὴν ἣν προεῖπε τὸ πνεῦμα τὸ ἅγιον διὰ στόματος Δαυὶδ περί ... (Acts 1.16), ὁ [sc. θεὸς] τοῦ πατρὸς ἡμῶν διὰ πνεύματος ἁγίου στόματος Δαυὶδ παιδός σου εἰπών (Acts 4.25 according to ℵ B A E, but this is ungrammatical;[1] Westcott and Hort suspected a primitive error here), ἐν Δαυὶδ λέγων (Heb. 4.7, with ὁ θεός as the subject).

In Pesaḥim 5.7 הַהַלֵּל occurs and in Yoma 7.1 the book of Numbers is referred to by name.

Two passages in the New Testament employ the dative case of a proper name to indicate the general location of the passage quoted: λέγει ἡ γραφὴ τῷ Φαραώ (Rom. 9.17) and ἡ γραφὴ ... προευηγγελίσατο τῷ Ἀβραάμ (Gal. 3.8).

(C)

The most precise formulas of quotation are those that involve an expression referring to a particular section of text. Lacking more definite divisions of chapters and verses, it was necessary, if one wished to refer to a special passage, to utilize catchwords or brief references to the contents of the passage. The only clear[2] example

---

[1] J. H. Ropes believes that the reading of the old uncial group "is probably to be adopted here." He continues, "To assume, as the Antiochian revisers appear to have done, that both του πατρος ημων and πνευματος αγιου were interpolated, imputes too great ineptitude to the supposed primitive interpolator, whose text was certainly widely adopted; and the hypothesis is intrinsically too easy to be safe," *The Text of Acts* (= *The Beginnings of Christianity*, Part I, *The Acts of the Apostles*, edd. F. J. Foakes Jackson and Kirsopp Lake, vol. III; London, 1926), p. 40.

[2] Perhaps Sanhedrin 6.2 approaches this usage, שֶׁכֵּן מָצִינוּ בְּעָכָן ("For so have we found it with [lit. in] Achan").

in the Mishnah is וְכֵן הוּא אוֹמֵר בְּדָוִד (Aboth 3.7), which Danby interprets, "And it is written in [the Scripture concerning] David." The
reference is to the history of David in I Chron. 29.14.

Two or three such examples are found in the New Testament.
The question, οὐκ ἀνέγνωτε ἐν τῇ βίβλῳ Μωϋσέως ἐπὶ τοῦ βάτου; (Mark
12.26), which Luke reproduces as Μωϋσῆς ἐμήνυσεν ἐπὶ τῆς βάτου
(20.37), refers to the narrative of the burning thorn bush in Exod.
3.6. Similarly Paul asks the question οὐκ οἴδατε ἐν Ἠλίᾳ τί λέγει ἡ
γραφή ...; (Rom. 11.2), referring to the narrative of Elijah in I Kings
19.10.[1] A third example is perhaps to be found in the introductory
phrase used in Mk. 10.9 to introduce a quotation from Gen. 1.27.
The words ἀπὸ δὲ ἀρχῆς κτίσεως have been taken to mean "at the
beginning of his book" or "at the beginning of Genesis," with
ἔγραψεν Μωϋσῆς understood.[2] A somewhat similar introductory
expression is used in the Damascus Document to introduce the
same passage from Genesis.[3]

The most precise of all such references is in Acts 13.33, which is
probably the earliest known citation of a Psalm by number. The
text is uncertain: 𝔓[74] א A B C Ψ 33 81 1739 read ὡς ἐν τῷ ψαλμῷ
γέγραπται τῷ δευτέρῳ, whereas certain Western witnesses, including
D d gig Origen Hilary Ps. Jerome and Latin manuscripts known
to Bede, read ὡς ἐν τῷ πρώτῳ ψαλμῷ γέγραπται. The latter reading
reflects a rabbinical practice of uniting the first and second Psalms.[4]

II

Both the New Testament and the Mishnah, as one would expect
in view of their origin, contain many similar or identical formulas
introducing quotations of Scripture.[5] When one compares the fre-

---

[1] Similarly Philo, De Agricultura, § 24, λέγει γὰρ ἐν ταῖς ἀραῖς, referring to
Gen. 3.15. Sections in the Homeric poems were likewise commonly identified
in antiquity by making brief references to the topic of a given section.
[2] So, e.g., J. Wellhausen, Das Evangelium Marci, 2te Aufl. (Berlin, 1909),
p. 76.
[3] See the discussion by J. de Waard, A Comparative Study of the Old
Testament Text in the Dead Sea Scrolls and in the New Testament (Leiden,
1965), pp. 31-33 and 83, note 3.
[4] For discussions of the textual problem in Acts 13.33 see Ropes (op. cit.,
pp. 263-265) and the present writer in his forthcoming Textual Commentary
on the Greek New Testament, in loc.
[5] In certain cases the similarity is to be explained on the basis of a common
dependence on formulas introducing literary references in the Old Testament,
as, e.g., Josh. 8.31, כַּכָּתוּב בְּסֵפֶר תּוֹרַת מֹשֶׁה, LXX (9.2b) καθὰ γέγραπται ἐν τῷ

quency of certain types of formulas, it is discovered that the Mishnah shows a great preference for those formulas involving a verb of saying, whereas in the New Testament the frequency of this type is more evenly balanced by the type containing a reference to the written record.

It is noticeable likewise that the New Testament makes use of a much greater variety of types of formulas than does the Mishnah. This is not surprising, for the writings of the New Testament include a much greater range of literary *genres* than does the Mishnah.

All varieties of formulas indicate that the contributors to the New Testament and to the Mishnah had the very highest view of the inspiration of the Scriptures which they quote.[1] Both corpora contain not a few examples where the subject of the verb of saying in the formula may be either the Scriptures or God.[2] Indeed, so habitual was the identification of the divine Author with the words of Scripture that occasionally personality is attributed to the passage itself (see p. 55 above).

On the other hand, both the Mishnah and the New Testament recognize the instrumentality of human authors in the production of the Scriptures which each quotes. The former refers, rather infrequently, to Moses, Joshua, David, and Ezekiel; the latter refers, with relatively greater frequency than does the Mishnah, to Moses, David, Isaiah, Jeremiah, Daniel, Hosea, Joel, and Enoch.

νόμῳ Μωϋσῆ; or with a verb of saying, Num. 21.14, עַל־כֵּן יֵאָמַר בְּסֵפֶר מִלְחֲמֹת יְהֹוָה, LXX, διὰ τοῦτο λέγεται ἐν βιβλίῳ Πόλεμος τοῦ κυρίου; see also Deut. 28.58, 61; Josh. 8.34; 10.13; 23.6; II Sam. 1.18, I Kings 11.41; 14.19; II Kings 13.12; 23.24, 28; I Chron. 9.1; 29.29; II Chron. 12.15; 20.34; 25.4; 35.12; Ezra 6.18; etc. As one would expect, certain of these Old Testament formulas, particularly those involving the idea of writing, reappear in Josephus; see Adolf Schlatter, *Die Theologie des Judentums nach dem Bericht des Josefus* (= *Beiträge zur Förderung christlicher Theologie*, 2. Reihe, 26. Band; Gütersloh, 1932), pp. 64f. It may also be mentioned that in the fragments of the so-called Zadokite Work a quotation is usually introduced by the formula "as He said," more rarely "as God said," or with the name of the human author, "as Moses [Isaiah, Ezekiel, Zechariah] said." See R. H. Charles in *The Apocrypha and Pseudepigrapha of the Old Testament*, II (Oxford, 1913), 789.

[1] Cf. B. B. Warfield, " 'It Says': 'Scripture Says': 'God Says,' " *Revelation and Inspiration* (New York, 1927), pp. 283-332; republished in *The Inspiration and Authority of the Bible* (Philadelphia, 1948), pp. 299-348.

[2] The author of Hebrews occasionally cites the words of Scripture as the words of God not only where the Old Testament does not so characterize them, but even where the words are in the third person about God (1.6, 7, 8; 4.4, 7; 7.21; 10.30b).

It is not surprising also that the New Testament and the Mishnah, though agreeing in the use of many formulas, differ in the choice of certain other formulas. Thus, as was pointed out above, the Mishnah makes use of a phrase, תַּלְמוּד לוֹמַר, which has no apparent parallel in the New Testament. This formula is particularly appropriate in a body of literature which became the basis of the Talmud (compare the first word of the formula).

Another characteristic difference is the relatively large number of occurrences in the New Testament (in Matthew and John) of formulas containing the verb πληροῦν, ἀναπληροῦν, or τελειοῦν. Whether the ἵνα with which these formulas are prefixed is to be interpreted as having a telic or an ecbatic force,[1] the significance of the formulas for the purposes of the present analysis is not greatly altered. In either case the occurrence of certain events was held to be involved in the predetermined plan of God revealed in the Scriptures. That the Mishnah makes no use of this formula[2] cannot be accounted for in terms merely of the difference between the literary *genre* of the New Testament as a whole and of the Mishnah as a whole. The real reason is far more deep-seated than that and is to be traced ultimately to two differing interpretations of history. More precisely, the characteristically Christian view of the continuing activity of

---

[1] It is probably telic, so Albert Debrunner, *Friedrich Blass' Grammatik des neutestamentlichen Griechisch*, 8te Aufl. (Göttingen, 1949), § 391, Anm. 5 (Engl. trans. by R. W. Funk, 1961, p. 198), and Emil Klostermann, *Das Matthäusevangelium (Handbuch zum Neuen Testament*, 4), 2te Aufl. (Tübingen, 1927), p. 9. This judgment is strongly supported by the occasional substitution of ὅπως for ἵνα in the formula.

[2] This statement is not contradicted by Sheqalim 6.6 and Baba Qamma 3.9 (quoted above p. 56), where the *pi'el* of קוּם, though properly translated "fulfilled," is used in a way quite unlike the πληροῦν-formula of the New Testament. In the Mishnah passages, the Scripture which is quoted is said to be fulfilled by anyone whenever he complies with the Mosaic precept; there is no suggestion of a divine agent effectually fulfilling at one period in history God's pre-disclosed plan, as is involved in the New Testament usage. Furthermore, even in later rabbinical writings the formula מַה (לְקַיֵּם) לְקַיֵּם־ שֶׁנֶּאֱמַר bears only a superficial resemblance to ἵνα πληρωθῇ τὸ ῥηθέν, *et sim.* It is significant that the three examples of this formula quoted by [H. L. Strack and] Paul Billerbeck (*Kommentar zum Neuen Testament aus Talmud und Midrasch*, I [1922], 74) from the Babylonian Talmud and the Siphre Deut. as parallels to Matt. 1.22 are, in their contexts, general and lacking in any theleological import. Bacher cites (*op. cit.*, p. 170) but one example (from Seder 'Olam, c. 27 *fin.*) where Jose b. Ḥalafta refers to the fulfillment of a prophetic word (Jer. 9.9) through an historical event. For an illuminating discussion of the meaning of the Talmudic קיים, see Alfred Guillaume, "The Midrash in the Gospels," *Expository Times*, XXXVIII (1925-26), pp. 394f.

God in the historical events comprising the life, death, and resurrection of Jesus of Nazareth, fulfilling and completing the divine revelation recorded in the Old Testament, is reflected even in the choice of formulas introducing quotations of Scripture in the New Testament.[1]

---

[1] In an extensive examination made by Fitzmyer of forty-four introductory formulas that occur in the Qumran literature (Joseph A. Fitzmyer, s.j., "The Use of Explicit Old Testament Quotations in Qumran Literature and in the New Testament," *New Testament Studies*, VII [1960-61], 297-333) the author concludes that "the famous formulae of fulfillment or realization which are frequently found in the New Testament have practically speaking no equivalent in the Qumran literature." According to Fitzmyer, the reason is to be found in the difference of outlook which characterizes the two groups: "The Qumran theology is still dominated by a forward look, an expectation of what is to come about in the *eschaton*, whereas the Christian theology is more characterized by a backward glance, seeing the culmination of all that preceded in the advent of Christ" (p. 303). For further comments on differences between formulas of quotation used at Qumran and those current elsewhere, see Krister Stendahl, *The School of St. Matthew* (Uppsala, 1954), pp. 183-202; A. S. van der Woude in *Oudtestamentische Studiën*, XIV (1965), pp. 360-361; Fitzmyer in *Journal of Biblical Literature*, LXXXVI (1967), 32-33 and 36; and C. F. D. Moule, "Fulfilment-Words in the New Testament: Use and Abuse," *New Testament Studies*, XIV (1967-68), 293-320, esp. 308-311.

It may also be mentioned that, according to Gottlob Schrenk, "Josephus does not have the concept of the fulfillment of Scripture" (Kittel's *Theologisches Wörterbuch zum Neuen Testament*, vol. I, s. v. γραφή, p. 758, note 52).

CHAPTER SIX

HOW MANY TIMES DOES 'ΕΠΙΟΥΣΙΟΣ OCCUR OUTSIDE THE LORD'S PRAYER?

Until about half a century ago the word ἐπιούσιος was unknown to theologians outside the context of the Lord's Prayer. Quite understandably this adjective (the only adjective in the Lord's Prayer) had been the object of much discussion as to its derivation and meaning.[1] Then in 1925 the classical philologist, Albert Debrunner, reported that the word had been found in a fragmentary Greek papyrus of a householder's account-book listing the purchase of provisions.[2] An astonishing aspect of Debrunner's announcement was the circumstance that this Greek papyrus had been published thirty-six years before its significance for the Lord's Prayer was appreciated.[3] When therefore in 1954 it was reported in *Biblica* that the Berlin palaeographer, Günther Klaffenbach, had discovered the second occurence of this word in a context other than the Lord's Prayer, one could not only rejoice because of that fact, but also because only four years had elapsed between the discovery and its announcement in a Biblical journal.[4] But this joy was short-lived, for, upon further investigation, it became apparent that Klaffenbach had pursued a will-o'-the-wisp. The following is a summary of the "discovery."

In 1941 Chr. Blinkenberg published a Greek inscription from the acropolis at Lindos, on Rhodes, in which there appeared the words τω ιερει τας Αθανας εν[ια]υσιω.[5] After having given sustained atten-

---

[1] For a selected list of patristic quotations and discussions of ἐπιούσιος, see G. W. H. Lampe, *A Patristic Greek Lexicon*, s. v. For articles published in journals, see B. M. Metzger, *Index to Periodical Literature on Christ and the Gospels* (Leiden, 1966), pp. 229ff. and 313.

[2] *Theologische Literaturzeitung*, 1925, col. 119.

[3] The papyrus was published by A. H. Sayce in W. M. Flinders Petrie, *Hawara, Biahmu, and Arsinoe* (London, 1889), p. 34, no. 245. The text of the papyrus was reprinted by Friedrich Preisigke in his *Sammelbuch griechischer Urkunden aus Ägypten*, I (Strassburg, 1915), no. 5224.

[4] See E. V[ogt] in *Biblica*, XXXV (1954), 136f.; Klaffenbach's article appeared in *Museum Helveticum*, VI, 4 (1949; published March, 1950), 216f.

[5] Chr. Blinkenberg, *Lindos. Fouilles de l'ácropole 1902-1914*; II, *Inscriptions*, ii (Berlin and Copenhagen, 1941), no. 419, col. 777, lines 17-18.

tion to the inscription, Klaffenbach argued that the sense of this phrase must be something like "to the coming, the next (i.e., chosen for the next year) priest of Athens." But since ἐνιαύσιος does not bear this meaning, Klaffenbach suggested that the correct reconstruction must be ἐπ[ιο]υσιῳ, dropping a footnote to the effect that "Blinkenberg hat also lediglich N und Π verlesen." What shall one say of this?

In checking the copious *index verborum* of Blinkenberg's magnificent edition of the hundreds of inscriptions discovered at Lindos, one finds that, although ἐνιαύσιος appears only once (namely in this disputed passage), ἐνιαυτός appears frequently (nineteen times). Furthermore, one observes that in the immediately succeeding context of the inscription reference is made to the τοι επισταται τοι αρχοντε[ς τ]ον επ ιερεων Καλλ[ιστρ]ατου και Ροδοπειθευς ενιαυ[τον] ...,which must mean something like "the Epistatai, who are in office during the year that Kallistratos and Rhodopeitheus are priests ..." Now, it turns out that this Kallistratos is the previously named ἱερεὺς ἐνιαύσιος. One begins to doubt, then, whether Klaffenbach was justified in urging that the context demands that ὁ ἐνιαύσιος ἱερεύς means "the coming, the next priest." A glance at Blinkenberg's tables of priests at Lindos[1] discloses the information that it was customary for each priest to serve for one year. There is, in fact, no reason to take the phrase in question in any other sense than "the priest for a year."

After having come to this conclusion, the present writer decided to request from the National Museum of Copenhagen, where the stela is now deposited, a squeeze of the line in question to determine whether Blinkenberg did or did not misread Π for N. Just before writing, however, it was discovered that Debrunner had already made a similar inquiry,[2] and had learned that there is no doubt that Blinkenberg had transcribed the word correctly![3] Thus one must regretfully conclude that there is still but one recorded

---

[1] *Op. cit.*, II, i, col. 143ff.

[2] Albert Debrunner, "'Epiousios' und kein Ende," *Museum Helveticum*, IX, 1 (January, 1952), 60-62. The significance of "kein Ende" can be appreciated when it is known that, over the years since his initial publication in 1925, Debrunner gave repeated attention to the word ἐπιούσιος; for a bibliographical list of eight other articles and notes which he published dealing directly with it, see *Sprachgeschichte und Wortbedeutung; Festschrift Albert Debrunner* ... (Bern, 1954), pp. 448ff.

[3] The Greek epigrapher, Marcus N. Tod, also called attention to Klaffenbach's erroneous reconstruction (*Church Quarterly Review*, CLVIII [1957], 49-51).

instance of ἐπιούσιος in a context other than the Lord's Prayer.

The word "recorded" in the preceding sentence has been chosen deliberately, for, according to information given the author by T. C. Skeat of the Department of Manuscripts in the British Museum, the papyrus householder's list cannot now be found! The document was one of the Hawara papyri which, it has been generally assumed, Petrie deposited in University College, London.[1] "Most of them," Skeat wrote to the present writer in a letter dated 12th August, 1956, "are still there but several, including this vital one, have disappeared (I expect Petrie lent them to friends who omitted to return them)." This is all the more distressing in view of the possibility that its editor, A. H. Sayce, may have misread the papyrus.[2] As Skeat pointed out in a subsequent letter (dated 6th March, 1957), Sayce's "shortcomings as a decipherer are generally recognised— see, e.g. Griffiths's balanced obituary notice in *Journal of Egyptian Archaeology*, 1929. Ample examples can be gleaned from almost any of Sayce's publications, e.g. the two papyri published by him in 1890 and recently re-discovered by [E. G.] Turner in University College (*Journ. Eg. Arch.*, 1952, pp. 132-133)."

Until this papyrus has been found again, therefore, the cautious lexicographer must perforce rely only on the context of the Lord's Prayer, on etymological considerations, and on patristic and versional evidence in seeking to ascertain the precise meaning of ἐπιούσιος.[3]

---

[1] According to Joseph W. Scott, Librarian, and Harry S. Smith, Department of Egyptology, University College, London, "there is in fact no certainty whether this particular papyrus [edited by Sayce] came to University College or not. It may be significant that in his article on the Hawara papyri in 1911, J. G. Milne made no mention of it. When the importance of Sayce's reading for the interpretation of ἐπιούσιον in the Lord's prayer was realized, searches were made by a number of scholars for the papyrus at University College without result" ("Letters to the Editor," *The* [London] *Times Literary Supplement*, April 18, 1966, p. 372). See also the letter from Prof. E. G. Turner (*ibid.*, May 5, 1966, p. 387), requesting librarians and curators seek for the lost document in their collections of papyri.

[2] Sayce reported that he found ἐπιουσι( ).

[3] Several scholars (most recently W. Foerster in Kittel's *Theologisches Wörterbuch*, II, 587 [Eng. trans., p. 591]) have called attention to the evidence cited by Holmes and Parsons in their edition of the Septuagint at II Macc. 1.8, to the effect that three Armenian manuscripts (the Codices Sergis) support the reading ἐπιουσίους. For a discussion of this "evidence" see D. Y. Hadidian, "The Meaning of ἐπιούσιος and the Codices Sergis," *New Testament Studies*, V (1958), 75-81, who concludes that, amid a wide variety of ill-founded and erroneous statements made by various scholars concerning these codices and their significance, in reality no further instance of ἐπιούσιος has come to light.

CHAPTER SEVEN

SEVENTY OR SEVENTY-TWO DISCIPLES?

Did Jesus send out seventy or seventy-two disciples? The narrative in chapter 10 of Luke involves, as is well known, textual variants in both of the verses where the number of the disciples is mentioned (verses 1 and 17). It is the purpose of the present chapter to collect the evidence for and against each variant reading and to list other groups of seventy or seventy-two mentioned in Jewish antiquities and early Christian literature. Though it may turn out to be difficult, in view of the evenly balanced evidence, to arrive at a firm decision in favor of one or the other variant reading, it will no doubt be useful to survey the evidence and to correct certain widespread misapprehensions as to what several early manuscripts actually read.

One of the earliest witnesses to this passage is the Chester Beatty Papyrus I, dating from about the middle of the third century. Though it is fragmentary at the beginning of the tenth chapter of Luke,[1] fortunately verse 17 is extant. Unhappily, however, its evidence for this verse has been incorrectly cited in many editions of the New Testament which include readings from the manuscript. The latest editions of the New Testament prepared by Bover (4th ed. 1959), the British and Foreign Bible Society (2nd ed. 1958), Merk (9th ed. 1964), Souter (2nd ed. 1947), as well as the Huck-Lietzmann-Cross Synopsis (9th ed. 1954) and Nelson's Gospel Parallels (2nd ed. [1957]), all cite $\mathfrak{P}^{45}$ as supporting the reading "72." Undoubtedly the editors of these editions have depended upon Sir Frederic G. Kenyon's transcription of $\mathfrak{P}^{45}$, which, admirable though it be in many respects, is, nevertheless, marred by occasional inaccuracies, and at this verse, as C. H. Roberts has pointed out, the reading of the papyrus is incorrectly given. Roberts's own suggestion, however, that $\mathfrak{P}^{45}$ reads "76" disciples,[2] is likewise an error. The present writer has examined the passage in $\mathfrak{P}^{45}$ under natural and artificial light, and has assured himself that the Greek character which follows the letter omicron (standing for "70") is neither β, as

[1] Merk erroneously cites $\mathfrak{P}^{45}$ in his apparatus for Luke 10.1.
[2] *Harvard Theological Review*, XLVI (1953), 236, n. 14.

Kenyon supposed, nor ς, as Roberts thinks, but merely the *diplé*, or space-filler (>), which scribes would use occasionally in order to bring an otherwise short line even with the right-hand margin of the column. In fact, by consulting Kenyon's volume of Plates of 𝔓⁴⁵ anyone can see the similarity between the disputed character and the *diplé* which appears on the same folio near the top of the column.

As regards versional evidence, at Luke 10.1 Tischendorf and von Soden wrongly cite the Old Latin manuscript *b* in support of "70." Von Soden cites Syrˢ for the addition of δύο in verse 17, but Burkitt declared that the evidence of this manuscript is not clear here.[1] Again, a palimpsest manuscript of the Acts dating from the sixth or seventh century (Codex Floriacensis, commonly designated by the siglum *h*) is sometimes cited as evidence for "72." Among the readings of this manuscript which one of its editors, E. S. Buchanan, thought he could decipher, supplementing the pioneer work of Samuel Berger, was Acts 14.6, [*et fugerunt*] *in Lycaoniae civitates, sicut ihs dixerat eis LX[XII in Lys]tra et Derben.* Although Berger's transcript gives no hint of the words *sicut ihs dixerat eis LX[XII]*, Buchanan was sure of them, and declared, "It is almost certain, from considerations of space, that our MS. read LXXII and not LXX."[2] In view of Buchanan's eccentricities (not to use a stronger word),[3] it would seem unwise to place much confidence in this reading and restoration,[4] and therefore it should not be cited as evidence for or against the variants in Luke 10.1 and 17.

---

[1] F. C. Burkitt, *Evangelion da-Mepharreshe*, I (Cambridge, 1904), 313.

[2] E. S. Buchanan, *The Four Gospels from the Codex Corbeiensis ... together with ... the Fleury Palimpsest* (*Old Latin Biblical Texts*, no. v; Oxford, 1907), p. 98.

[3] For an absurd debate instigated by Buchanan regarding a Latin palimpsest of the Gospels from Tarragona (which only he was able to decipher by going to the top of a sky-scraper building in New York!), see the (sometimes acrimonious) papers by Camille Pitollet and Pierre Batiffol in *The Oldest Text of the Gospels, with an Introduction by E. S. Buchanan* (New York, 1924). An edition of this palimpsest, prepared by Buchanan, was printed by G. P. Putnam's Sons, New York, but was subsequently suppressed. See also Henry A. Sanders, "Buchanans Publikationen altlateinischer Texte, eine Warnung," *Zeitschrift für die neutestamentliche Wissenschaft*, XXI (1922), 291-9, and publications referred to under items 384, 420, and 459-61 in the present writer's *Annotated Bibliography of the Textual Criticism of the New Testament* (Copenhagen, 1955).

[4] In his review of Buchanan's volume F. C. Burkitt expresses a *caveat*: although "it is quite possible that he has read *h* correctly in Ac. xiv. 6 ... this startling reference to Lc. x. 17 (or rather Matt. x. 23) is not legible in the

The early evidence for "70" and "72" in Luke 10.1 and 17 may now be set out.

ἑβδομήκοντα

GREEK EVIDENCE: 𝔓⁴⁵ (extant for only v. 17) ℵ A C K L M (v. 17 only) W X Γ Δ Θ Λ Ξ Π Ψ 0115 (extant for only v. 17) fam. 1 fam. 13 28 (v. 17 only) 33 (v. 17 only) 565 700 892 1009 1010 1071 1079 1195 1216 1230 1241 1242 1253 1344 1365 1546 1646 2148 2174

VERSIONAL EVIDENCE: f q i (extant for only v. 1) Syrᶜ (v. 17), ᵖᵉˢʰ, ʰᵃʳ, ᵖᵃˡ Copᵇᵒ Goth Ethiop Old Slavonic

PATRISTIC EVIDENCE: Iren ⁱⁱ. ²¹. ¹ ᵃⁿᵈ ⁱⁱⁱ. ¹³. ² Tert adv Marc iv. 24 Clem ʰʸᵖᵒᵗ ᵛⁱⁱ (ᵃᵖ ᴱᵘˢ ʰⁱˢᵗ ⁱⁱ.¹.⁴) Orig ʰᵒᵐ ⁷, ³ ⁱⁿ ᵉˣᵒᵈ Eus ʰⁱˢᵗ ⁱ.¹⁰.⁷; ¹³.⁴; ⁱⁱⁱ.²⁴. ⁵; ᵈᵉᵐ ᵉᵛ ⁱⁱⁱ.².²⁴ᶠ.; ⁴.³⁷; ᵗʰᵉᵒᵖʰ ˢʸʳ ᵛ.²² Amb ⁱⁿ ᴸᵘᶜ. ˣ.³ Tit Bostr ᵃᵖ ᶜᵃᵗ ᵒˣ ⁸² Cyr Al ᵍʳ ᵉᵗ ˢʸʳ Hier ᵉᵖ ⁶⁹. ⁶: ⁷⁸. ⁶ Bas ᵐᵒʳ ²⁹¹

ἑβδομήκοντα δύο

GREEK EVIDENCE: 𝔓⁷⁵ B D M (v. 1 only) R (ex indice capitum) 0181 (v. 1 only) 28 (v. 1 only) 33 (v. 1 only)

VERSIONAL EVIDENCE: a b c d e l r² aur Vulg Syr ˢ, ᶜ (ᵛ. ¹), ʰ ᵐᵍ (ᵛ. ¹⁷) Copˢᵃ Arm Georgian Persian

PATRISTIC EVIDENCE: [Tatian's] Diatess ⁽ᴱᵖʰʳ⁾, ᴸⁱèᵍᵉ, ᴾᵉʳˢ, ᵀᵒˢᶜ, ⱽᵉⁿ Doctr App³⁴ Act Jud Thom¹⁷⁶ Doct Addai⁵ Orig ʰᵒᵐ ²⁷, ¹¹ ⁱⁿ ᴺᵘᵐ Ephr ⁱⁿ ᴾᵃᵘˡ Clem Recog ⁱ. ⁴⁰ Adamant ᵈⁱᵃˡ ⁸⁰⁶, ⁸²⁸ Aug ᶜᵒⁿˢᵉⁿˢ ⁱⁱ. ²³, ⁵⁴ Ambrst ʳᵒᵐ ⁸¹

Before discussing the weight of the evidence cited above, the following observations should be made.

I

In Luke 10.1 Syrˢ,ᶜ read "72", whereas in verse 17 Syrᶜ reads "70," and, though Burkitt (Evang. da-Meph., vol. I, p. 313) was inclined to think that Syrˢ reads "72," he indicates that "the reading is not quite clear." In Luke 10.1 Syrᵖᵃˡ is extant only in

---

photograph, and I think still needs verification before any argument can be built upon it. In the case of a Palimpsest the old rule holds good, that in the mouth of two or three witnesses every word must be established" (Journal of Theological Studies, IX [1908], 305f.). Likewise A. C. Clark expressed himself with due caution: "If this reading is correct (it does not appear in Berger's transcript), I can only regard the words sicut ... LX [XII] as a note which has got into the text" (The Acts of the Apostles [Oxford, 1933], p. 248).

Codex A, which reads "70." In verse 17 all three codices read "70." Zohrab's Armenian text (followed by the American Bible Society ed.) prints "72" but gives "70" in a footnote.

Twice Ephraem in his comments on Tatian's Diatessaron (preserved in Armenian) refers to "72" (pp. 59 and 160, Moesinger; pp. 50 and 140, Leloir), but in the Appendix one finds "70" (p. 287, Moesinger; p. 248, Leloir). Fortunately a Syriac manuscript (dating from the end of the fifth or the beginning of the sixth century) containing about three-fourths of Ephraem's Commentary on the Diatessaron has recently become available. Although it is defective in the section corresponding to p. 50 of Leloir's Latin translation, and has a different Appendix from that in the Armenian text, the passage that corresponds to p. 140 reads "Et ideo elegit septuaginta duos statim, et misit eos a se, et sanarunt mirabiliter ..." (p. 127, Leloir's trans.). Thus, although Ephraem does not happen to quote the Diatessaron's text concerning the number of disciples mentioned in Luke 10.1 and 17, he does make a comment himself about the number, and this, in the Syriac tradition of the Commentary proper, is "72."

In the Latin translation made by the Mechitharist Fathers of Ephraem's Commentary on Paul's Epistles (Venice, 1893) three times reference is made to the "72" disciples (in comments on I Cor. 15.7; II Cor. 8.23 and 11.15). Though it is true, as Molitor[1] and Klijn[2] have indicated, that the Latin rendering of scriptural passages in this edition has frequently been conformed to the text of the Latin Vulgate, in this case the Armenian text itself apparently reads "72."[3] Origen, as frequently, supports both readings. In his homily 7, 3 in Exod. (preserved only in Latin) he argues on the basis of the seventy palm trees that there were seventy disciples. On the other hand, in his homily 27, 11 in Num. he finds the seventy-two palms a type of Jesus' seventy-two disciples.

In the later Patristic period Christian imagination was busy with the identity of the seventy or seventy-two disciples, and various lists were drawn up. Indexes of the names of the seventy are given

---

[1] Joseph Moliter, *Der Paulustext des hl. Ephräms* ... (Rome, 1938), pp. 19*-24*.

[2] A. F. J. Klijn, *Journal of Theological Studies*, n.s., v (1954), 76.

[3] Unfortunately the Armenian text of Ephraem is not available to me; for its testimony I depend upon Joseph Schäfers, *Evangelienzitate in Ephräms der Syrers Kommentar zu den Paulinischen Schriften* (Freiburg im B., 1917), p. 24, who refers to I Cor. 15.7 and II Cor. 8.22f.

in texts attributed to Dorotheus and Epiphanius. Other lists of the Seventy-two are supplied by pseudo-Hippolytus and pseudo-Logothetes, as well as in an Index Anonymus Graeco-Syrus.[1] Still later is another list of the Seventy incorporated in the Byzantine Painter's Manuel of Dionysius, monk of Fourna d'Agrapha.[2]

II

In analysing the external evidence, one observes that many (though not all) early Syriac witnesses, including Tatian, testify to the predominance in Syria of the tradition that there were seventy-two disciples. With this agree the chief representatives of the Alexandrian and Western texts, B and D, as well as Jerome's Vulgate. (The capitula, however, in several manuscripts of the Vulgate read LXX [see Wordsworth and White, I, p. 286], and in two of his epistles Jerome himself speaks of seventy disciples). Among the versions, part of the Old Latin, the Syr[s, h mg], the Sahidic, and the Georgian support "72."

On the other hand, other Alexandrian evidence of moderately great weight ($\aleph$ L Δ Λ Ξ) as well as so-called Caesarean witnesses ($\mathfrak{P}^{45}$ Θ *fam.* 1 *fam.* 13) and W join in support of the number "70." Several Western witnesses (part of the Old Latin as well as Irenaeus and Tertullian) also read "70." Among the Greek and Latin Fathers, it appears that "70" enjoyed a somewhat wider currency than "72."

The factors bearing upon the evaluation of the internal evidence, whether involving transcriptional or intrinsic probabilities, are singularly elusive. Did Jesus' action have any symbolic import? Did he wish to convey some symbolic meaning by the number of disciples? Which number, "70" or "72," appears to be better suited to further his intention? Moreover, the view of certain scholars (for example, Creed, Easton, Klostermann, Luce, Manson, etc.), that part or all of Luke's account is unhistorical, being in fact but another version of the sending out of the Twelve, does not solve the textual problem. Whether or not the narrative rests upon an actual event in Jesus' ministry, certainly many of those who transmitted

---

[1] All these have been edited by Theodor Schermann in his Teubner edition, *Prophetarum vitae fabulosae* ... (Leipzig, 1907), pp. 132ff. For a discussion of the several lists, see R. A. Lipsius, *Die apokryphen Apostelgeschichten und Apostellegenden*, 1 (Braunschweig, 1887), 193ff.

[2] See Athanasios Papadopoulos-Kérameus, ed., *Manuel d'iconographie chrétienne* ... (St.-Pétersbourg, 1909), pp. 151-3; another list is given on pp. 298f.

the account were likely to find a parallel to instances of seventy or seventy-two in Jewish antiquities—of which there are many. These include the following (in some cases the literary evidence is late, but the tradition embodied may go back to an earlier date).

(*a*) There were seventy elders appointed by Moses to assist him (Num. 11.16-17, 24-5).[1]

(*b*) The several nations of the earth total seventy (Gen. 11); but in the LXX the number comes to seventy-two.[2]

(*c*) According to the Talmud, every commandment that God gave to Moses on Mt. Sinai "divided itself and could be heard in all seventy languages" (*B. Shabbat* 88*b*).

(*d*) The *Alphabet of Rabbi Akiba*, a semi-mystical treatise of the early post-Talmudic period, goes one step further, declaring that "during the forty days Moses spent [on Sinai] he was taught the Torah in the seventy aspects of the seventy languages" (*Othioth de-rabbi Akiba*, ed. Wertheimer [1914], p. 12).

(*e*) Still later the reference to seventy languages was dropped, and in the Zohar the seventy aspects stand for the inexhaustible totality of the divine Torah (*Zohar*, I, 140*a*; *Zohar hadash*, fol. 8*b*).

(*f*) Josephus appointed and installed a council of seventy magistrates in Galilee (*Jewish War*, II.xx.5 (570), and *Life*, 14 (79)), and during the War of the Jews the Zealots set up a tribunal of seventy (*Jewish War*, IV.v.4 (336)).

(*g*) According to the Mishnah, the supreme Sanhedrin consisted of seventy-one members (*Sanhedrin*, 1.5f.; 2.4; *Shebuth*, 2.2). In other passages reference is made to a (local?) council of seventy-two elders (*Zebahim*, 1.3; *Yadaim*, 3.5; 4.2).

(*h*) According to the *Letter of Aristeas* (sections 46-50) six elders were chosen from each of the twelve tribes in order to prepare a Greek translation of the Torah. Aristeas concludes the list of names of those selected with the statement: οἱ πάντες ἑβδομήκοντα δύο. (It also chanced, he says, that the work of translation was completed

---

[1] On rabbinic legends concerning how Moses selected seventy out of the twelve tribes without incurring ill-will and envy, see [Strack-] Billerbeck, *Kommentar*, ii, 166 *in loc.*

[2] For a wide selection of rabbinic comments, see [Strack-] Billerbeck's *Kommentar* on Rom. 1.23 (iii, 48-51). Furthermore, according to Appendix I to the Testaments of the XII Patriarchs (8.3f.), "When the nations were divided in the time of Phaleg ... the Lord, blessed be he, came down from his highest heaven, and brought down with him seventy ministering angels, Michael at their head. He commanded them to teach the seventy families which sprang from the loins of Noah seventy languages."

in seventy-two days; sect. 307). Josephus repeats this story, though in the following sentence he gives the number as seventy (*Antiq.*, XII.ii.5 (49-57)). Subsequent authors refer to this version as "the Seventy" (οἱ ο′) or occasionally, with greater precision, "the Seventy-two" (οἱ οβ′).[1]

In manuscripts of the Septuagint, κατὰ τοὺς ἑβδομήκοντα stands in the subscription to Genesis in Codex B; παρὰ ἑβδομήκοντα stands at the end of Proverbs in MS. C; and ἡ τῶν ἑβδομήκοντα ἔκδοσις appears in a note before Isaiah in MS. Q.

(*i*) In the ritual of the Feast of Tabernacles, seventy bullocks were offered on behalf of the Gentile nations. The rabbis said, "They offer seventy bullocks for the seventy nations, to make atonement for them, that the rain may fall upon the fields of all the world; for, in the feast of tabernacles, נידונין על המים, *judgment is made as to the waters* [that is, God determines what rains shall be for the year following]."[2]

(*j*) There were seventy sons of Jerubbaal (Judg. 9.2), seventy sons of Ahab (II Kings 10.1), and seventy priests of Bel (Bel and Dragon, 10).

(*k*) According to I Enoch the Jews were distributed among seventy (*v.l.* seven) [angelic] shepherds (89.59ff.), but subsequently (90.1) some versions represent half of them as thirty-six. In III Enoch, however, the number of princes of kingdoms on high is seventy-two, corresponding to the seventy-two tongues of the world (17.8; cf. 18.2f., 30.2; in 48.C.9, however, reference is made to seventy princes). It may be mentioned also that in the same book Metatron is said to have seventy names (48. D, but the subsequent enumeration includes over one hundred names).

(*l*) Ezra is commanded by God to keep hidden the seventy [apocryphal] books (II Esdr. 14.46).

(*m*) According to the Jerusalem Targum, seventy angels accompanied God at his descent to see the Tower of Babel.[3]

---

[1] See the *testimonia* collected by Paul Wendland in the Teubner edition of Aristeas (Leipzig, 1900), pp. 90-166. For a still wider-ranging list of references in the Fathers, see Constantine Oikonomos, Περὶ τῶν ο′ ἑρμηνευτῶν τῆς Παλαιᾶς Θείας Γραφῆς, II (Athens, 1845), 268-285.

[2] Gloss on *Bemidbar Rabba*, sect. 21 (quoted by J. Lightfoot on John 7.37, in *Horae hebraicae et talmudicae*, III [Oxford, 1859], 320).

[3] For a list of other (mostly still later) instances of groups of seventy, see Moritz Steinschneider, "Die kanonische Zahl der muhammedanischen Secten und die Symbolik der Zahl 70-73, aus jüdischen und muhammedanisch-arabischen Quellen nachgewiesen," *Zeitschrift für die morganländische Gesell-*

(*n*) The newly discovered Coptic Gospel of Philip states that "the Lord went into the dye-works of Levi. He took seventy-two colors and threw them into the vat. He took them out all white ..." (logion 54).

Which of these instances of seventy or seventy-two may have influenced Jesus and/or those who formed and transmitted the account in Luke 10, it is difficult to determine. Certainly many of the opinions of commentators on this passage are arbitrary and fanciful, as, for example, the view of those who assume that the appointment of the Seventy took place about the time of the Feast of Tabernacles, when seventy bullocks were sacrificed for the Gentile nations, and that therefore the ritual of the feast may have had something to do with the number. Again, some think that since the disciples probably went to Transjordan, where many Gentiles lived, it was appropriate that the number should correspond to the seventy Gentile nations on earth. On the other hand, still other scholars point out that the context offers no hint that such an allegory was intended, and since Luke and Theophilus were not Jews they could neither have expressed nor understood such a thought simply by the use of the number 70.

CONCLUSIONS

So many factors must be taken into account, and so many influences may have been at work, that the utmost caution should be observed in drawing fixed conclusions.

From the standpoint of external evidence, it is obvious that both readings were widely current from a very early period. On the one hand, it appears that "72" is read by witnesses that are generally accounted to be primary representatives of each of several text-types. Thus B (Alexandrian text) unites with D and part of the Old Latin (Western text) as well as Syr^s (early Antiochian text) and Sah (text of Upper Egypt). Furthermore, the Bodmer codex of Luke ($\mathfrak{P}^{75}$) carries the date of the reading "72" back into the early third century. The emergence of the number "70" could be explained either psychologically (it is more likely that the precise number should be transformed into the round number 70, than that

---

schaft, IV (1850), 145-70; and "Nachtrag," *ibid.*, LVII (1903), 474-507. Much of the material collected by P. Saintyves in *Deux mythes évangéliques, les douze apôtres et les 72 disciples* (Paris, 1938), is disappointingly irrelevant.

the "solemn" number 70 should be transformed into 72) or palaeo-graphically (a scribe accidentally omitted δύο because δύο (or the variant reading δύο δύο) occurs in the immediate context of verse 1). Thereafter "70" spread far and wide in subsequent witnesses, being aided by the patristic exegesis which saw a parallel to the seventy palm trees at Elim.

On the other hand, however, the interpretation of this testimony is not absolutely certain. What appears to be independent diversity of types of text that support "72" may be illusory, for it is possible that Tatian, who seems to have read "72," may have influenced Syr^s, D, part of the Old Latin, and many of the Syrian Fathers. The evidence of the Bodmer Papyrus, B, and the Sahidic may be the result of a mathematical penchant of an Alexandrian recensionist who altered "70" to "72" for, so to speak, "scholarly" reasons. Furthermore, it can be argued on palaeographical grounds that in verse 1 the word δύο was accidentally added to ἐβδομήκοντα because of the presence of δύο [δύο] a few words later. As far as the external evidence goes, therefore, perhaps all that one can say with assurance is that both "70" and "72" were widespread in the early centuries.

As regards internal evidence, if it be granted that Jesus sent out a large group of disciples "two by two into every town and place where he himself was about to come," the number may have been intended (by Jesus and/or by those who transmitted the account) to suggest some symbolic significance. But what this symbolism was is exceedingly difficult to ascertain. On the one hand, if the mission is to be understood as a mission to Israel, the number may have been determined as a multiple of the twelve tribes of Israel. On the other hand, since several authors in the New Testament find a parallel between Jesus and Moses,[1] it may be that this group of Jesus' disciples is intended to correspond to the seventy elders who gave assistance to Moses. So evenly balanced are these two possibilities that it is hazardous to dogmatize as to which is the more probable.

In short, though the reading "72" is supported by a combination of witnesses that normally carries a high degree of conviction as to originality, yet the age and diversity of the witnesses which support "70" are so weighty, and the internal considerations so evenly

---

[1] For the passages, see Jeremias in Kittel, *Theologisches Wörterbuch*, IV, 871-8.

balanced, that the investigator must be content with the conclusion that (1) on the basis of our present knowledge the number of Jesus' disciples referred to in Luke 10 cannot be determined with confidence, and (2) if one is editing the text the least unsatisfactory solution is to print ἑβδομήκοντα [δύο].

CHAPTER EIGHT

THE ASCENSION OF JESUS CHRIST

Among the chief anniversaries in the Church's calendar of holy days the ascension of Jesus Christ probably causes modern Christians more embarrassment than joy. Coming forty days after Easter, Ascension Thursday used to be observed with special services and the cessation of ordinary work-a-day activities. But in the second half of the twentieth century most church members are either entirely unaware of the religious significance of the day, or are vaguely uneasy that somehow a Christian is expected to believe that Jesus Christ returned to God in heaven by a kind of celestial elevator. No other story of the New Testament creates for the modern reader a greater sense of conflict between what he knows of astrophysics and what he thinks the Biblical account necessarily implies.

I. APOSTOLIC TESTIMONY TO THE ASCENSION

The testimony in the New Testament relating to the ascension of Jesus Christ can be set forth in three categories.

(1) Descriptive accounts of the ascension are confined to Luke-Acts and to the long ending of Mark. The text of the conclusion of the third Gospel (24.51) has been transmitted in two forms, the longer of which reads: καὶ ἐγένετο ἐν τῷ εὐλογεῖν αὐτὸν [sc. Ἰησοῦν] αὐτοὺς διέστη ἀπ' αὐτῶν καὶ ἀνεφέρετο εἰς τὸν οὐρανόν. This text is supported by 𝔓⁷⁵ A B C K L W X Θ Π Ψ *fam.* 1, *fam.* 13, 28 *al.* The shorter text, which omits καὶ ἀνέφετο εἰς τὸν οὐρανόν, is supported by ℵ* D *a b e ff² j l* geo¹.[1] According to Westcott and Hort the explicit reference to the ascension is a Western non-interpolation (i.e. an Alexandrian interpolation),[2] which therefore is to be re-

---

[1] Although the Sinaitic Syriac manuscript is sometimes cited as evidence supporting the reading which makes no explicit reference to the ascension, verse 51 in this witness reads ܘܟܕ ܒܪܟ ܐܢܘܢ ܐܬܦܪܫ ܡܢܗܘܢ ("And while he blessed them, he was lifted up from them"); i.e. instead of διέστη the version implies the reading ἀναφέρετο (or, perhaps, ὑψώθη).

[2] See Hort in "Notes on Select Readings," p. 73 in B. F. Westcott and F. J. A. Hort, *The New Testament in the Original Greek*, [vol. II,] *Introduction [and] Appendix*, 2nd ed. (London, 1896).

garded as a secondary modification of the text. During the past
generation, however, a growing number of textual critics have
expressed dissatisfaction with Hort's judgment concerning so-called
Western non-interpolations, and in the present instance have been
inclined to explain the origin of the shorter, Western text as either
(1) a harmonization introduced in order to relieve the apparent
contradiction between this account and the account in Acts 1.3ff.
of the forty-day interval between Easter and the ascension mentioned, or (2) an accidental scribal oversight occasioned by homoeo-
arcton (ΚΑΙΑ ... ΚΑΙΑ).[1] Whatever may be the outcome of the
current debate on the evaluation of Western non-interpolations,[2] in
the present passage it should be noted that even if one prefers the
shorter form of text, which makes no explicit mention of the ascension, the description of the joyful return to Jerusalem on the
part of the disciples after Jesus left them seems to suggest a parting
of more than ordinary significance.

It is in the book of Acts that the account of the ascension is told
with circumstantial detail. Having made the general statement (1.3)
that Jesus "presented himself alive after his passion by many
proofs, appearing to them [the disciples] during forty days, and
speaking of the kingdom of God," the author reports that Jesus
appeared to a group of his followers on the mount called Olivet,
which is near Jerusalem. The narrative continues: "as they were

---

[1] The following scholars argue for the originality of the longer form of
the text of Luke 24.51: W. Bauer, *Das Leben Jesu im Zeitalter der neutestamentlichen Apokryphen* (Tübingen, 1909), p. 275; L. Brun, *Die Auferstehung
Christi in der urchristlichen Überlieferung* (Oslo, 1925), p. 91; G. Bertram,
"Die Himmelfahrt Jesu vom Kreuz aus und der Glaube an seine Auferstehung," *Festgabe für Adolf Deissmann* (Tübingen, 1927), p. 205; A. Fridrichsen, "Die Himmelfahrt bei Lukas," *Theologische Blätter*, VI (1927), 339;
M. Goguel, *La foi à la résurrection de Jésus dans le christianisme primitif*
(Paris, 1933), p. 348, n. 2; A. C. Clark, *The Acts of the Apostles* (Oxford, 1933),
p. 407; A. N. Wilder, "Variant Traditions of the Resurrection in Acts,"
Journal of Biblical Literature, LXII (1943), 311; M.-J. Lagrange, *Critique
textuelle*; II, *La critique rationnelle* (Paris, 1935), p. 69; Benoit, "L'Ascension," *Revue Biblique*, LVI (1949), 189; J. Jeremias, *Die Abendmahlsworte Jesu*,
3te Aufl. (Göttingen, 1960), p. 144, Engl. trans., *The Eucharistic Words of
Jesus* (London, 1966), p. 152; and K. Aland, *New Testament Studies*, XII
(1966), 208-210 (= *Studien zur Überlieferung des Neuen Testaments und seines
Textes* [Berlin, 1967], pp. 170f.).

[2] For recent discussions of Western non-interpolations, see Aland, *op. cit.*,
pp. 195-210 (= pp. 162-172), and Carlo M. Martini, s.j., *Il problema della
recensionalità del codice B alla luce del papiro Bodmer XIV* (Rome, 1966),
pp. 151ff.

looking on, he was lifted up, and a cloud took him out of their sight (βλεπόντων αὐτῶν ἐπήρθη, καὶ νεφέλη ὑπέλαβεν αὐτὸν ἀπὸ τῶν ὀφθαλμῶν αὐτῶν). And while they were gazing into heaven as he went, behold, two men stood by them in white robes, and said, 'Men of Galilee, why do you stand looking into heaven? This Jesus, who was taken up from you into heaven, will come in the same way as you saw him go into heaven' " (1.9-11). The verisimilitude of the account is enhanced by the presence of a little touch that suggests a veritable reminiscence of what one may be sure was the disciples' real attitude at the moment, though it soon ceased to be. When they asked, "Lord, will you at this time restore the kingdom to Israel?" (Acts 1.6), their thoughts were still running in the groove of the old Jewish expectation.

The long ending of Mark's Gospel (16.19) also contains an explicit reference to the ascension: "So then the Lord Jesus, after he had spoken to them, was taken up into heaven, and sat down at the right hand of God (ἀνελήμφθη εἰς τὸν οὐρανὸν καὶ ἐκάθισεν ἐκ δεξιῶν τοῦ θεοῦ)." Though not part of the original form of the second Gospel, the long ending has been generally recognized by the church as part of the canonical text of Mark.

(2) The Gospel according to John twice refers to the ascension in an anticipatory manner. In 6.62 Jesus is represented as asking, "What if you were to see the Son of man ascending where he was before?" and in 20.17 Jesus cautions Mary Magdalene, "Do not hold me, for I have not yet ascended to the Father; but go to my brethren and say to them, I am ascending to my Father and your Father, to my God and your God." Whatever one may believe concerning the genuineness of these statements as sayings of Jesus, there can hardly be reasonable question that the tradition recorded in the opening chapter of Acts was before the evangelist's mind as he wrote these words.

(3) Besides direct and anticipatory references to the ascension, many other New Testament passages reflect the widespread currency in the early Church of what may be called a doctrine of the ascension of Christ. Sometimes the doctrine is introduced in connection with Jesus' resurrection, and sometimes it is developed in terms of his glorification and session at the right hand of God. Characteristic words which are used in the New Testament to describe the ascension and glorification of Christ include the following:

ἀναβαίνειν   Jn. 3.13; 6.62; 20.17; Acts 2.34; Eph. 4.8-10.
ἀναλαμβάνειν   [Mk.]16.19; Acts 1.2, 11, 22; 1 Tim. 3.16.
ἀνάλημψις   Lk. 9.51.
εἰσέρχεσθαι   Heb. 6.20; 9.12, 24.
καθίζειν   (trans.) Acts 2.30; Eph. 1.20.
                          (intrans.) Heb. 1.3; 8.1; 10.12; 12.2.
πορεύεσθαι   Jn. 14.2, 12, 28; 16.7, 28; 1 Pet. 3.22.
ὑπάγειν   Jn. 7.33; 8.14, 21; 13.33; 14.4; 16.5, 10, 17.
ὑψοῦν   Acts 2.33; 5.31.
ὑπερυψοῦν   Phil. 2.9.

In these passages a variety of authors indicate that Jesus was
taken up, exalted, highly exalted; that he went up, entered, and
sat down at the right hand of the Majesty on high. In the choice
of this language it is probable that two Old Testament passages
exercised a molding influence upon the church's vocabulary: (a) the
account of the assumption of Elijah[1] in II Kings 2.11, and (b) the

---

[1] The *Religionsgeschichtlicher* has combed Jewish and secular literature for
parallels to the account of Christ's ascension. Besides Enoch and Elijah Old
Jewish parallels have been found in the accounts of Baruch (II Bar. 46.7;
48.30), Ezra (IV Ezr. 14.9, 49), Moses (Josephus, *Antiq.* IV.viii.48), Zephaniah
(Clement, *Strom.* 5.11), Abraham (*Apocal. of Abraham*, 15-29), Isaiah (*Ascens.
of Is.*, 6-11), and Adam (*Life of Adam and Eve*, 25-29). (For parallels in
pre-Israelitish cultures, see Georg Bertram, "Die religionsgeschichtliche Hin-
tergrund des Begriffs der 'Erhöhung' in der Septuaginta," *Zeitschrift für
alttestamentliche Wissenschaft*, LXVIII [1956], 57-71). Non-Jewish parallels have
been found in the manner of departure of the king Etana, the worship of
king Sulgis, the apotheosis of Heracles, of Titus, of Germanicus, of Antoninus
and Faustina, of Sappho, and others. Still other personages have been
reported as leaving the earth in an unusual manner at death, such as Romu-
lus, Mithras, Julius Caesar, Apollonius of Tyana, Mani, Mohammed, and the
Virgin Mary. (For other non-Jewish parallels see Richard Holland, "Zur
Typik des Himmelfahrt," *Archiv für Religionswissenschaft*, XXIII (1925), 207-
220; and Elias Bickermann, "Die römische Kaiserapotheose," *ibid.*, XXVII
(1929), 1-34, esp. 9-13.
There seems to be no need for the purposes of the present study to analyze
the accounts of these so-called parallels. It is enough to mention here that
(1) a vigorous, scientific methodology will not be satisfied with mere surface
analogies, but will demand evidence of substantial parallelism; (2) when
such parallelism has been established, an inquiry must be made as to the
nature of the parallelism (i.e. whether it is genetic or merely analogical); and
(3) if genetic, it must not be uncritically assumed that the direction in which
the influence operated was always upon Christianity (cf. pp. 9-11 above).
Furthermore, the question whether the New Testament account of Christ's
ascension is or is not similar to other accounts of ascensions or assumptions
from earth to heaven is subordinate to the question of the significance of
Christ's ascension; the latter remains *sui generis* in that it reveals the signifi-

proof-text from Psalm 110.1 (which New Testament writers use more frequently than any other single verse from the Old Testament), "The Lord says to my lord, 'Sit at my right hand, till I make your enemies your footstool.'"

In addition to the explicit account in chap. 1, the book of Acts contains several allusions to the exaltation of Christ. Thus, in his sermon at Pentecost, before quoting Psalm 110.1, Peter declares, "This Jesus God raised up, and of that we all are witnesses. Being therefore exalted at the right hand of God ..., he has poured out this which you see and hear" (2.32f.). Later, Peter and the apostles say to the high priest, "The God of our fathers raised Jesus whom you killed by hanging him on a tree. God exalted him at his right hand as Leader and Savior" (5.30f.).

In the apostolic Letters more than once the resurrection and the exaltation of Christ are linked together. Thus, in Rom. 8.34 Paul speaks of "Christ Jesus, who died, yes, who was raised from the dead, who is at the right hand of God, who indeed intercedes for us." In Col. 3.1 references to Christ's resurrection and heavenly session are brought together ("If then you have been raised with Christ, seek the things that are above, where Christ is, seated at the right hand of God"; compare Eph. 1.19f.). In I Pet. 3.21f. another apostolic author combines allusions to the resurrection, the ascension, and the present *sessio ad dextram*: "through the resurrection of Jesus Christ, who has gone into heaven and is at the right hand of God."

The doctrine of Christ's exaltation after his death and mediatorial work in heaven is emphasized in the Letter to the Hebrews. Though there is but one reference to Christ's resurrection (13.20), several

---

cance of Christ's own unique person and work. The investigation of literary parallels is to some extent analagous to that of tracing the adoption and the adaptation of iconographic imagery by Christian artists from pagan protypes in order to represent pictorially the ascension of Christ; see, e.g. Ernest T. DeWald, "The Iconography of the Ascension," *American Journal of Archaeology*, 2nd ser., XIX (1915), pp. 227-319; Hubert Schrade's monograph, *Zur Ikonographie der Himmelfahrt Christi*, in *Vorträge der Bibliothek Warburg, 1928-29*, ed. Fritz Saxl (Berlin, 1930), pp. 66-190; and G. Kretschmer, "Himmelfahrt und Pfingsten," *Zeitschrift für Kirkengeschichte*, LXVI (1954-55), 209-253. For comments on differences between Jewish and pagan accounts of ascensions and the Lukan account, see P. A. van Stempvoort, "The Interpretation of the Ascension in Luke and Acts," *New Testament Studies*, V (1958), 38; Ernst Haenchen, *Die Apostelgeschichte*, 5te Aufl. (Göttingen, 1965), p. 116; and J. Heuschen, *The Bible on Ascension*, trans. by F. Vander Heijden (De Père, Wisconsin, 1965), pp. 90-92.

passages speak of his entering the heavenly sanctuary (6.20; 9.12, 24) and his sitting down at God's right hand (1.3; 8.1; 10.12; 12.2), where, the author states, Christ has fully accomplished his priestly and kingly work on our behalf.

From these passages, and others which might also be cited, it appears that the apostolic teaching did not always sharply differentiate the ascension or glorification of Christ from his resurrection. Apparently in some parts of the early church the resurrection and ascension were regarded as two episodes in the same process of the exaltation of Christ. In the passages mentioned in sections (1) and (2) above, however, the ascension is clearly distinguished from the resurrection.

It is perhaps not surprising that it is Luke the theologian and the historian who is concerned to inform his readers more precisely concerning the length of time between Easter and the final appearance of Jesus to his disciples. Having condensed his narrative at the close of his "former treatise" (24.51), at the beginning of his second book he indicates that forty days elapsed between the first and the last appearances of Jesus to his followers (Acts 1.3). Whether the "forty" is intended to be taken as exactly forty or as a round number, and whether it has a mystical significance, are questions to which diverse answers have been given.[1] It deserves to be mentioned, however, that most of the numerals employed by Luke throughout the Gospel and the Acts give the impression of being intended in an exact sense.

By way of summary one can say that the testimony of several New Testament authors links Christ's ascension and glorification closely to his resurrection. The special contribution which Luke makes is to suggest that the ascension was an event as real and objective as the other appearances of the risen Lord.

---

[1] For a summary of differing opinions reference may be made to Victorien Larrañaga, *L'Ascension de Notre-Seigneur dans le Nouveau Testament* (Rome , 1938), pp. 603-628 [= *La Ascensión del Señor en el Nuevo Testamento*, II (Madrid, 1943), 248-275]. For other literature (up to 1961) not cited by Larrañaga, see A. J. Mattill, Jr., *A Classified Bibliography of Literature on the Acts of the Apostles* (Leiden and Grand Rapids, 1966), being vol. VII of *New Testament Tools and Studies*, pp. 325ff., to which may be added P.-H. Menoud, " 'Pendant quarante jours' Actes 1.3," *Neotestamentica et Patristica* [Cullmann Festschrift] (Leiden, 1962), pp. 148-156.

II. IMPLICATIONS OF THE ASCENSION OF JESUS CHRIST

The narrative of Christ's ascension in Acts 1 is similar in many respects to the other accounts of Christ's post-resurrection appearances. It is neither more nor less difficult to explain than they are.[1] The impression which the New Testament accounts of the ten or eleven appearances[2] of Christ make upon the reader is that the risen Lord was not subject to the ordinary laws of nature. Taken as a whole the narratives of the resurrection imply that Jesus' body had passed into a condition new to human experience. He could appear suddenly and unexpectedly from the hiddenness of God, and he could disappear again just as suddenly and unexpectedly. As one modern exegete puts it, the implication of such texts as Jn. 20.19-20 is that the risen Jesus was "at once sufficiently corporeal to show his wounds and sufficiently immaterial to pass through closed doors."[3]

The post-resurrection accounts suggest that the risen Lord was not living at any one place in Jerusalem or Galilee. Instead they imply that he had passed into a mode of being out of which he "appeared" in whatever form he willed, superior to all obstacles, and into which he disappeared again. Since we have no category from personal experience of this mode of being, theologians are accustomed to speak of the mystery of Christ's resurrection. It is not the purpose of the present study to attempt to probe that

---

[1] Cf. the argument of W. A. Whitehouse, *Christian Faith and the Scientific Attitude* (Edinburgh and London [1952], pp. 87-89, where he points out that "what creates the difficulty [for modern readers of the life of Jesus] is the assertion of His bodily resurrection from the dead, and this can only be eliminated from the life-story (or explained away as a mythological mode of expression) by violating the integrity of the New Testament witness and the religion which is true to it. The final item in the life-story, the Ascension, does not add to the difficulty ... The intellectual difficulty about the physical facts entailed by His bodily resurrection and His appearances is not increased by this last withdrawal. What the story does is to underline the importance of taking this post-crucifixion life as a part of His earthly history, with its own limited duration" (p. 88). A similar point is made by A. W. Argyle, "The Ascension," *Expository Times*, LXVI (1955), 240ff.

[2] If the reference in I Cor. 15.6 to Jesus' appearing "to more than five hundred brethren at one time" is identified with his appearing on a mountain in Galilee in Matt. 28.17 (which, by the statement "but some doubted," may suggest that more persons were present than merely the eleven disciples), there are ten appearances reported in the New Testament; if they are not identified, there are eleven appearances.

[3] C. K. Barrett, *The Gospel According to St. John, an Introduction with Commentary and Notes on the Greek Text* (London, 1962), p. 472.

mystery, but merely to explore what, given the mystery of Christ's resurrection, Luke's account of the ascension is intended to teach.[1]

It should be said at the outset that the ascension of Jesus follows necessarily as part of the logic of his bodily resurrection.[2] For, if Jesus rose from the dead not with a natural, but with a spiritual (or glorified) body—and this is undoubtedly the teaching of the New Testament—then it would appear to be inappropriate for him to remain permanently on earth. The translation of his resurrected body to that sphere of existence to which it properly belonged can be said to be both natural and necessary.

In interpreting the significance of the ascension, one may profitably begin by considering the incarnation. It is perhaps too obvious to be mentioned that one would be on the wrong track if he tried to reckon the number of minutes, or days, or months, or years that it took the eternal Christ to leave heaven and come to earth, to be incarnated.[3] As the incarnation is not to be thought of as the passage from God's space into ours, so, on the other hand, the ascension is not to be regarded as a journey from earth to heaven which required a certain number of minutes, days, months, or years to be accomplished. In other words, the ascension, properly understood, has no more to do with Ptolemaic astronomy than does the incarnation. That Jesus "ascended up on high" does not mean that he was elevated so many feet above sea-level, but that he entered a higher sphere, a spiritual existence, what the Christian

---

[1] Compare the carefully phrased statement of Heuschen: "The resurrection of Christ is a real event which, being a mystery of faith, is not a reality which can be ascertained by using criteria of historical science. So too the ascension of the Lord, taken in the sense in which we speak [i.e. "ascension" means first of all "exaltation of Christ"], is a real event, which however because of its supernatural and unearthly character cannot be strictly proved, but only believed. That which can be proved historically is the faith of the disciples in this ascension of the Master. We can also historically prove that this conviction of their faith was well founded" (J. Heuschen, op. cit., p. 74.)

[2] On this point see C. F. D. Moule, "The Ascension—Acts 1.9," Expository Times, LXVIII (1956/57), 208, and Hugh Anderson's discussion of the ascension in his chapter on "The Easter Witness of the Evangelists," in The New Testament in Historical and Contemporary Perspective, Essays in Memory of G. H. C. Macgregor, ed. by Hugh Anderson and William Barclay (Oxford, 1965), pp. 49-51.

[3] Whatever other early theologians thought about the incarnation, there is no suggestion in the Fourth Gospel that the "enfleshment" of the Logos (1.14) required a certain lapse of time or the traversing of a certain distance in stellar space to earth, such as is recounted in later gnostic speculations.

calls heaven, where God is and whence he had come to visit the earth in humility. When a school boy says that he has been promoted to a higher class, we would do him an injustice if we took him to mean no more than that he was transferred from a classroom on the ground floor to one upstairs. Similarly, the New Testament writers use ordinary language of physical elevation to suggest a metaphorical or analogical meaning. In short, to speak, as the Bible and the Apostles' Creed do, of Christ's ascending to heaven and of his sitting on the right hand of God, is to employ symbolic language.

The point was made above that the appearance of the risen Christ to his followers on Mount Olivet (Acts 1.3-11) is represented as an episode as real and objective as his other appearances during the period of approximately six weeks after the crucifixion. The only difference between the ascension and the previous withdrawals is that the ascension was the last of them. All of the post-resurrection appearances were intended to convince his followers that he had conquered death and was indeed accredited as God's Messiah. How was he to make certain that they would understand that the period during which he had "manifested himself" to them was now coming to an end, and that they should not expect further appearances of the same kind? He could, of course, have told them that this was now the last time he would appear to them, and that they should not wait for him to appear yet again. Human nature being what it is, however, it is not hard to imagine that, without some decisive and dramatic symbol suggesting the terminus of the transitional period, the disciples would have continued to live in suspense, hoping against hope that at any instant their Master would appear again. Later, when no subsequent manifestation occurred, such expectation would have been supplanted by all kinds of doubts and perplexities as to what had finally become of their Lord. What is being suggested, therefore, is that though Jesus did not need to ascend in order to return to that sphere which we call heaven, yet in fact he did ascend a certain distance into the sky,[1]

---

[1] According to Hugh Montefiore (in *Novum Testamentum*, IV [1960], 309-310, reprinted in his book, *Josephus and the New Testament* [London, 1962], pp. 30-31), Jesus' ascension may be alluded to by Tacitus (*Hist.*, v.13) and by Josephus (*Jewish War*, VI.v.3), both of whom refer to miraculous portents seen in the sky at a time that corresponds roughly to the chronology of Acts 1. Such a supposition, however, runs counter to the testimony of the New Testament, namely that after his resurrection and before his ascension Christ

until a cloud took him out of sight. By such a miraculous sign he impressed upon his followers the conviction that this was now the last time he would appear to them, and that henceforth they should not expect another manifestation, but should realize that the transitional period had ended.

The symbolism which Jesus employed was both natural and appropriate. The transcendent realm of the Spirit is frequently referred to by the idea of height. The expression "the Most High" is a surrogate for God in the thinking of many peoples. At Jesus' final appearance to his followers he rose from their midst, not because he had to do so in order to go to the Father, but for didactic reasons, in order to make his last act symbolically intelligible.

That the lesson was learned by the early Church seems to be clear from the fact that the records of the first and second centuries indicate that the disciples suddenly ceased to look for any manifestation of the risen Lord other than his second coming. It appears that something had taken place which assured them that the period of his post-resurrection appearances had definitely come to an end.

In addition to conveying the sense that his departure was final, his act of ascending conveyed the clear impression that he had gone to his Father and that all power was put into his hands.[1] Very likely those whose minds were first impressed by Jesus' ascension believed, as we no longer believe, that heaven as a place is above our heads, and that the path of the ascending Jesus was the way thither.[2] But still today, with our superior knowledge of the cosmic

---

appeared to none but his followers, with the exception, perhaps, of James (I Cor. 15.7).

[1] On the distinction between the event of the ascension itself (which was surely as unseen to mortal eyes as was the incarnation) and the miraculous outward sign with which the last post-resurrection appearance ended, Barth writes: "Ascension as visible exaltation—i.e. exaltation that is perceptible as vertical elevation in space—of Jesus Christ before the bodily eyes of His disciples is obviously not the way to the session at the right hand of God. For the right hand of God is no place, least of all a place to be reached by some sort of natural or supernatural way through astronomic space. As sign and wonder this exaltation is a *pointer* to the revelation, that occurred in his resurrection, of Jesus Christ as the bearer of all power in heaven and earth," *Credo, a Presentation of the Chief Problems of Dogmatics with Reference to the Apostles' Creed* (London [1936], p. 113; compare Barth, *Dogmatics in Outline* (London [1949], pp. 124-128.

[2] During the patristic and medieval period the implications of the ascension for current theories of the cosmos were often discussed. Augustine (*Haeres.*, 59) opposed the view of those who taught that the body of Christ ascended no farther than the sun, in which it was deposited ("Negant

system, there is no other symbolical action that can be imagined which could convey the desired impression. In short, whatever else Jesus' final withdrawal may be thought to involve, it is certain that he parted from his followers in such a way that they thereby became even more certain of his royal power and rule.

One may ask, in conclusion, what is meant by the symbolic language used by several New Testament theologians (e.g. Eph. 1.20; I Pet. 3.22; Heb. 1.3; etc.) that Christ is seated at the right hand of God on high. What is God's right hand? This is metaphorical language for the divine omnipotence. Where is it? Everywhere. To sit, therefore, at the right hand of God does not mean that Christ is resting; it affirms that he is reigning as king, wielding the power of divine omnipotence.[1]

Salvatorem in carne sedere ad dexteram Patris, sed ea se exuisse perhibent, eamque in sole posuisse, accipientes occasionem de Psalmo, *In sole posuit tabernaculum suum*"). On the assumption made by many of the Scholastics that the outermost sphere (of the Ptolemaic cosmos) was made of impenetrable material, a special miracle had to be postulated for Christ to pass bodily through this sphere. Furthermore, this outside shell of the universe was sometimes regarded as the limit beyond which there could be nothing worthy of the name of locality but where a complete vacuum prevailed. The idea that Christ in glory existed bodily in that void led Durandus and others to make the objection that sensation would be impossible to him, as no sense-impressions can be transmitted where there is no medium through which they can pass. (St. Thomas's views on this matter changed, and the Leonine ed. of his works omits his discussion and solution of this difficulty, which appear in other editions as 3a:57:4:@2). For an account of the history of the doctrine of the ascension down to the late Middle Ages, see J. G. Davies's Bampton Lectures, *He Ascended into Heaven* (London, [1958]); for Luther's view, see Albrecht Oepke, "Unser Glaube an die Himmelfahrt Christi," *Luthertum*, XLIV (1938), 161-186, especially 174ff.

[1] The *sessio ad dextram* is, as Calvin observes, "a similitude borrowed from princes," and refers, "not to the posture of his [i.e. Christ's] body, but to the majesty of his dominion" (*Institutes of the Christian Religion*, II.xvi.15).

CHAPTER NINE

EXPLICIT REFERENCES IN THE WORKS OF ORIGEN TO VARIANT READINGS IN NEW TESTAMENT MANUSCRIPTS

Of all the ante-Nicene Fathers Origen is by far the most important source of information regarding the text of the Bible. Reared in the literary tradition prevailing at Alexandria, he was one of the first scholars of the Christian Church to give sustained attention to the transmission of the Scriptures. His work on the text of the Old Testament, the monumental Hexapla, surpasses in sheer magnitude all similar projects in textual criticism down to comparatively recent times.

The question whether Origen ever attempted to edit a critical text of the New Testament has been answered quite diversely. On the one hand, several scholars,[1] impressed by Origen's concern over the deplorable condition of Biblical manuscripts of his day, have supposed that, since he sought to remedy these conditions in the Old Testament by the employment of critical symbols invented by Homeric commentators, he would have been likely to do the same for the text of the New Testament. They point, for example, to Origen's complaint concerning the variant readings in manuscripts of the Gospels: "The differences among the manuscripts have become great, either through the negligence of some copyist or through the perverse audactiy of others; they either neglect to check over what they have transcribed, or, in the process of checking, they make additions or deletions as they please."[2] In support of the

---

[1] E.g., J. L. Hug, *Einleitung in die Schriften des Neuen Testaments*, I (3rd ed., Stuttgart and Tübingen, 1826), 119-200, 223-37 (Eng. trans. by David Fosdick [Andover, 1836], pp. 117, 131-8); Caspar René Gregory, *Prolegomena* to Tischendorf's *Novum Testamentum graece*, III (8th ed., Leipzig, 1884), 1146; *idem, Textkritik des Neuen Testamentes*, II (Leipzig, 1902), 763-4, and III, 1004.

[2] *Comm. in Matt.* xv, 14 (*Griechische Christliche Schriftsteller*, Origenes x, 387, 28-338, 7, Klostermann): πολλὴ γέγονεν ἡ τῶν ἀντιγράφων διαφορά, εἴτε ἀπὸ ῥαθυμίας τινῶν γραφέων, εἴτε ἀπὸ τόλμης τινῶν μοχθηρᾶς <εἴτε ἀπὸ ἀμελούν-των> τῆς διορθώσεως τῶν γραφομένων, εἴτε καὶ ἀπὸ τῶν τὰ ἑαυτοῖς δοκοῦντα ἐν τῇ διορθώσει <ἢ> προστιθέντων τῶν ἀφαιρούντων. The words within angular brackets are not in the Greek manuscripts of Origen but have been supplied by editors (e.g. Koetschau, Eltester, and Klostermann) on the basis of the

hypothesis that Origen prepared a recension of the New Testament, attention is sometimes drawn to two passages in the works of Jerome in which he appeals with deference to *exemplaribus Adamantii*.[1] In one passage Jerome declares: *Legitur in quibusdam codicibus: "Quis vos fascinavit non credere vertati?" Sed hoc quia in exemplaribus Adamantii non habetur, omisimus*.[2] The other passage, which has been a *crux interpretum*,[3] is: *In quibusdam Latinis codicibus additum est, "neque Filius": cum in Graecis, et maxime Adamantii et Pierii*[4] *exemplaribus, hoc non habeatur ascriptum: sed quia in nonnullis legitur, disserendum videtur*.[5]

On the other hand, other scholars have argued that these passages contain no clear evidence to support the theory that Origen prepared an edition of the Greek New Testament. Jerome's references to *exemplaribus Adamantii* need be understood as nothing more than copies of the New Testament (or Gospels) once possessed by Origen and here and there, perhaps, annotated with critical comments.[6] Moreover, if Origen really had prepared a recension of the New Testament text, it is passing strange, these scholars argue, that no trace of it remains. It is pointed out, furthermore, that, in the same context in which Origen refers to his critical labors on the text of

---

Latin translation. A. D. L[oman] proposed another emendation: εἴτε ἀπὸ μοχθηρίας τῆς διοθώσεως τῶν γραφομένων εἴτε καὶ ἀπὸ τόλμης τινῶν τῶν τὰ ἑαυτοῖς δοκοῦντα (*Theologisch tijdschrift*, VII [1873], 233).

[1] Adamantius, it need scarcely be mentioned, was Origen's surname; see Eusebius, *Hist. eccl.*, VI, xiv, 10; Epiphanius, *Panarion*, LXIV, 1.

[2] *Comm. in Gal.*, I (Migne, *Patrologia Latina*, XXVI, 373 C).

[3] The problem arises from the circumstance that, though Jerome asserts that the words in question, namely οὐδὲ ὁ υἱός, were absent from the approved copies of Origen, yet Origen nowhere appears to doubt their genuineness, nor does he indicate that he knows of any manuscripts which omitted them. Cf. the perplexity over this passage expressed by Wordsworth and White, *Novum Testamentum ... latine*, ed. maior, I (Oxford, 1898), 658-9, and Eberhard Nestle, *Einführung in das griechische Neue Testament* (2nd ed., Göttingen, 1899), pp. 152ff. (Eng. trans. [London, 1901], p. 187).

[4] The Pierius referred to here is doubtless the disciple of Origen by this name, known as "the younger Origen," who was head of the Catechetical School at Alexandria *c*. 255; see Eusebius, *Hist. eccl.*, VII, xxxii, 26f. and Jerome, *De vir. illustr.*, 76.

[5] *Comm. in Matt.*, iv (Migne, *Patrologia Latina*, XXVI, 188B).

[6] E.g. [Westcott and] Hort, *The New Testament in the Original Greek*, [II] *Introduction* (Cambridge, 1881), 182, § 249; F. H. A. Scrivener, *A Plain Introduction to the Criticism of the New Testament*, 4th ed., II (London, 1894), 271ff.; Oscar von Gebhardt, "Bibeltext des N.T." in Herzog-Hauck, *Realencyklopädie für protestantische Thelogie und Kirche*, 3te Aufl., II (Leipzig, 1897), 25; and B. H. Streeter, *The Four Gospels*, 5th impr. (London, 1936), pp. 594ff.

the Old Testament, he declares quite explicitly that he had not dared to do the same for the text of the New Testament: *In exemplaribus autem Novi Testamenti hoc ipsum me posse facere sine periculo non putavi. Tantum suspiciones exponere me debere et rationes causasque suspicionum, non esse inrationabile existimavi.*[1]

In light of these considerations, it is not difficult to draw the conclusion that, so far as is known, Origen never attempted to prepare a formal edition of the New Testament. At the same time, in all his writings, and particularly in his exegetical treatises, Origen shows great interest in and solicitude for critical details in the Biblical text. A succession of scholarly investigations of Origen's quotations of the New Testament[2] bears testimony to the wealth of textual information which the voluminous writings of this Father provide.

In addition to the usual mode of citation of texts for comment or example, Origen occasionally makes reference to variant readings in New Testament manuscripts current in his day. Thus, as will be seen from the list of passages given below, he refers to variant readings found in "few," "other," "certain," "many," "most," or "almost all" of the manuscripts.[3] In spite of the many studies on Origen's contribution to the textual criticism of the New Testa-

---

[1] *Comm. in Matt.*, xv, 14 (x, 388, 31-389, 5, Klostermann). (It should be pointed out that this statement is lacking in the Greek tradition of Origen, being preserved only in the Latin recension). The date of this evidence must be placed within the last decade of Origen's life, for according to Eusebius (VI, xxvi, 2) Origen wrote his Commentary on Matthew toward the end of his life, under the rule of Philip the Arabian (i.e. after A.D. 244).

[2] E.g. J. J. Griesbach, *De codicibus quatuor evangeliorum Origenianis* (Halle, 1771), reprinted in his *Opuscula academica*, ed. J. P. Gabler, 1 (Jena, 1824), 226-317; *idem, Novi Testamenti loci ab Origene et Clemente Alex. in scriptis eorum quae graece supersunt allegati cum textu vulgari collati* (= *Symbolae criticae ad supplendas et corrigendas variarum N. T. lectionum collectiones ...,* II [Halle, 1793]); J. P. P. Martin, "Origène et la critique textuelle du N. T.," *Revue des questions historiques,* xxxvII (1885), 5-62; Paul Koetschau, "Bibelzitate bei Origenes," *Zeitschrift für wissenschaftliche Theologie,* xLIII [N. F., VIII] (1900), 321-77; Erwin Preuschen, "Bibelcitate bei Origenes," *Zeitschrift für die neutestamentliche Wissenschaft,* IV (1903), pp. 67-74; Ernst Hautsch, *De quattuor evangeliorum codicibus Origenianis* (Diss., Göttingen, 1907), translated with additions as *Die Evangelienzitate des Origenes* (= *Texte und Untersuchungen,* 3te Ser., IV, 2a [xxxIV, 2a]; Leipzig, 1909); and Frank Pack, "Origen's Evaluation of Textual Variants in the Greek Bible," *Restoration Quarterly,* IV (1960), 139-46.

[3] In referring to Old Testament manuscripts he uses, in addition, such expressions as "the more (most) accurate," "the ancient," "the majority," and "the common" manuscripts.

ment, this class of explicit references to variant readings has been strangely neglected. It is obvious, however, that an analysis of the evidence presented in such passages should cast light upon several important matters, notably: (1) the evaluation of the sagacity of Origen as a textual critic, and (2) the proportion of manuscript evidence for and against a given variant reading extant today as compared with the proportion of manuscript evidence known to Origen.

The following is a collection of passages in Origen's works in which he refers to variant readings in New Testament manuscripts, with the citation of the support for these variants which has been preserved today in New Testament manuscripts.

No. 1. Matt. 4.17. In the great mass of witnesses the theme of Jesus' preaching is represented as being identical with that of John the Baptist (3.2), namely μετανοεῖτε· ἤγγικεν γὰρ ἡ βασιλεία τῶν οὐρανῶν. According to Origen, however, in certain manuscripts the word μετανοεῖτε does not appear.[1] In his comments he shows that he is quite prepared to accept the longer text, for "if the Saviour says the same things that John did, God who sent both is one." At the same time Origen shows his preference for the variant reading that omits μετανοεῖτε [and γάρ], arguing as follows: "John, on the one hand, making ready for God a prepared people, probably says at first 'Repent ye'; but Jesus, receiving those that have been made ready and no longer needing repentance, does not say 'Repent ye.' " Today μετανοεῖτε and γάρ are lacking in the Sinaitic and Curetonian Syriac as well as in Clement and Eusebius.

(Matt. 6.1; see p. 101 below).

No. 2. Matt. 8.28-32 (parallels in Mark 5.1-17 and Luke 8.26-37). In his comment on John 1.28 Origen acknowledges that "in the matter of proper names the Greek copies are often incorrect,"[2] and then cites an example drawn from the Synoptic Gospels. "The transaction (οἰκονομία) about the swine, which were driven down a steep place by the demons and drowned in the sea, is recorded to

---

[1] Ἔν τισι τὸ μετανοεῖτε οὐ κεῖται, *Matt. frag.,* 74 (XII, iii, 1, 45, Klostermann).

[2] *Comm. in Ioan.,* vi, 41 (24) (IV, 150, 3 seq., Preuschen). R. G. Clapp's careful analysis, "A Study of the Place-Names Gergesa and Bethabara," *Journal of Biblical Literature,* XXVI (1907), 62-83, is still exceedingly valuable; cf. also F. C. Burkitt, "Gergesa—A Reply," *ibid.,* XXVII (1908), 128-33, and José M. Bover, "Dos casos de toponimia y de crítica textual," *Sefarad,* XII (1952), 271-82.

have taken place in the country of the Γερασηνῶν. Now, Γέρασα is a town of Arabia, and has near it neither sea nor lake. ... But in a few copies we have found εἰς τὴν χώραν τῶν Γαδαρηνῶν." This reading, however, does not suit Origen any better than the one which was apparently in the majority of manuscripts known to him, because, though Gadara is in the neighborhood of "the well-known hot springs," no lake is there with overhanging banks, nor any sea. He suggests, therefore, a third place, Γέργεσα, because it "is an old town in the neighborhood of the lake now called Tiberias, and on the edge of it there is a steep place abutting on the lake." In support of this suggestion Origen argues on the basis of local tradition (it is the place "from which, it is pointed out, the swine were cast down by the demons") and of etymology ("the meaning of Gergesa is 'dwelling of the casters-out,' " and thus the name "contains a prophetic reference to the conduct shown the Saviour by the citizens of those places, who 'besought him to depart out of their territory' ").

Unfortunately Origen does not indicate which Synoptic account it is that he is discussing. Moreover, though he declares that the words Gerasenes and Gadarenes are witnessed by manuscripts, he does not actually say that the name which he prefers (Γεργεσαῖοι) was found in any manuscripts known to him. Today the evidence in all three Synoptics is divided:

Matt. 8.28

Γαδαρηνῶν ℵ* B C* M Θ Σ 566 713 1189 1555 syr[s,p,h].

Γεργεσηνῶν ℵ[c] C[3] fam. 1 fam. 13 22 157 565 700 𝔎.

Gerasenorum it vg syr[h mg] cop[sa].

Mark 5.1

Γερασηνῶν ℵ* B D it vg.

Γεργεσηνῶν ℵ[c] L U Δ Θ fam. 1 22 33 565 700 syr[s] cop[bo] arm geo eth.

Γαδαρηνῶν A C Π Σ Φ fam. 13 157 𝔎 syr[p,h].

Γεργυστηνῶν W.

Luke 8.26, 37

Γερασηνῶν 𝔓[75] B C* (only vs. 37) it vg syr[h mg] cop[sa] geo.

Γεργεσηνῶν ℵ* [cb] (only vs. 37) C[2] (only vs. 37) L X 1 33 157 syr[pal] cop[bo] geo eth.

Γαδαρηνῶν ℵ[ca] (only vs. 37) A R W Δ Π Ψ fam. 13 28 565 syr[s,p,h] goth.

No. 3. Matt. 16.20. In discussing the meaning of Jesus' injunction to his disciples that they should tell no one that he was the Messiah,[1] Origen mentions a variant reading in Matthew's account, where, he says, "according to some of the manuscripts (κατά τινα τῶν ἀντι-γράφων)" Matthew has διεστείλατο, but "some other manuscripts (τινα τῶν ἀντιγράφων)" have ἐπετίμησεν. Since Origen's explanation of the significance of the passage does not depend upon the difference of the verbs, after mentioning the existence of the variant reading he has nothing more to say about it. Apparently he preferred the reading διεστείλατο, for in his discussion this verb is used constantly, while ἐπετίμησεν is mentioned only once (when he points out that the verb used in the Synoptic parallels [Mark 8.30; Luke 9.21] also appears in "some of the manuscripts of Matthew"). Today ἐπετί-μησεν is preserved in only B* D d (comminatus est) e (increpauit) syr[c] eth, and διεστείλατο appears in unc rell, minusc omn, f ff[1] g[1] l aur vg (praecepit) a b c ff[2] q r[2] (imperauit) syr[p,h] cop[sa,bo] geo Aug.

No. 4. Matt. 18.1. Before commenting on the disciples' question as to who is the greatest in the kingdom of heaven, Origen mentions that "according to some of the manuscripts (κατὰ μέν τινα τῶν ἀντι-γράφων)" the Evangelist prefixed the phrase ἐν ἐκείνῃ τῇ ὥρᾳ, "whereas according to others (κατὰ δὲ ἄλλα)" the expression ἐν ἐκείνῃ τῇ ἡμέρᾳ appears.[2] For Origen's purpose it makes no difference which reading is original, and he expresses no opinion on the matter. Among witnesses today ὥρᾳ is read by unc pler, minusc pler d f g[2] l q vg syr[p,h] cop[sa,bo] eth arm[codd] Aug, and ἡμέρᾳ is read by Θ 1 33 517 700 713 954 1424 1675 a b c e ff[1,2] g[1] n aur syr[s,c] arm[edd] geo Hil.

No. 5. Matt. 21.5. In commenting on this passage Origen draws attention to Jesus' fulfillment of Zechariah's prophecy by riding into Jerusalem ἐπὶ ὄνον καὶ πῶλον υἱὸν ὑποζυγίου.[3] He notes that there is a variant reading here, and says that "in some [manuscripts] (ἔν τισι)" the word υἱόν does not appear. Today the word is lacking in ℵ[a] L Z and in a scattering of Old Latin witnesses.

No. 6. Matt. 24.19. Origen's comment on this verse (Vae autem praegnantibus et nutrientibus in illis diebus) is preserved only in Latin.[4] After discussing the meaning of praegnantibus he turns to

---

[1] Comm. in Matt., xii, 15 (X, 103, 1 seq., Klostermann).

[2] Comm. in Matt., xiii, 14 (X, 213, 22-26, Klostermann).

[3] Comm. in Matt., xvi, 14 (X, 522, 12-17, Klostermann). The text of part of Origen's comment is corrupt, but the reference to the variant reading appears to be firm; see Hautsch, op. cit., XXXIV, 2ᵃ (1909), 72ff.

[4] In Matt. Comm. ser., 43 (XI, ii, 87, 28-30, Klostermann).

consider the second part of the statement and writes: *Si autem (sicut in multis exemplariis) scriptum est "vae sugentibus," dicendum est quoniam animae sunt quae lactantur adhuc.* It is difficult to imagine what variant in Greek (if any) may lie behind Origen's *sugentibus*— which has the appearance of a translational variant in Latin. The only variants of θηλαζούσαις extant today are θηλαζομέναις in D and ἐν θηλαζούσαις in L.

No. 7. Matt. 27.16-17. In this famous passage Origen is our earliest witness for the existence of manuscripts which prefix the name "Jesus" to the name "Barabbas". He declares that "in many copies it is not stated that Barabbas was also called Jesus, and perhaps [the omission is] right."[1] The consideration which weighs with Origen in deciding that the text which lacks Barabbas's *praenomen* is correct is basically a dogmatic one; he does not think that the name "Jesus" was ever applied to evil-doers, and therefore the variant reading is the work of heretics (*in multis exemplaribus non continetur quod "Barabbas" etiam "Iesus" dicebatur, et forsitan recte, ut ne nomen Iesu conveniat alicui iniquorum. In tanta enim multitudine scripturarum neminem scimus Iesum peccatorem. ... Et puto quod in haeresibus tale aliquid superadditum est*). The witnesses which today read Ἰησοῦν Βαραββᾶν in verses 16 and 17 are Θ *fam.* 1 22 (only in vs. 17) 229 1582 syr[s,pal] arm geo[2].

No. 8. Mark 2.14; 3.18. In rebutting Celsus' allegation that Jesus had gathered about him a group of "ten or eleven persons of notorious character, the very wickedest of tax-collectors and sailors," Origen declares that Matthew alone was a tax-collector. A little later, however, he indicates that "Levi also, who was a follower of Jesus, may have been a tax-collector; but he was in no wise of the number of the apostles, except according to a statement in some of the copies of the Gospel according to Mark (κατά τινα τῶν ἀντιγράφων ...)."[2] Although Origen does not explicitly say so, he probably knew and preferred the variant reading in Mark 2.14 where Ἰάκωβον replaces Λευείν in D Θ *fam.* 13 543 565 *a b c e ff g*[1]* Ephr Photius.

---

[1] *In Matt. Comm. ser.*, 121 (XI, ii, 255, 24-31, Klostermann).

[2] *Contra Celsum*, i, 62 (I, 113, 19-22, Koetschau). The manuscripts vary in reading Λευης, Λευΐς and Λεβης. In Origen's comments on Ἰάκωβος Ἀλφαίου in Matt. 10.3 he remarks that ἔν τισι δὲ τοῦ κατὰ Μᾶρκαν εὐαγγελίου εὑρίσκεται " Ἰάκωβον τὸν τοῦ Ἀλφαίου" <ἀντὶ τοῦ "Λευὶ τὸν τοῦ Ἀλφαίου">, *In Matt. frag.*, 194 (XII, iii, 1, 93, Klostermann); Klostermann's insertion of the words between angular brackets is undoubtedly justified.

(Mark 5.1-17; see no. 2 above).

No. 9. Luke 1.46. In the Latin translation of Origen's homilies on Luke (the Greek text is not extant), reference is made to the variant readings regarding the authorship of the *Magnificat*. The name of the blessed Mary, he says, stands here "in some copies," while "according to other manuscripts" it is Elizabeth who prophesies.[1] Elsewhere in this and the following homily Origen takes for granted that the familiar text with "Mary" is correct. Among extant witnesses "Elisabeth" is read by only *a b l** Iren[lat], Nicetas of Remesiana, and Cyril of Jerusalem.

(Luke 8.26-37; see no. 2 above).

No. 10. Luke 9.48. In the course of discussing Jesus' teaching regarding true greatness Origen notices that Jesus' declaration, "He who is least among you all, the same is great," stands also in other manuscripts (καὶ ἐν ἄλλοις) with the future tense, "... the same shall be great."[2] Though Origen makes no explicit statement as to which reading he prefers, it may be supposed that he favored the present tense, for he uses it when citing the same passage twice some chapters later.[3] The future tense of the verb, which is probably an interpretative alteration, is preserved in A D Γ Δ Λ Π unc[9] al pler *e q* syr[c,p] arm.

No. 11. Luke 14.19. While commenting on Jesus' parable concerning the excuses offered by those who had been invited to the great feast, Origen uses a variant reading to make a point in his interpretation. He introduces his comment with the observation that "in some [manuscripts] instead of 'I pray you,' there stands 'And because of this I am not able to come' " (καὶ ἔν τισιν, ἀντὶ τοῦ " Ἐρωτῶ σε," "Καὶ διὰ τοῦτο οὐ δύναται ἐλθεῖν" κεῖται).[4] The only Greek manuscript which preserves this variant today is Codex Bezae (διὸ οὐ δύναμαι ἐλθεῖν), with the support of *a b c ff² i q*.

No. 12. Luke 23.45. The generally accepted text of this passage describing the failure of the sun's light at the time of Jesus' crucifixion (τοῦ ἡλίου ἐκλιπόντος) has given much trouble to ancient and modern commentators alike. In the Latin translation of Origen's

---

[1] *In Luc. Hom.*, vii (IX, 47, 19-48, 3, Rauer). According to Zahn (*Komm.*, Exk. III, pp. 748ff.) the significant words regarding the variant are due to Jerome and do not represent Origen's original homily; see also Zahn in *Neue kirchliche Zeitschrift*, XXII (1911), 253-68.
[2] *Comm. in Matt.*, xiii, 19 (X, 233, 14-15, Klostermann).
[3] *Ibid.*, 29.
[4] *In Luc. frag.*, 68 (IX, 268, 15-17, Rauer).

commentary on Matthew he notices that, "according to most copies (*secundum pleraque exemplaria*)" Luke reads *et obscuratus est sol* (i.e. καὶ ἐσκοτίσθη ὁ ἥλιος).[1] Some copies, however (*in quibusdam autem exemplariis*), read *sole deficiente*, a reading which Origen first suggests may have arisen from a desire for greater explicitness on the part of someone who assumed that the darkness could not be due to anything but an eclipse. But later he prefers to say that the enemies of the church altered the text in order to be able to use it as a point of attack on the Gospels. The reading ἐσκοτίσθη ὁ ἥλιος occurs in D W Θ *fam.* 13 28 157 700 𝕶 lat syr eth geo Marcion Tatian. Since elsewhere Origen follows the generally accepted text, and assumes the occurrence of an eclipse,[2] it is probable, as Hort pointed out, that in his commentary on Matthew he was "under the influence of the Western MS or MSS which have so largely affected the text of this work elsewhere."[3]

No. 13. John 1.3-4. In common with most ante-Nicene writers Origen favored that punctuation of these two sentences which places a full stop after οὐδὲ ἕν. In commenting on this text he mentions an alternative reading which substitutes ἐστίν for ἦν (1) in verse 4. He writes, "Some of the copies ... have a reading which is not devoid of probability, 'What was made is life in him' " (τινὰ μέντοι τε τῶν ἀντιγράφων ἔχει, καὶ τάχα οὐκ ἀπιθάνως· "ὃ γέγονεν ἐν αὐτῷ ζωή ἐστιν").[4] This variant reading is supported today by ℵ D it syr[c] cop[sa].

No. 14. John 1.28. Origen's well known preference for Bethabara as the place of John's baptizing was based on geographical and etymological grounds. He writes: "We are aware of the reading which is found in almost all the copies (σχέδον ἐν πᾶσι τοῖς ἀντιγράφοις κεῖται), 'These things were done in Bethany.' This appears, moreover, to have been the reading at an earlier time; and in Heracleon we read 'Bethany.' We are convinced, however, that we should not read 'Bethany' but 'Bethabara.'[5] We have visited the places to inquire as to the footsteps of Jesus and his disciples and

---

[1] *In Mt. Comm. ser.*, 134 (XI, ii, 274, 4-25, Klostermann).

[2] *Comm. in Cant.* and *Contra Celsum*, ii, 33, 35.

[3] *Introduction [and] Appendix*, "Notes on Select Readings," p. 70.

[4] *Comm. in Ioan.*, ii, 19 (13) (IV, 76, 23-24, Preuschen).

[5] The form in the extant manuscripts of Origen's tractate varies; most have Βηθαρά, others have Βαθαρά or Βηθαραβά. (The last is the reading at John 1.28 in ℵ[cb] syr[h mg] eth.) His interpretation of the meaning of the name as οἶκος κατασκενῆς suggests that he intended to write Βηθαβαρά.

of the prophets. Now, Bethany ... is fifteen stadia from Jerusalem, and the Jordan river is about one hundred and eighty stadia distant from it. Nor is there any other place of the same name in the neighborhood of the Jordan, but they say that Bethabara is pointed out on the banks of the Jordan. ... The etymology of the name, too, corresponds with the baptism of him who made ready for the Lord a people prepared for him—for it yields the meaning 'House of preparation,' while Bethany means 'House of obedience.' "[1]

Among present-day witnesses to the reading Βηθαβαρᾷ are C² K U Λ 083 1 22 33 syr[s,c] cop[sa] arm geo.

No. 15. John 3.34. The ordinary text of this verse reads, "for it is not by measure (ἐκ μέτρου) that he gives the Spirit." Origen comments, without expressing any preference, that "in other copies (ἐν ἑτέροις ἀντιγράφοις) one finds the reading ἐκ μέρους."[2] This variant reading is preserved in U 12 40 63 238 253.

No. 16. Rom. 3.5. In this passage, according to the generally accepted text, Paul raises several questions: "If our wickedness serves to show the righteousness of God, what shall we say? Is God unjust who visits with wrath? (I speak in a merely human way). God forbid." Origen, according to his Latin translator, comments on this passage as follows: *Sciendum sane est, quod in quibusdam etiam Graecis exemplaribus sic invenitur, "Numquid iniquus Deus, qui infert iram adversum homines?" Et magis secundum hunc sensum videbuntur quae diximus convenire. Secundum hoc vero quod in Latinis exemplaribus et nonnullis Graecorum invenimus, "Numquid iniquus Deus, qui infert iram?—secundum hominem dico—absit," ita intelligendum videtur.*[3] A little later Origen reverts to the variant reading again. He says, *Haec de eo quod dictum est, "Numquid iniquus Deus qui infert iram," vel "adversum homines," ut in quibusdam exemplaribus legi diximus, vel, ut nos habemus, "secundum hominem dico; absit," prout occurrere nobis potuit, dicta sunt.*[4]

According to Origen, the variation in this passage involves κατὰ ἄνθρωπον λέγω and κατὰ τῶν ἀνθρώπων. The latter, he says, is found "in certain Greek copies." Today it is preserved only in the margin

---

[1] *Comm. in Ioan.*, vi, 40 (24) (IV, 149, 12ff., Preuschen). For discussions of the passage, see M.-J. Lagrange, "Origène, la critique textuelle et la tradition topographique," *Revue Biblique*, IV (1895), 501-24; see also R. G. Clapp's article (cited above, p. 91, note 2).

[2] *Comm. in Ioan. frag.*, 48 (IV, 523, 16-18, Preuschen).

[3] *Comm. in Rom.*, iii, 1 (Migne, *Patrologia Graeca*, XIV, 923D-924A).

[4] *Ibid.*, 926 B.

of 1739 (in the hand of the scribe or a contemporary) and in the Sahidic version.

No. 17. Rom. 5.14. In the commonly received text of this passage Paul declares that "death reigned from Adam to Moses, even over those whose sins were not like the transgression of Adam." Origen, however, quotes the sentence five times without the negative, and once says that "in some copies (*in nonnullis exemplaribus*)" it is read with the negative.[1] The overwhelming bulk of extant manuscripts have the negative, and only 384 385 424ᶜ 1739 and l^{+a}54 (along with several Latin fathers) omit the negative.

No. 18. Rom. 7.6. In Paul's discussion of the Christian's freedom from the law he declares, "Now we are discharged from the law, having died to that which held us captive (νυνὶ δὲ κατηργήθημεν ἀπὸ τοῦ νόμου, ἀποθανόντες ἐν ᾧ κατειχόμεθα)." Some manuscripts, however, read "we are discharged from the law of death, by which we were held captive (... τοῦ νόμου τοῦ θανάτου ...)." Origen knows this latter reading (*Scio et in aliis exemplaribus scriptum "a lege mortis in qua detinebamur"*),[2] but on exegetical grounds he prefers the reading *mortui* (= ἀποθανόντες), declaring that this is "both truer and better (*et verius est et rectius*)." Today τοῦ θανάτου is read by D E F G it vgᶜˡ.

No. 19. Rom. 14.23; 16.25-27. For the purposes of this study it is unnecessary to deal at length with the tangle of evidence and the welter of opinions regarding the position(s) of the doxology at the close of the Epistle to the Romans.[3] It will be sufficient to mention that Origen declares that Marcion had struck out not only the paragraph containing the doxology (16.25-27) but the last two chapters also (*Caput hoc Marcion, a quo scripturae evangelicae atque apostolicae interpolatae sunt, de hac epistola penitus abstulit; et non solum hoc, sed et ab eo loco ubi scriptum est, "Omne autem quod non est ex fide, peccatum est* [14:23]*," usque ad finem cuncta dissecuit*).[4]

---

[1] *Comm. in Rom.*, v, 1 (Migne, *Patrologia Graeca*, XIV, 1019A).

[2] *Comm. in Rom.*, vi, 7 (Migne, *Patrologia Graeca*, XIV, 1075B).

[3] It is enough here to refer to R. Schumacher, *Die beiden letzten Kapitel des Römerbriefes* (= *Neutestamentliche Abhandlungen*, XIV, 4; Münster in Westf., 1929), and T. W. Manson, "Paul's Letter to the Romans—and others," *Bulletin of the John Rylands Library*, XXXI (1948), 224-40.

[4] *Comm. in Rom.*, xvi, 24-27 (Migne, *Patrologia Graeca*, XIV, 1290). This is the common interpretation of Origen's statement about Marcion; see J. B. Lightfoot, *Biblical Essays* (London, 1893), pp. 288ff. For a different interpretation, see F. J. A. Hort, *ibid.*, pp. 329ff., and "Notes on Select Readings," pp. 112f.

Origen goes on to say that in other copies which have not been corrupted by Marcion this whole section (i.e. 16.25-27) is placed differently; in some manuscripts it stands after 14.23, whereas in other manuscripts it stands at the close of the Epistle (*In aliis vero exemplaribus, id est in his quae non sunt a Marcione temerata, hoc ipsum caput diverse positum invenimus. In nonnullis etenim codicibus post eum locum quem supra diximus, hoc est "Omne autem quod non est ex fide peccatum est," statim cohaerens habetur "Ei autem qui potens est vos confirmare." Alii vero codices in fine id, ut nunc positum est, continent*). From what follows it appears that Origen regarded the weight of the manuscripts as nearly evenly balanced. Whether the words *ut nunc positum est* refers to the position of the doxology which Origen himself adopts in his commentary, or to the position which was most common in his day, is not easily decided.[1] In any case, Origen knew of two forms of the text of Romans as regards the position of the doxology.

Today the evidence for the position of the doxology is as follows:

After 14.23—L Ψ 0209^{vid} minusc^{200} it^{dem} syr^h.
After 16.24—𝔓^{61} ℵ B C D E 81 1739 *al* it vg syr^p cop$^{sa, bo}$ eth.
After both 14.23 and 16.24—A P 5 33 104 arm^{codd}.
After 15.33—𝔓^{46}.
Omitted entirely—F^{gr} G 629 it^g gothic.

No. 20. Col. 2.15. Instead of the usual text of this verse (θριαμβεύσας αὐτοὺς ἐν αὐτῷ) Origen, through his Latin translator, indicates that some Greek manuscripts read ἐν τῷ ξύλῳ (*Audi ergo, de his quid ipse pronuntiat: "Quod erat," inquit, "contrarium nobis tulit illud de medio, affigens cruci suae, exuens principatus et potestates traduxit libere, triumphans eas in ligno crucis," licet in aliis exemplaribus habeatur: "triumphans eas in semet ipso," sed apud Graecos habetur "in ligno"*).[2] No Greek manuscript is known to preserve this reading today.

No. 21. 2 Tim. 4.6. Origen, according to his Latin translator, refers to a variant in Greek manuscripts of which nothing further is known today: *audi eum [Paulum] et in aliis dicentem, "Iam enim ego im-*

---

[1] It is clear, however, that Origen read and commented on the passage at the end of the Epistle (see the text of ms. 1739, in the Laura on Mt. Athos, which preserves a text of Romans drawn directly from Origen's commentary; ed. von der Goltz in *Texte und Untersuchungen*, N.F., II, 4a, 1899).

[2] *Hom. in lib. Iesu Nave*, viii, 3 (VII, 338, 14-18, Baehrens).

molor, et tempus resolutionis"—vel, ut in graecis codicibus legimus, "reversionis"—"meae instat."[1]

No. 22. Heb. 2.9. Origen comments on this verse, "He [Christ] is a great high priest, having offered himself up in sacrifice once for all, and not for human beings alone, but for the rest of rational creatures as well (ἀλλὰ καὶ ὑπὲρ τῶν λοιπῶν λογικῶν [i.e. angels and other heavenly creatures]). 'For without God he tasted death for everyone' (χωρὶς γὰρ θεοῦ ὑπὲρ παντὸς ἐγεύσατο θανάτου). In some copies of the Epistle to the Hebrews the words are 'by the grace of God' (ὅπερ ἔν τισι κεῖται τῆς πρὸς Ἑβραίους ἀντιγράφοις 'χάριτι θεοῦ')."[2] It is plain from the continuation of Origen's comments that he is not interested in deciding between χωρὶς θεοῦ and χάριτι θεοῦ. Presumably he found the former reading to be the common text; today it survives only in 0121b 424[c] 1739* and 3 mss. of syr[p].

In a different category from the examples cited above are the instances when, because of some exegetical difficulty, Origen suggests that perhaps all of the manuscripts existing in his day may have become corrupt. The following are three or four examples. Of Matt. 5.45 ("That you may be sons of your Father who is in heaven") he says, "You [the reader] will inquire whether this was said as it stands or whether the word 'your' is present as a result of a mistake in the manuscripts."[3] In his *Commentary on Matthew* he suggests that the discrepancy between the Septuagint text of Ps. 118.25 and Matthew's quotation of it (21.9) is to be accounted for by the theory that the Evangelist had quoted the Hebrew text of the Psalm, but that it was corrupted by copyists: "So my opinion is that the Gospels in being copied over and over again by persons who did not know the language became confused at this point in the quotation from the Psalm mentioned above."[4] In the same commentary Origen notices the difference between Matthew's report (26.63) of the question put by the High Priest to Jesus at his trial and Mark's report (14:61), and suggests that the difference may be owing to a blunder (*mendum*) in the manuscripts.[5] In his comment on the eighth Psalm Origen implies that the only reading of Matthew 21.9

---

[1] *Hom. in Num.*, xxiv, 1 (VII, 226, 1-3, Baehrens).
[2] *Comm. in Ioan.*, i, 35 (40) (IV, 45, 19-20, Preuschen), cf. J. Scherer, *Entretien d'Origène* ... (Cairo, 1946), pp. 45 and 172 f.
[3] *Comm. in Ioan.*, xx, 17 (V, 349, 11-19, Preuschen).
[4] *Comm. in Matt.*, xvi, 19 (X, 542, 1-6, Klostermann).
[5] *Comm. in Matt. ser.*, 118 (XI, ii, 251, 27-30, Klostermann).

and 15 known to him had οἴκῳ in one verse and υἱῷ in the other.[1]
Whether he means to attribute this discrepancy to scribes (as Audet
argues)[2] or to the Evangelist himself is an open question.[3]

Mention should be made of a comment on Matt. 6.1, which,
because it is of doubtful authenticity, is not included in its place in
the list above. Origen (or Apollinaris) apparently was accustomed
to read this verse, "take heed that you do not your alms (ἐλεημο-
σύνην) before men," for he states that "in other copies it says
'righteousness' (ἐν ἄλλοις ἀντιγράφοις τὴν δικαιοσύνην φησί)."[4] Today
most editors favor the variant δικαιοσύνην, which is read by ℵ* B D
1 209 372 660 1424* 1582 it(pler) vg syr[s,pal].

Finally, attention should perhaps be drawn to Origen's categorical
statement in his refutation of Celsus' condescending gibe about
Jesus as carpenter, that "in none of the Gospels current in the
churches is Jesus himself ever described as being a carpenter."[5]
Griesbach argued[6] that Origen would not have made so dogmatic a
statement unless he were certain that in no passage is Jesus called
a carpenter, and that therefore he did not know the commonly
received text of Mark 6.3 (ὁ τέκνων, ὁ υἱὸς τῆς Μαρίας) but only the
variant, ὁ τέκτονος ὁ υἱὸς τῆς Μαρίας, which is preserved today in
𝔓[45] fam.13 33 472 565 579 700 it[pt] arm geo[1] eth. But it is more
probable that his denial rests upon a lapse of memory,[7] for he was
apparently less well acquainted with the Gospel of Mark than with
the other Gospels.[8]

---

[1] Comm. in Ps., 8 (XII, 16, Lommatzsch) ζητήσεις δὲ πρότερον ταὐτόν ἐστιν
οἶκος Δαυὶδ καὶ υἱὸς Δαυίδ, καὶ εἰ μὴ ταὐτόν ἐστιν, ἡμάρτηται τὸ κατὰ Ματθαῖον
γραφικῶς· ὀφειλον ἔχειν ἤτοι δίς· τῷ οἴκῳ Δαυὶδ, ἤτοι· τῷ υἱῷ Δαυίδ.

[2] Jean-Paul Audet, La Didachè (Paris, 1958), pp. 63ff., 420.

[3] The Coptic version of Did. 10.6 is a witness to the phrase ὡσαννὰ τῷ
οἴκῳ Δαυίδ, but whether this implies the existence of copies of Matthew with
the reading is not certain.

[4] Catena frag., 113 (XII, iii, 1, 61, Klostermann). In MS C[a] fol. 11a the
statement is attributed to Apollinaris (XII, ii, 73, fr. 113, Klostermann and
Früchtel). When Origen wrote his commentary on Rom. iii, 7 he read
δικαιοσύνην in Matt. 6.1 (Migne, Patrologia Graeca, XIV, 943 A).

[5] Contra Celsum, vi, 36.

[6] Opusc. I, 263, Anm. 26.

[7] So Paul Koetschau in the introduction to his edition of Origen's Contra
Celsum, I, p. xxxiv.

[8] Proof for this last statement is perhaps to be found in de Orat., xviii, 3
(II, 341, 9-11, Koetschau) where Origen says, with reference to the Matthean
and Lucan forms of the Lord's Prayer, "We have also searched Mark for
some such similar prayer that might have escaped our notice, but we have
found no trace of one."

The above-cited instances of Origen's explicit references to variant readings in New Testament manuscripts lead one to conclude that he was an acute observer of textual phenomena but was quite uncritical in his evaluation of their significance. In the majority of cases he was content merely to make the observation that certain other copies present a different reading, without indicating his preference for one or the other variant. This tantalizing nonchalance is so unlike his careful procedure in dealing with the Greek text of the Old Testament that some special explanation must be sought. Doubtless the primary reason is to be found in the circumstance that there was a Hebrew original against which the Septuagint and other Greek versions could be compared. Lacking any such convenient norm by which to determine the validity of variant readings in the New Testament documents, Origen hesitated in most instances to pass judgment upon the genuineness of this or that reading. In several instances, however, he more or less definitely indicates his preference (e.g. Nos. 1, 2, 7, 14, 18). In these cases his criteria were not derived from a study of the manuscripts themselves, but from various more or less inconsequential and irrelevant considerations. He was especially gratified when the supposed etymological derivation of a place-name yielded an edifying interpretation (e.g. Nos. 2 and 14). Only rarely does Origen make a textual decision solely on exegetical grounds (No. 18). On the whole his treatment of variant readings is most unsatisfactory from the standpoint of modern textual criticism. He combines a remarkable indifference to what are now regarded as important aspects of textual criticism with a quite uncritical method of dealing with them.

If the modern scholar is disappointed in Origen as a textual critic, he must be grateful to him for describing some of the conditions of the New Testament text of the second and third centuries. Origen knows of the existence of variant readings that fall within each of the main families of manuscripts that modern scholars have isolated. Although Origen occasionally testifies to the existence of copies in his time which contained readings that no longer survive in any manuscript today (e.g. Nos. 20 and 21), on the whole most variants which he mentions have been preserved also by other witnesses. In other words, the diversities of texts in his day are generally represented in their descendants today. It should be noted, however, that what Origen indicates to be the proportion of manuscripts current in the third century for and against a reading is not always the same as the proportion among extant manuscripts today. For example, the reading "Elizabeth" as the subject who speaks the *Magnificat* (No. 9) is supported today, outside of Origen and other patristic witnesses (Irenaeus, Nicetas, and Cyril of Jerusalem), only by old Latin manuscripts; and in such passages as John 3.34 and Heb. 2.9 (Nos. 15 and 22) only a few of the later manuscripts happen to preserve the reading which Origen implies was rather widespread in his day. In these cases our knowledge of the existence and circulation of such variants is carried back several hundred years earlier than the date of the non-Origenian witnesses. It should further be observed that this kind of patristic testimony may be relied upon with far greater assurance than the ordinary quotations of Scripture made by way of homiletical comment or illustration. In the latter, the evidence is always open to the suspicion that subsequent scribes may have modified the citation in order to bring it into harmony with later manuscripts. Such a possibility is reduced to a minimum, however, when the author explicitly refers to the existence of manuscripts containing such and such a variant reading current in his own day. Thus the evidence derived from this kind of patristic testimony is of extremely great value for both the accurate localizing and the precise dating of the emergence and circulation of variant readings. It is no less imperative today than it was more than half a century ago—when Eberhard Nestle suggested the *desideratum*[1]—that a collection of *testimonia patristica*, arranged according to time and locality, be made of all those passages in which the Fathers appeal to manuscripts current in their own day.

---

[9] Eberhard Nestle, *Einführung in das griechische Neue Testament*, 2nd ed. (Göttingen, 1899), pp. 266-7 (Eng. trans. [London, 1901], pp. 340-1); 3rd ed. (1909), pp. 165-7.

CHAPTER TEN

A MAGICAL AMULET FOR CURING FEVER

Among the Greek papyri in the Princeton University Collections is a magical talisman designed to rid the wearer of fever.[1] This charm, which is written on a cheap grade of coarse papyrus[2] by an unlettered hand, measures about 2⅜ inches wide and about 5¼ long (see Plate I B). When discovered it was still folded in a narrow compass, presumably to be placed in a small container and worn on the body of the patient.[3] From the style of the handwriting the amulet can be dated in the third or fourth Christian century.

The first third of the papyrus contains a meaningless string of mysterious-sounding syllables, arranged in seven lines, the first of which reads ζαγουρηπαγουρη. In each of the following six lines the formula is written in such a way that the first letter and the last letter of the preceding line are dropped, thus forming a triangular pattern. The ancients attached a good deal of significance to the shape of this pattern (which was known as βοτρυοειδής "shaped like a bunch of grapes"), the theory being that the shortening of the incantation in successive lines would be effective in lessening the malady.[4] The barbaric sound of the formula, composed of syllables

---

[1] It is no. 159 in the Princeton University Collections, and was first edited by the present writer in *Papyri in the Princeton University Collections*, vol. III, ed. by Allen Chester Johnson and Sidney Pullman Goodrich (Princeton, 1942), 78-79. Princeton University Press, the holder of the original copyright, has granted permission to incorporate this material, in greatly expanded form, in the present study.

[2] The papyrus is palimpsest, and illegible traces of the earlier writing remain in the upper left-hand and right-hand margins.

[3] On fever amulets see Ulrich Wilcken, *Archiv für Papyrusforschung*, I (Leipzig, 1901), 420-27; Preisendanz's collection of magical Greek papyri (cf. p. 105, note 2 below); and, for a Gnostic fever amulet (dating from the fourth or fifth century) published since Preisendanz, Edmund H. Kase, Jr., *Papyri in the Princeton University Collections*, II (Princeton, 1936), no. 107.

[4] Another common pattern, formed by dropping a letter in successive lines from either the right-hand or the left-hand margin, thus producing the shape of a triangle, was called πτερυγοειδής ("shaped like a wing"). For examples found in papyri, see Gerhard Kropatscheck, *De amuletorum apud antiquos usu*, Diss. (Greifswald, 1907), p. 29; Franz Dornseiff, *Das Alphabet in Mystik und Magie*, 2te Aufl. (= ΣΤΟΙΧΕΙΑ, *Studien zur Geschichte des antiken Weltbildes und des griechischen Wissenschaft*, VII; Leipzig, 1925), pp. 55-67; and P. Michaelidae 27 (ed. D. S. Crawford; London, 1955).

that convey no meaning, no doubt produced a desirable psychological effect upon the patient.[1] The first part of the Princeton
charm, ζαγουρη, was evidently regarded as highly efficacious, for
nearly a dozen other incantations have been found which make
use of it, either alone or in combination with other magical expressions.[2]

The superstitious use of amulets and charms, so prevalent in the
ancient world,[3] was the object of more than one "scientific" examination. For example, Pliny the Elder discussed the question whether
words and formulated incantations (*verba et incantamenta carminum*)
possess any efficacy,[4] and Lucian, in his typically mocking manner,

---

[1] Iamblichus (*De Mysteriis*, vii, 5; ed. Thomas Taylor, 2nd ed. [London,
1845], pp. 294ff.) answers Porphyry's question why charms and incantations
are couched in barbaric and outlandish words, replying that they lose their
potency if they are translated.

[2] For ζαγουρη see Karl Wessely, *Ephesia Grammata* (Vienna, 1886), nos. 36,
206, 207, 209, 335, and Karl Preisendanz, *Papyri Graecae Magicae*, ii (Leipzig
and Berlin, 1931), no. xxxvi, lines 10, 64, 309, 350. On the other hand παγουρη
is less common; for examples (with ζαγουρη) see Preisendanz, *op. cit.*, no. xxxvi,
lines 309 and 350.

[3] From a vast literature on the subject, and in addition to the several
titles which are mentioned in other footnotes of the present study, the
following surveys and monographs may be mentioned: Campbell Bonner,
Studies in Magical Amulets, Chiefly Graeco-Egyptian (Ann Arbor, 1950); E.
A. Wallis Budge, *Amulets and Superstitions* (London, 1930); Ernst von Dob-
schütz, "Charms and Amulets (Christian)," Hastings' *Encyclopædia of Re-
ligion and Ethics*, iii (1911), 413-430; F. Eckstein and J. H. Waszink,
"Amulett," *Reallexikon für Antike und Christentum*, i (1950), cols. 397-411;
S. Eitrem and A. Fridrichsen, *Ein christliches Amulett auf Papyrus* (= *Vi-
denskapsselskapets Forhandlinger for 1921*, No. 1; Kristiania, 1921); Sam
Eitrem, "Aus 'Papyrologie und Religionsgeschichte': Die magischen Papyri,"
Papyri und Altertumswissenschaft, ed. Walter Otto and Leopold Wenger
(= *Münchener Beiträge zur Papyrusforschung und antiken Rechtsgeschichte*,
xix; Munich, 1934), pp. 243-263; Johannes Ficker, "Amulett," Herzog-
Hauck, *Realencyclopädie für protestantische Theologie und Kirche*, 3te Aufl.,
i (1896), 467-476 (with a full list of extant early Christian objects); Theodor
Hopfner, *Griechisch-ägyptischer Offenbarungszauber* (= *Studien zur Palaeo-
graphie und Papyruskunde*, ed. C. Wessely, xxi; Leipzig, 1921); M. P. Nilsson,
Die Religion in den griechischen Zauberpapyri (Lund, 1948); A. D. Nock,
"Greek Magical Papyri," *Journal of Egyptian Archaeology*, xv (1929) 219-235;
Ernst Reiss, "Religious Gleanings from the Magical Papyri," *Classical
Weekly*, xxviii (1934-35), 105-111; B. R. Rees, "Popular Religion in Graeco-
Roman Egypt," *Journal of Egyptian Archaeology*, xxxvi (1950), 86-100; and
T. Schrire, *Hebrew Amulets, Their Decipherment and Interpretation* (London,
1966). Likewise reference may be made to two bibliographies of Greek and
Roman folklore and magic, compiled by Eugene S. McCartney and Richard
H. Crum in *Classical Weekly*, xl (1946-47), 99-101, and *ib.*, xlii (1948-49),
234-236.

[4] Pliny, *Natural History*, xxviii, 3.

ridiculed those who thought that an external amulet or charm would cure an internal ailment.[1]

The early Church looked with severe disfavor upon such charms and incantations. According to the account in the Acts of the Apostles, after Paul had preached at Ephesus, a city known far and wide for being hospitable to magicians, sorcerers, and charlatans of all kinds,[2] "a number of those who practiced magic arts brought their books together and burned them[3] in the sight of all; and they counted the value of them and found it came to fifty thousand pieces of silver" (Acts 19.19).

The popularity of what were known as Ἐφέσια γράμματα, however, could not be so easily suppressed. Indeed, to judge from the repreated remonstrance of Church Fathers and Synodical pronouncements against such magical charms, the use of amulets continued to be widely prevalent. Thus, Augustine differentiates between a medicinal and a magical use of herbs as follows: "It is one thing to say: If you bruise down this herb and drink it, it will remove the pain from your stomach; and another to say: If you hang this herb around your neck, it will remove the pain from your stomach. In the former case the wholesome mixture is approved of, in the latter the superstitious charm is condemned; although indeed, where incantations and invocations and marks are not used, it is frequently doubtful whether the thing tied or fixed in any way to the body to cure it, acts by a natural potency, in which case it may be freely used; or acts by a sort of charm, in which case it becomes the Christian to avoid it the more carefully the more efficacious it may seem to be."[4]

---

[1] Lucian, *The Lover of Lies*, § 7f.

[2] Shakespeare draws upon this notorious aspect of Ephesian culture when he has Antipholus describe Ephesus in the following terms:

> They say this town is full of cozenage,
> As, nimble jugglers that deceive the eye,
> Dark-working sorcerers that change the mind,
> Soul-killing witches that deform the body,
> Disguised cheaters, prating mountebanks,
> And many such-like liberties of sin.
> *A Comedy of Errors*, I.ii.97-102.

[3] For other examples of the burning of books in antiquity, see Clarence A. Forbes, "Books for the Burning," *Transactions and Proceedings of the American Philological Association*, LXVII (1936), 114-125, and A. S. Pease, "Notes on Book-Burning," in *Munera Studiosa*, ed. by M. H. Shepherd, Jr., and S. E. Johnson (Cambridge, Massachusetts, 1946), pp. 145-160.

[4] Augustine, *De doctrina christiana*, II, xxix, 45 (Migne, *Patrologia Latina*,

Chrysostom often inveighed against the use of amulets, adducing, among other arguments, the example of Job, Lazarus, and the infirm man at the pool of Bethesda. The last mentioned, for instance, "never betook himself to any diviner, or enchanter; he tied no amulets to his body (οὐκ ἐπέδησε περίαπτα), but expected help only from the Lord."[1]

In the fourth century the Synod of Laodicea[2] considered the matter to be of such importance that it issued a separate canon proscribing the manufacture and use of amulets. Canon XXXVI declares: "They who are of the priesthood, or of the clergy, shall not ... make what are called amulets (τὰ λεγόμενα φυλακτήρια), which are chains for their own souls. And those who wear such, we command to be cast out of the Church."[3]

So inveterate, however, was the belief in the efficacy of charms that Christians began to make amulets from portions of the Scriptures—a verse or two of the Psalms or a phrase from the Gospels.[4]

---

xxxiv, 56f.). On another occasion, however, Augustine apparently was prepared to permit a copy of the Gospel [of John] to be laid on the head of one who suffered pain in his head (*in Johannis Evangelium*, tract. vii.12 [Migne, *Patrologia Latina*, xxxv, 1443]). Of all the books of the Scriptures the Gospel of John seems to have been regarded as the most effective in such curative powers, and particularly its opening chapter; see Edmond Le Blant, "Le premier chapître de Saint Jean et la croyance à ses vertus secrètes," *Revue archéologie*, xxv, 2 (1894), 8-13. See also footnote 4 below.

[1] John Chrysostom, *Adv. Judaeos*, hom. viii, 5 (Migne, *Patrologia Graeca*, xlviii, 935). For other instances of Chrysostom's repeated condemnation of magical talismans and incantations, see *ad Pop. Antioch.*, hom. xix, 4 [*ib.* xlix, 196]; *ad Illum. Catech.*, ii, 5 [*ib.* xlix, 239]; hom. *in I Cor.* 7.2 [*ib.* li, 216]; *in Ps.* 9, ch. 7 [*ib.* lv, 132]; *in Joh.* hom. xxxvii and lv [*ib.* lix, 207 and 301]; *in I Cor.* hom. xii, 8 [*ib.* lxi, 105]; *in Gal.* com. i, 7 [*ib.* 623]; *in Col.* hom. viii, 5 [*ib.* lxii, 358]; and *in I Thess.* hom. iii, 5 [*ib.* 412].

[2] The date of the Synod cannot be fixed within narrower limits than sometime after A.D. 341 and before 381 (K. J. von Hefele, *Histoire des Conciles*, ed. Henri Leclercq, I, 2 [Paris, 1907], pp. 989f.).

[3] *The Nicene and Post-Nicene Fathers of the Christian Church*, Second Series, ed. by Philip Schaff and Henry Wace, vol. xiv, *The Seven Ecumenical Councils*, ed. by Henry R. Percival (New York, 1900), p. 151. For other references to conciliar condemnation of magic, see Joseph Bingham, *The Antiquities of the Christian Church*, Bk. xvi, chap. v, sect. 6ff.

[4] See Paul Collart, "Psaumes et amulettes," *Aegyptus*, xiv (1934), 463-467; Claire Préaux, "Une Amulette chrétienne," *Chronique d'Égypte*, xx (1935), 361-370; Edmund H. Kase, Jr., *op. cit.* (p. 104, note 3), pp. 102f.; Igino Cecchetti, "Un interessante documento dei primi tempi del Christianesimo in Egitto," in *Miscellanea Giulio Belvederi* (Città del Vaticano, 1954-55), pp. 557-578; and especially H. Mulder, "De Canon en het volksgeloof. Een onderzoek van de amuletten der eersten Christenen," *Gereformeerd theologisch tijdschrift*, liv (1954), 97-138, who lists twenty-nine items (pp. 103ff.), most containing Biblical verses.

These were suspended around the neck during the day or hung on the bed for protection during the night.[1] In later generations Christians began to wear *arculae*, small boxes containing bits of the remains of saints.[2]

The following is the text of the Princeton amulet, dating, as was mentioned earlier, from about the third or fourth Christian century.

P. Prin. 159

ζαγουρ[η]παγουρη
αγουρηπαγουρ
γουρηπαγου
ουρηπαγο
5   υρηπαγ
ρηπα
ηπ
ππ
κύριοι ἄγγελοι
10 καὶ ἀγαθοὶ παύ-
σατε [. .]διαν ὃν
ἔτεκεν [Σ]οφία
ἀπὸ τ[οῦ] ἀνέ-
χοντος αὐτὸν
15 πυρετοῦ ἐν τῇ
σήμερον ἡμέρᾳ
ἐν τῇ ἄρτι ὥρᾳ
[ἤδη ἤ]δη τα-
[χὺ τα]χύ.

FREE TRANSLATION

[Magical charm] "Good angels who rule over us, allay the fever of .. dias, whom [S]ophia bore, this very day, this very hour, this very moment, at once, at once!"

COMMENTS

Line 8. The character is apparently intended as a ligature of the two letters in the preceding line.

---

[1] See passages cited by J. C. Suicer in his *Thesaurus Ecclesiasticus*, I (Amsterdam, 1728), 1227, and II, 1465f.

[2] For examples see Du Cange, *Glossarium*, s. vv. *encolpium* and *phylacterium*.

Line 9. The combination κύριοι ἄγγελοι is unusual; it has turned up also in a lead curse-tablet, edited by Richard Wünsch in *Archiv für Religionswissenschaft*, XII (1909), 38 lines 5f., and in P. Osloenses I, edited by S. Eitrem, 1925, lines 44 and 246 (I am indebted to Professor Morton Smith of Columbia University for directing my attention to the examples in the Oslo papyrus).

The identity of the angels that are invoked may be surmised by comparing other charms in which angels are mentioned by name; e.g. Μιχαήλ, Γαβριήλ, Οὐριήλ, Ῥαφαήλ (*Revue des Études Grecques*, IV [1891], 228; XVI [1903], 47); Ἀρχάφ (*id.*, v [1892], 76), otherwise called Ἀρλάφ or Ἀραάφ. For the names of other angels (e.g. Arakiel, Ramiel, Samiel, Urjan, Saraqael, Fanuel, etc.), mentioned in apocryphal literature, see Enoch, chaps. 20 and 40; Apocalypse of Baruch (Syriac), 55.2; Apocalypse of Moses, 2; and the Sibylline Oracles, ii, 214. For names of angels in Syria see Wm. K. Prentice, "Magical Formulae on Lintels of the Christian Period in Syria," *American Journal of Archaeology*, Second Series, x (1906), 137-150, especially p. 143, and Hermann Gollancz, *The Book of Protection, Being a Collection of Charms ... from Syriac MSS.* (London, 1912), p. lxxv.

Lines 10-11. The copyist of the charm, confusing vowels which were pronounced alike, wrote ἀγαθὴ παύσαται.

Line 11. The name, apparently masculine, cannot be ascertained. There is space in the lacuna for one broad letter or two narrow letters. Only the tops of the next two letters are visible, and they may be read as δρ, αρ, δι, or λι.

Line 12. In magical papyri maternal rather than paternal relationships predominate. One of the very few clear instances of a patronymic is in a curse-tablet from Cumae (cf. Augustine Audollent, *Defixionum Tabellae* [Paris, 1904], no. 198, lines 14, 27, and 32, and John G. Winter, *Papyri in the University of Michigan Collections, Miscellaneous Papyri* [Ann Arbor, 1936], no. 155).

Line 18. The reiteration[1] expresses the urgency of the suppliant; for other examples, see Wessely, *op. cit.*, p. 176; Preisendanz, *op. cit.*, II, nos. xviii *b*; xxxvi, lines 11, 84, 113f., 132, 319f., 360; and xxxix, line 21. Wilcken (*op. cit.*, p. 426) remarks that ταχὺ ταχύ, a popular formula in Greek amulets, was taken over into Coptic and Latin texts; as an example of the latter he refers to *tacs tacs* in

---

[1] On reiterated formulae (cf. Paul's repeated ἀνάθεμα ἔστω, Gal. 1.8), see Eduard Norden's comments in his *P. Vergilius Maro Aeneis Buch VI*, 3te Aufl. (Berlin and Leipzig, 1926), pp. 136f.

Inscriptiones Graecae; *Corpus Inscriptionum Atticarum*, III, 3, Appendix ed. Richard Wünsch (Berlin 1897), p. xxviii. For examples in Coptic, see Adolf Erman and Fritz Krebs, *Aus den Papyrus der königlichen Museen* (Berlin, 1899), pp. 259ff., and A. M. Kropp, *Ausgewählte koptische Zaubertexte*, I (Brussels, 1931), 12, line 25.

CHAPTER ELEVEN

THE CHRISTIANIZATION OF NUBIA AND THE OLD NUBIAN VERSION OF THE NEW TESTAMENT

During the past few years[1] attention throughout the world has been focused on the preservation of hundreds, if not thousands, of ancient monuments in Nubia threatened with destruction in the waters of the Nile. The new high dam, now under construction near Aswân, will turn the lands of Egyptian and Sudanese Nubia into an inland lake three hundred miles long. The rising waters will destroy what has been described as a unique open-air museum, containing scores of ancient Egyptian and Nubian monuments, tombs by the thousands, and untold prehistoric remains. The cost of removing or protecting temples and fortresses, and of excavating hitherto unknown treasures of ancient civilizations on the scale demanded, is far beyond the resources of the United Arab Republic and the Sudan. Most appropriately, the United Nations Education-al, Scientific and Cultural Organization (UNESCO) has marshalled the forces of finance and archaeology throughout the world in an effort to rescue the threatened monuments and sites.[2]

It is fitting that, with the rise of contemporary interest in ancient Nubian monuments, attention should also be given to the remains of the Old Nubian version of the New Testament.[3] Curiously

---

[1] This chapter was originally presented as a paper at the Fourth Inter-national Conference on Patristic Studies held at Christ Church, Oxford, in 1963.

[2] For popularly written accounts of these efforts one may consult the volume entitled *A Common Trust; the Preservation of the Ancient Monuments of Nubia* (UNESCO, 1960), and Rex Keating, *Nubian Twilight* (New York, 1963). Among many scientific reports of recent archaeological excavations in Nubia mention may be made of those by William Y. Adams and H.-Å. Norström in *Kush*, XI (1963), 10-46; by B. B. Piotrovski in *Vestnik drevnoi istorii*, II (84, 1963), 185ff.; and by Adams in *Kush*, XII (1964), 216-248; XIII (1965), 148-176.

[3] The term Old Nubian is used in order to distinguish this version from modern translations of portions of the New Testament, prepared by mission-aries in several contemporary Nubian dialects. For brief descriptions of these modern versions, see T. H. Darlow and H. F. Moule, *Historical Catalogue of the Printed Editions of Holy Scripture in the Library of the British and Foreign Bible Society* (London, 1903-1908), and Eric M. North, *The Book of a Thou-sand Tongues* (New York, 1935). On modern Nubian dialects in general see

enough, though these fragments (see Plate II) were published more than half a century ago,[1] as yet the textual affinities of the version remain unanalyzed. It is hoped that in what follows a beginning may be made in ascertaining the textual complexion of this ancient version of the New Testament.

Before examining the text of the fragments themselves, however, it will not be out of place to sketch what is known of the Christianization of the ancient Nubian kingdoms. The plural of the word "kingdom" is used deliberately, for in the period which concerns this study Nubia was composed of three distinct and independent kingdoms, each with its own king or chieftain.[2] These territories, the exact boundaries of which are not known today, lay between Egypt on the north and Abyssinia on the south. They comprised Nobadia (Nobatia; Arabic Nūbā) in the north, between the First and Second Cataracts, with its capital at Pakhoras (now Faras), and Alodia (Arabic 'Alwah) in the south, with its capital at Sōba, near the modern city of Khartūm. Between the two lay Makuria (Arabic Maḵurrah), having its capital at (Old) Dongola. The conversion of Nobadia and Alodia to the Monophysite form of Christianity and the conversion of Makuria to the Catholic (or Melkite) faith make an interesting and tangled chapter in the history of the expansion of Christianity in Africa.[3] Ecclesiastical links with Byzantium were continued for several centuries after the period of systematic missionary activity in the sixth century, and gravestones have been found inscribed in Greek (albeit very bad Greek) as late as A.D. 1243.[4]

Ernst Zyhlarz, "Das meroitische Sprachproblem," *Anthropos*, xxv (1930), 409-463. According to S. Hillelson (s. v. "Nūba," *Encyclopædia of Islam*, III [1936], 943), the language of the Old Nubian Christian texts approximates most closely to modern Maḥas, although the provenance of most of the existing remains is the northernmost part of Nubia where Kenzī is spoken.

[1] They were edited in 1906-1907 by Heinrich Schäfer and Carl Schmidt in "Die ersten Bruchstücke christlicher Literatur in altnubischer Sprache," *Sitzungsberichte der königlich Preussischen Akademie der Wissenschaften*, phil.-hist. Kl., 8 Nov.. 1906, pp. 774-785, and "Die altnubischen Handschriften der königlichen Bibliothek zu Berlin," *ibid.*, 20. Juni 1907, pp. 602-613, especially pp. 602-606. For the dialect, see Ernst Zyhlarz, *Grundzüge der nubischen Grammatik im christlichen Frühmittelalter* (= *Abhandlungen für die Kunde des Morgenlandes*, XVIII, 1; Leipzig, 1928).

[2] Cf. L. P. Kirwan, "Notes on the Topography of the Christian Nubian Kingdoms," *Journal of Egyptian Archaeology*, xxi (1935), 57-62, with a map.

[3] For references to modern studies of the Christianization of Nubia, see below, p. 114, note 3.

[4] See Herbert Junker, "Die christlichen Grabsteine Nubiens," *Zeitschrift*

When it was that Christianity first reached Nubia is not known. Before 373, however, there must have been a number of Christians living at Philae, just north of Nobadia near Aswân, for Athanasius (who died in 373) says that he consecrated a certain Marcus as bishop of Philae.[1] During the first centuries of Christianity the vast stretches south of Philae would have given shelter to more than one Christian driven from Egypt during the persecutions ordered by Diocletian and other Roman emperors. According to Duchesne and Harnack it was not until the fourth century that the Gospel penetrated this wide territory south of Philae, though it is possible that Christianity was preached prior to this date to certain "Ethiopians" on the border.[2] Before 450 Bp. Apion of Syene (modern Aswân) called for military help for the churches at Philae, which were being pressed by marauding tribes known as the Nobadae and Blemmyes.[3] Aid came in the person of Maximinus, commander of the Roman forces in Egypt, who marched to the south, routed the invaders with great slaughter, and compelled them to give hostages as a pledge of their future good behavior. On the death of Maximinus, however, the restless tribes once again joined forces and invaded Egypt, recovering their hostages.

After further disturbances, the power of the Blemmyes was broken by a powerful chieftain of the Nobadae named Silkō. Fortunately for the historian, Silkō's victories are recounted at length in a Greek inscription which he caused to be cut about A.D. 500 on a wall in the temple of Talmis (i.e. Kalābshah).[4]

---

für ägyptische Sprache, LX (1925), 111-148, and Togo Mina, *Inscriptions coptes et grecques de Nubie* (Cairo, 1942).

[1] Athanasius, *Letter to the Antiochians*, 10 (Migne, *Patrologia Graeca*, XXVI, 808).

[2] Louis Duchesne, "Les missions chrétiennes au sud de l'Empire romain," *Mélanges d'archéologie et d'histoire*, XVI (1896), 79-122, and Adolf von Harnack, *The Mission and Expansion of Christianity in the First Three Centuries*, Eng. trans., 2nd ed., II (London, 1908), 179.

[3] The evidence is preserved in a Greek papyrus dating from c. A.D. 425-450 and edited by Ulrich Wilcken, "Heidnisches und Christliches aus Ägypten," *Archiv für Papyrusforschung*, I (1901), 396-407. See also J. Krall, *Beiträge zur Geschichte der Blemyer und Nubier* (= *Denkschrift der kais. Akademie der Wissenschaften zu Wien*, phil.-hist. Kl., XLVI, No. 4; 1898), and Louis Bréhier, "Blemmyes," *Dictionnaire d'histoire et de géographie ecclésiastiques*, IX (1937), cols. 183-185.

[4] W. Dittenberger, *Orientis Graeci inscriptiones selectae*, I (Leipzig, 1903), 303-310. For a discussion of this and related inscriptions, see Günther Roeder, "Die Geschichte Nubiens und des Sudans," *Klio*, XII (1912), 51-82, and L. P. Kirwan, "Studies in the Later History of Nubia," *University of Liverpool Annals of Archaeology and Anthropology*, XXIV (1937), 69-105.

Some years later (perhaps about 535 or shortly thereafter) the temple of Isis at Philae, which had remained a center of pagan worship despite the edict of Theodosius I against paganism, was finally closed by order of Justinian I. According to Procopius of Caesarea, the Emperor sent a certain Narses to Philae to reduce this last stronghold of the ancient gods in the Roman Empire. Narses carried out his instructions with thoroughness, for he seized the priests of Isis and Osiris and cast them into prison, confiscated the revenues of the great temple on behalf of his master, and carried off the statues of the gods, which were of precious metal, to Constantinople.[1] Not long afterwards the bishop of Philae, Theodore, rededicated the temple of Isis in honor of St. Stephen the Martyr, covering the walls with a coating of plaster to hide the figures of the pagan gods.[2]

Though there doubtless were, as is clear from what has been said above, not a few Christians in that part of Nubia just south of Philae, it was only after the temple of Isis at Philae had been closed that the systematic conversion of Nubia as a whole was undertaken.[3] In fact, the efforts at evangelization were prosecuted by two rival groups of missionaries sent out simultaneously by Justinian and by the Empress Theodora. The Emperor and his wife differed, it will be remembered, in theology, the latter being an ardent champion of Monophysitism. The story of how the Empress outwitted her husband and established Monophysite churches in Nubia is told with picturesque detail by John, bishop of Ephesus (sometimes called John of Asia).

About A.D. 545 a Monophysite priest named Julian, being deeply

---

[1] Procopius, *History of the Wars*, I, xix, 36f. Procopius, who was private secretary to Belisarius, wrote his history about A.D. 545.

[2] An inscription recording the rededication has survived on the temple walls; see Gustave Lefebvre, *Recueil des inscriptions grecques chrétiennes d'Égypte* (Cairo, 1907), no. 587 (see also no. 591).

[3] For discussions of the stages of the Christianization of Nubia, see G. Roeder, "Die christliche Zeit Nubiens und des Sudans," *Zeitschrift für Kirchengeschichte*, XXXIII (1912), 117-146; Johann Kraus, *Die Anfänge des Christentums in Nubien* (Mödling bei Wien, 1930); L. P. Kirwan, "A Contemporary Account of the Conversion of the Sudan to Christianity," *Sudan Notes and Records*, XX (1937), 289-295; Ugo Monneret de Villard, *Storia della Nubia cristiana* (= *Orientalia christiana analecta*, CXVIII; Rome, 1938); L. P. Kirwan's Appendix entitled "The Nature of Nubian Christianity" in his volume, *The Oxford University Excavations at Firka* (Oxford, 1939), pp. 49-51; and W. Y. Adams, "Post-Pharaonic Nubia in the Light of Archaeology," *Journal of Egyptian Archaeology*, LI (1965), 169-178.

concerned for the spiritual condition of the Nobadae, sought the advice and assistance of his patroness, the Empress, who promised to do everything in her power for the conversion of the Nubian tribes from paganism. Rather injudiciously, however, she informed the Emperor Justinian of her plans to send Julian as a missionary to Nubia. When her husband learned that the person she intended to send was opposed to the Council of Chalcedon, he decided to send a rival mission of his own so that the heathen might be saved from the errors of heresy. According to the historian, John of Ephesus,[1]

> "He [Justinian] entered upon the matter with great zeal, and sent, without a moment's delay, ambassadors with gold and baptismal robes, and gifts of honor for the king of that people, and letters for the Duke of the Thebaid, enjoining him to take every care of the embassy, and escort them to the territories of the Nobadae."

When, however, the Empress learned of these things, she quickly wrote to the same Duke of the Thebaid the following orders,

> "Inasmuch as both his majesty and myself have purposed to send an embassy to the people of the Nobadae, and I am now dispatching a blessed man named Julian, it is my will that my ambassador should arrive at the aforesaid people before his majesty's. Be warned that if you permit his ambassador to arrive there before mine, and do not hinder him by various pretexts until mine shall have reached you, and have passed through your province, and arrived at his destination, your life shall answer for it; for I will immediately send and take off your head."

The Empress's letter had its intended effect. When the missionaries who had been dispatched by Justinian arrived they were told, "You must wait a little, while we look out and procure beasts of burden, and men who know the deserts; and then you will be able to proceed."

In due time Julian and his companions sent by the Empress also arrived, and, finding the requisite horses and guides awaiting them, were the first to proceed. The Duke, having planned this move with typical eastern guile, had the following excuse ready for the Emperor's party, who were impatient to be off, saying,

---

[1] *The Third Part of the Ecclesiastical History of John, Bishop of Ephesus,* now first translated from the original Syriac by R. Payne Smith (Oxford, 1860), iv, 6-9 and 49-53 (pp. 251ff. and 315ff.). The Syriac text is most conveniently available in the edition prepared by E. W. Brooks in *Corpus Scriptorum Christianorum Orientalium,* vol. cv; *Scriptores syri,* Tom. 54 (Louvain, 1936; reprinted 1952).

> "Lo! When I had made my preparations, and was desirous of sending you onward, ambassadors from the Empress arrived, and fell upon me with violence, and took away the beasts of burden I had got ready, and have passed onward. ... But abide with me, until I can make fresh preparations for you, and then you shall go in peace."

In the meantime Julian arrived at Nobadia, where "he taught and baptized the king and the nobles, informing them concerning the schism which the Chalcedonians had made, and how they had reviled the holy men, and established a new faith besides that of Nicaea."[1]

Having been instructed how they should receive the Emperor's men it is not surprising that the King of the Nobadae and his nobles showed little enthusiasm for their message. They said,

> "We accept the honorable gift of the Emperor and we will send back gifts twofold in return, but we do not cleave to persecutors and calumniators. For behold, we have already received holy baptism from this excellent man [Julian] and we cannot receive a second baptism."[2]

For two years Julian continued his evangelistic work in Nobadia, though he suffered greatly, the historian tells us, from the extreme heat of that country. According to John's account,

> "From nine o'clock until four in the afternoon he was obliged to take refuge in caverns, full of water, where he sat undressed and girt only in a linen garment, such as the people of that country wear. And if he left the water his skin, he said, was blistered by the heat. Nevertheless, he endured it patiently, and taught them, and baptized both the king and his nobles, and much people also."[3]

At the close of two years of missionary work among the Nobadae Julian returned to Constantinople to report the success of his work to the Empress. This must have been prior to A.D. 548, for in that year Theodora died. Before her death, however, she appointed as his successor another Monophysite priest, named Longinus, to continue spiritual ministrations to the Nobadae.

Justinian, however, was determined that Longinus should not go to Nubia, and gave orders for his arrest. After some three years of constantly eluding the Emperor's spies, Longinus found an oppor-

---

[1] This sentence is quoted from a condensed version of John of Ephesus's account, preserved in Gregory Bar Hebraeus, *Chronicon ecclesiasticum*, edd. J. B. Abbeloos and T. J. Lamy, i (Louvain, 1872), col. 232.

[2] This is also Bar Hebraeus's condensed version.

[3] *Op. cit.*, iv, 7 (p. 255).

tunity to leave the country; "he disguised himself, and put a wig on his head, for he was very bald, and taking with him two servants, he fled."

Arriving in Nubia about the year 569, Longinus was welcomed with enthusiasm, and for six years he instructed the Nobadae afresh in the tenets of Monophysitism, building them a church, ordaining clergy, and teaching them the order of the Eucharist.

The story of the conversion of the people of Alodai and Makuria, the other two Nubian kingdoms, can be told still more briefly. According to John of Ephesus,

> "When the people of the Alodae heard of the conversion of the Nobadae, their king sent to the king of the Nobadae, requesting him to permit the bishop who had taught and baptized them to come and instruct them in like manner. ... The Lord therefore stirred up the spirit of Longinus to go to them; and though the Nobadae were grieved at being separated from him, they nevertheless sent with him nobles and princes and men well acquainted with the desert."[1]

After a journey filled with troubles arising from the hazards and heat of the desert, as well as the machinations of his enemies, at length Longinus arrived at Sōba, the capital of Alodia, and was received with joy by the king. According to the historian, "after a few days' instruction, both the king himself was baptized and all his nobles; and subsequently, in the process of time, his people also." These events took place, says John, in the year 891 (= A.D. 580).[2]

Although John of Ephesus says nothing about the conversion of the Makoritae, who inhabited the country between Nobadia and Alodia, it appears that about this same time orthodox missionaries brought the knowledge of Christianity to that land. Just before Longinus arrived in Alodia, the patriarch of Alexandria, hearing that the people of Alodia were eager for Christianity, sent two bishops to that country to baptize converts and to warn them against Longinus. According to the account of John of Ephesus, their mission to Alodia failed, for the princes there, being fore-warned by the Monophysite king of Nobadae against the Chalce-donian doctrine, drove them from the country under threat of death and would have none but Longinus as their spiritual leader.[3]

---

[1] *Op. cit.*, iv, 49ff. (pp. 316ff.).
[2] *Op. cit.*, iv, 53 fin. (p. 327).
[3] *Op. cit.*, iv, 50 (p. 318). That the Monophysite doctrine continued to

There is a hint, however, that the activities of these Melkite missionaries among the peoples of Nubia were not altogether fruitless. A contemporary historian, John of Biclarum in Spain, in recording events that occurred in the third year of Justin II (i.e. about 569), states: *Maccuritarum gens his temporibus Christi fidem recepit.*[1] Reading between the lines, it is altogether probable that, while en route to Alodia, the Melkite missionaries found opportunity to introduce orthodox Christianity among the neighboring tribes, including the Makoritae.[2] One should also bear in mind, in this connection, the presence on Nubian tombstones of Greek inscriptions that resemble many features of the Byzantine prayers for the dead.[3]

Such is an outline of the conversion of the several peoples of Nubia to Christianity. During the following generations the numbers of churches increased and were counted, we are told, by the hundreds.[4] For about five centuries Christianity flourished in Nubia.[5] Its decline coincided with the inroads made by Arab invaders pressing southward from Muslim Egypt. For centuries the Nubian kingdoms were compelled to pay tribute to the Arab rulers of Egypt. "At the end of the fourteenth century," as William Y. Adams points out, "both the documentary and the archaeological records fall silent, and we are left in ignorance of the ultimate fate of the Christian population. ... Recent excavations have shown that there was still a bishop at Qaṣr Ibrîm in 1372, but the fact that his see had been combined with that of Faras is a measure of the

---

prevail is the testimony of Eutychius, Patriarch of Alexandria (middle of tenth century), in his *Annals*, ii, 387 (Migne, *Patrologia Graeca*, CXI, cols. 1122f.).

[1] *Chronica Joannis abbatis monasterii Biclarensis*, ed. Th. Mommsen (= *Monumenta Germaniae Historica, Auctores antiquissimi*, XI [Berlin, 1894]), 212, line 7. By "Christi fidem" John means, of course, the orthodox Christian faith.

[2] The suggestion is made by L. P. Kirwan in his article, "Christianity and the Kura'án," *Journal of Egyptian Archaeology*, XX (1934), 201-203.

[3] See the literature referred to above, p. 112, note 4.

[4] See A. J. Butler in B. T. A. Evetts's edition of the early thirteenth century treatise by Abû Ṣâliḥ, *The Churches and Monasteries of Egypt and Some Neighbouring Countries* (Oxford, 1895), pp. 263f. For a recent study see William Y. Adams, "Architectural Evolution of the Nubian Church, 500-1400 A.D.," *Journal of the American Research Center in Egypt*, IV (1965), 87-139.

[5] Cf. Yu. M. Kobishchanov, "Soobshcheniya srednevekovykh efiopskikh istochnikov khristianskoj Nubii [Medieval Ethiopic Records on Christian Nubia]," *Palestinskij sbornik*, VII (70, 1962), 35-43.

diminished size of his flock.¹ Probably Christianity had already vanished from a large part of Nubia by this time, and we know that the 'royal' church at Dongola had been transformed into a mosque fifty years earlier."² By the end of the fourteenth century, having been cut off for centuries from the rest of the Christian world, the Nubian Church ceased to exist. The growing power of the Arabs hemmed in the Nubian Christians on the north, east, and west, and the whole population apostatized and embraced Islam.

When it was that the Scriptures were translated into Nubian, no one knows. If, however, the pattern of evangelization was similar to that in other lands, it is probable that, soon after the introduction of Christianity on a wide scale in the sixth century, a vernacular version would have been called for by the new converts.

In 1906 Dr. Carl Schmidt purchased in Cairo some Old Nubian fragments which had come from Upper Egypt. At first he and Heinrich Schäfer were inclined to date the fragments in the eighth century, but on further study they assigned them to the tenth or eleventh century.³ The document consists of a quire of sixteen mutilated pages from a parchment codex containing a portion of a lectionary for Christmastide (see Plate II). The appointed lessons extend from the 24th of Choiak to the 30th of Choiak, corresponding to December 20th to 26th. For each day a pericope is supplied from the Apostolos and the Gospel. The identity of the Gospel passage is marked by the name of the Evangelist and by the Ammonian number of the first section. The contents of the fragment are as follows:

[24 Choiak Epistle ...]
       Gospel, Matt. 1.22-25 (cf. 28th of Choiak)
[25 Choiak] Epistle, Phil. 2.12-18
       Gospel, Matt. 5.13-19

---

¹ At this point Adams refers to an article by J. Martin Plumley, *Illustrated London News*, 11 July 1964, p. 51. It may also be added that the archaeological remains have been studied from the point of view of the history of art by Kazimierz Michałowski, *Faras, Fouilles Polonaises 1961* (Warsaw, 1962), pp. 91-122, and *id.*, *Faras, Fouilles Polonaises 1961-1962* (Warsaw, 1965), pp. 48-240. For a chronological and artistic study of Nubian fresco paintings in the Cathedral at Faras, see Michałowski, "Die wichtigsten Entwicklungsetappen der Wandmalerei in Faras," in *Christentums am Nil* (Recklingshausen, 1964), pp. 79-94.

² William Y. Adams, "Post-Pharaonic Nubia in the Light of Archaeology," *Journal of Egyptian Archaeology*, LI (1965), 177.

³ *Op. cit.*, 20. Juni 1907, p. 606.

[26 Choiak] Epistle, Rom. 11.25-29
             [Gospel ...]
 27 Choiak Epistle, Heb. 5.4-10
             Gospel, John 16.33-17.25
 28 Choiak Epistle, Heb. 9.1-5
             Gospel, Matt. 1.18-25 (by reference; cf. 24th of Choiak)
 29 Choiak Epistle, Gal. 4.4-6
             Gospel, Matt. 2.1-12
[30 Choiak] Epistle, Rom. 8.3-7 (or more)
             [Gospel ...]

Except for one instance (the lessons for Dec. 25), the order and
choice of the lessons find no parallel in the Greek or Coptic lectionaries hitherto examined. The exception involves the two passages
appointed for Dec. 25 (Gal. 4.4-7 and Matt. 2.1-12), which coincide
with those of Greek menologia. Since the extant sheets of the
lectionary are numbered 100-115 and contain daily lessons for the
24th to the 30th of Choiak (= Dec. 20 to 26), it appears that
originally the lectionary began with lessons for Sept. 1st (as do
also the Greek menologia). The presence of the Ammonian section
numbers makes it probable that the lectionary was constructed
from a non-lectionary text, at least so far as the Gospel pericopes
are concerned.

Like other texts of Old Nubian, the lectionary is written in an
alphabet that is essentially Coptic, reinforced by several additional
letters needed to represent the peculiar sounds of the language.
Unlike later Nubian dialects, which include many words borrowed
from the Arabic, the language of the lectionary is characterized by
the presence of Grecised forms of peculiarly biblical words. It is
perhaps significant that in a related Nubian text recounting the
miracle of St. Mena,[1] the proper names Alexandria and Mareotis
appear under their Greek forms, and not the Coptic equivalents
ⲣⲁⲕⲟⲧⲉ and ⲡⲁⲛⲓⲣ̅ⲃⲁⲓⲁⲧ. As Griffith[2] points out, these features
indicate that Nubians translated their religious literature from
Greek, not Coptic. In accord with this conclusion is the statement

---

[1] See *Texts relating to Saint Mêna of Egypt and Canons of Nicaea in a
Nubian Dialect*, ed. by E. A. Wallis Budge (London, 1909).
[2] F. L. Griffith, *The Nubian Texts of the Christian Period* (= *Abhandlungen
der königl. preuss. Akademie der Wissenschaften*, phil.-hist. Classe, 1913, No. 8),
p. 71.

made by Abû Ṣâliḥ that the liturgy and prayer in the Nubian churches were in Greek.[1]

The textual affiliations of the Nubian version are difficult to ascertain with precision. The chief reason for this is the paucity of text which has been preserved; only about seventy verses are extant, and some of these are very imperfectly represented. Furthermore, one must bear in mind the distinction between renderings and readings, of which only the latter are of primary assistance in determining the textual analysis of a version. In spite of these circumstances, however, it is possible to draw tentative conclusions regarding the broad classification of the version.

The following is a list of variant readings disclosed by collating Griffith's reconstructed Greek text against the Textus Receptus and against the text of Westcott and Hort.

1. (Matt. 1.24) ἐγερθείς (WH)] διεγερθείς (TR) Nubian, with D L W Γ Δ Π Σ

2. (Matt. 1.24) παρέλαβεν τὴν γυναῖκα αὐτοῦ (TR and WH)] Nubian, "took to himself the Virgin"

3. (Matt. 1.25) υἱόν (WH)] + αὐτῆς τὸν πρωτότοκον (TR) Nubian, with C D* N W Γ Δ Π Σ min[pl] f ff[1] aur vg sy[p,h]

4. (Jn. 17.8) ὅτι τὰ ῥήματα ἃ ἔδωκάς μοι δέδωκα αὐτοῖς (TR and WH)] Nubian, "the like thou gavest unto them"

5. (Jn. 17.11) καθὼς ἡμεῖς (TR and WH)] + ἕν ἐσμεν Nubian, with 33 al[5] g sy[h] arm

6. (Jn. 17.12) μετ᾽ αὐτῶν (WH)] + ἐν τῷ κόσμῳ (TR) Nubian, with A C[3] X Y Γ Δ Θ Λ Π unc[7] f q sy arm eth

7. (Jn. 17.12) ᾧ (WH)] οὕς (TR) Nubian, with A C[3] D X Y Γ Δ Θ Λ Π unc[7] vg goth sy[p,h] eth

8. (Jn. 17.20) περί (TR and WH)] + πάντων Nubian, with X Π 1 247 al[10] arm sy[hmg]

9. (Jn. 17.22) ἡμεῖς ἕν (WH)] + ἐσμεν (TR) Nubian, with ℵ[c] A C[3] X Y Γ Δ Θ Λ Π unc[7] vg sy[p,h] cop[sah] goth arm

10. (Gal. 4.6) υἱοί (TR and WH)] + τοῦ θεοῦ Nubian, with D E F G d e f g m cop[sah (2 mss)]

11. (Gal. 4.6) ὁ θεός (TR and WH)] Nubian om, with B 1739 t cop[sah (1 ms)]

12. (Phil. 2.15) μέσον (WH)] ἐν μέσῳ (TR) Nubian, with D[b] E K L cop[sah] arm eth

---

[1] Op. cit.

An examination of these variants reveals that the Nubian version agrees with the Textus Receptus against the Westcott-Hort text in six of the twelve variants (nos. 1, 3, 6, 7, 9, and 12), but it never agrees with Westcott-Hort against the Textus Receptus. In six variants the Nubian goes against both the Textus Receptus and Westcott-Hort (nos. 2, 4, 5, 8, 10, and 11); two of these instances are unique readings (nos. 2 and 4).

If the variants are examined from the standpoint of the textual characteristics of supporting witnesses, one finds that several have Western and/or Caesarean affinities (nos. 1, 3, 7, and 10). Though occasionally the Sahidic version (or some of the Sahidic manuscripts) supports the Old Nubian (nos. 9, 10, 11, and 12), in most cases it does not. In one instance (no. 11) codex Vaticanus and 1739 agree with the Old Nubian in an omission.[1]

If one may generalize on the basis of such a limited amount of textual data, it appears that the Old Nubian version was made from a Greek text which was predominately Byzantine in character, but which preserved a mixture of other readings as well.

---

[1] Unfortunately no part of the surviving Old Nubian text coincides with any of the portions of the Greek lectionary text that have been critically established in the fascicles published thus far by the University of Chicago Press.

CHAPTER TWELVE

WHEN DID SCRIBES BEGIN TO USE
WRITING DESKS?

When did scribes begin to use tables or writing desks in the copying of manuscripts? To those who take for granted that present-day habits of writing in the Western world must have prevailed also in antiquity, this question will no doubt seem to be unnecessary or even perverse. "Did not the ancient scribe," (so the reply may be framed), "did not the ancient scribe instinctively recognize from the very beginning the convenience of writing on a table?" It is a fact, however, that a variety of evidence supports the conclusion that in antiquity scribes were not accustomed to write on tables or desks. On the contrary, an accumulation of artistic, archaeo-logical,[1] and literary evidence indicates that when a scribe was making relatively brief notes on a wax tablet or on a sheet of papyrus or parchment, he would usually stand and write while holding the writing material in his left hand. When a scribe had a more extensive task, such as the copying of a rather lengthy manu-script, he would sit, occasionally on the ground but more often on a stool or bench, supporting the scroll or codex on his knees, which were sometimes raised the higher by the use of a footstool or dias under the scribe's feet.

Since these conclusions have been generally recognized by schol-ars,[2] it is unnecessary to develop here the chief lines of proof, but it will be sufficient to mention only a few typical examples representing different kinds of evidence.

I. *Scribes writing while standing.*

(a) The Papyrus of Ani (c. 1570—c. 1350 B.C.), containing the

---

[1] For a discussion of the several pieces of furniture used in the Scriptorium at Qumran by the Dead Sea, see appendix, pp. 135-137 below.

[2] E.g., Theodor Birt, *Die Buchrolle in der Kunst; archäologisch-antiquari-sche Untersuchungen zum antiken Buchwesen* (Leipzig, 1907), p. 209; William Sanday, *Studies in the Synoptic Problem by Members of the University of Oxford* (Oxford, 1911), pp. 16ff.; A. Dain, *Les Manuscrits* (Paris, 1949), p. 22; Jaroslav Černý, *Paper and Books in Ancient Egypt* (London, [1952]), p. 14; and T. C. Skeat, "The Use of Dictation in Ancient Book-Production," *Proceedings of the British Academy*, XLII (1956), 138.

Theban recension of the Book of the Dead, shows Thoth, the scribe
of the gods, recording the weight of Ani's soul in a tablet held in
his left hand.[1]

(b) An ivory diptych (at Berlin) in honor of Rufius Probianus
(*vicarius urbis Romae*, A.D. 399-402) shows two *notarii* writing in
wax tablets, held in their left hands (see Plate III).[2]

(c) The sculptured sarcophagus of Flavius Gorgonius from the
second half of the fourth century (now in the Cathedral at Ancona)
depicts Gorgonius dictating to two scribes, who are writing in
tablets held in their left hands.[3]

(d) An ivory of the sixth century (now in the Archiepiscopal
Museum at Ravenna) shows Joseph in Egypt supplying his brethren
with grain, while a scribe stands by keeping a record in a book
which he holds in his left hand.[4]

(e) In the Rossano Gospels Codex, dating from the sixth century,
a miniature on folio 8[v] depicts Christ before Pilate, with a *notarius*
to one side writing with a stylus in a tablet which he holds in his
left hand.[5]

II. *Scribes writing while seated.*

(a) A limestone statuette, now in the Louvre, dating from
c. 2700—c. 2600 B.C. shows an Egyptian scribe,[6] who perhaps bore

---

[1] British Museum, Papyrus 10470; picture in E. A. Wallis Budge, *The Book of the Dead; the Papyrus of Ani, a Reproduction in Facsimile*, I (London, 1913), plate 3.

[2] For Rufius Probianus, see Pauly-Wissowa-Kroll-Mittelhaus, *Realencyclopädie der classischen Altertumswissenschaft*, XXIII, i [= XLV Halbband] (1957), 42. For a discussion of the diptych, see Daremberg-Saglio, *Dictionnaire des antiquités grecques et romaines*, II, i, 273f. and fig. 2457, and Richard Delbrueck, *Die Consulardiptychen und verwandte Denkmäler* (Berlin, 1929), pp. 250-256.

[3] For a picture see Josef Wilpert, *I sarcofagi cristiani antichi*, I (Rome, 1929), plate xiv (1).

[4] For a picture see Cabrol and Leclercq, *Dictionnaire d'archéologie chrétienne et de liturgie*, III, i (1914), fig. 2410; and Joseph Natanson, *Early Christian Ivories* (London, 1953), plate 41.

[5] For a picture see Antonio Muñoz, *Il codice purpureo di Rossano* (Rome, 1907), Plate XIV; reproduced in B. M. Metzger, *The Text of the New Testament, Its Transmission, Corruption, and Restoration* (Oxford, 1964), Plate VII.

[6] For sculptures of Egyptian scribes see F. W. von Bissing, *Einführung in die Geschichte der ägyptischen Kunst von den ältesten Zeiten bis auf die Römer* (Berlin, 1908), Tafel XIII, 2; *idem, Denkmäler ägyptischen Sculptur* (Munchen, 1914), Tafel XI B; and *Fondation Eugène Piot, Monuments et mémoires*, I, I (Paris, 1894), Pl. I.

the name Kai,¹ seated on the ground with his legs crossed beneath
him, and writing on a sheet of papyrus lying upon his short kilt,
which is tightly stretched over his legs, thus forming a support for
the writing material (see Plate IV A).²

(b) A colophon on a sheet of papyrus at the close of a scroll
containing portions of the third and fourth books of the Iliad,
dating from the third Christian century,³ speaks of the cooperation
of the stylus, the right hand, and the knee in writing. The first two
lines, as restored by Wifstrand, read as follows:

Ἐγὼ κορωνίς εἰμι γραμμάτων φύλαξ.
κάλαμός μ' ἔγραψε δεξιὰ χεὶρ καὶ γόνυ.⁴

That is, because the scribe held the sheet of papyrus on his lap
while he wrote, it could be said that the knee as well as the stylus
and the right hand cooperated in producing what was written.

(c) A mosaic in the Church of San Vitale, Ravenna, which was
consecrated A.D. 547, shows St. Matthew seated on a bench and
writing in an open codex which he holds on his lap.⁵

(d) A terra-cotta ampulla, now in the Louvre, dating from the
sixth or seventh Christian century, shows on one side a male figure
seated and writing in a book held on his knees.⁶

(e) The Codex Amiatinus, dating from the end of the seventh or
beginning of the eight century, has on folio 5ʳ a miniature of Ezra
the scribe, seated on a bench and with his feet on a footstool, while
holding on his lap an open codex in which he is writing with a
stylus (see Plate IV B).⁷

¹ See Jean Capart, "The Name of the Scribe of the Louvre," *Journal of Egyptian Archaeology*, VII (1921), 186-190.
² For other examples of Egyptian scribes at work, either standing or seated upon the ground, see Theodor Birt, *Die Buchrolle in der Kunst; archäologisch-antiquarische Untersuchungen zum antiken Buchwesen* (Leipzig, 1907), p. 1off.; Heinrich Schäfer [und Walter Andrae], *Die Kunst des alten Orients*, 3te Auflage (Berlin [1925]), no. 238 and 341, 4; and *Gads Danske Bibel Leksikon*, ed. by Eduard Nielson and Bent Noack, II (Copenhagen, 1966), 799.
³ British Museum, inventory no. 136; see H. J. M. Milne, *Catalogue of the Literary Papyri in the British Museum* (London, 1927), pp. 21-22.
⁴ Albert Wifstrand, "Ein metrischen Kolophon in einem Homerpapyrus," *Hermes*, LXVIII (1933), 468-472; see also Bror Olsson in *Zentralblatt für Bibliothekswesen*, LI (1934), 365-367. For a discussion of the bearing of this colophon on problems relating to the habits of scribes, see Skeat, *op. cit.*, pp. 183ff.
⁵ For a picture see Santi Muratori, *I mosaici ravennati della Chiesa di S. Vitale* (Bergamo [1942]), Plate 25.
⁶ For pictures see the *Art Bulletin*, XX (1938), figures 19 and 20, p. 275.
⁷ For an untouched picture of the miniature see Guido Biagi, *Reproductions from Illuminated Manuscripts* (Florence, 1914), Plate VI. The retouched

Besides these examples there are many, many other representations of scribes writing in scrolls or codices held on their knees,[1] as well as some other literary evidence,[2] but that which has been cited here will doubtless be sufficient for the present purpose.

If then it be granted that in antiquity scribes usually performed their duties in the two ways described above, the question naturally arises when it was that the custom of using writing desks came into general use. Surprisingly enough, handbooks of palaeography make no attempt to answer this simple question, and when an occasional scholar offers a comment on the matter, one looks in vain for the citation of evidence. Thus, for example, in 1949 M. Dain was content to remark that "sauf de très rares exceptions, ... ce n'est que dans les derniers siècles du moyen âge que l'on trouve des représentations figurées de copistes écrivant sur un pupitre ou même sur une table, cette dernière parfois inclinée sur le côté."[3] From the data which are cited below it will be seen that scribes begin to be represented as writing at tables considerably earlier than "the last centuries of the Middle Ages," as Dain thought.[4]

---

picture in John Willis Clark, *The Care of Books* (Cambridge, 1909), frontispiece, Strikingly similar is the representation of Matthew in the Lindisfarne Gospels; see ed. by E. G. Millar (London, 1923), or by T. D. Kendrick, *et al.*, I (Oltun, 1960), fol. 25 (color plate).

[1] For many other examples of persons represented as writing on their lap, see A. M. Friend, Jr., "The Portraits of the Evangelists in Greek and Latin Manuscripts," *Art Studies*, v (1927), 115-146; vii (1929), 3-29; Dimitri Tselos, "Unique Portraits of the Evangelists in an English Gospel-Book of the Twelfth Century," *ib.*, xxxiv (1952), 257-277; David Diringer, *The Illuminated Book, its History and Production* (London [1958]); and Sirarpie Der Nersessian, *The Chester Beatty Library, a Catalogue of the Armenian Manuscripts* ..., II (Dublin, 1958), mss. 554 and 557.

[2] See a line in Callimachus's *Aetia*, known previously through Apollonius Dyscolus's discussion of anastrophic ἐπί (= *Grammatici graeci*, II, 2, ed. G. Uhlig [Leipzig, 1910], p. 442) and now known also through *Papyrus Oxyrhynchos*, 2079, lines 21f., in which the poet refers to placing a writing-tablet on his knees preparatory to composing his poem, καὶ γὰρ ὅτε πρώτιστον ἐμοῖς ἔπι δέλτον ἔθηκα γούνασιν. Perhaps in imitation of Callimachus (so R. Pfeiffer, *Hermes*, LXIII [1928], 319), in the Prooemium to the *Batrachomyomachia* (v.3) the poet appeals to the muses to give aid, ἥν (scilicet ἀοιδὴν) νέον ἐν δέλτοισιν ἐμοῖσ' ἐπὶ γούνασι θῆκα (though it is possible that here the aid is not for the writing but for the recitation of the poem; see O. Crusius, *Philologus*, LVIII [1899], 592f.). Another piece of literary evidence is the interesting description of Jos. Bryennios of the means and manner of writing during the Byzantine period, including reference to δακτύλων κίνησις, γονάτων κάμψις (quoted by V. Gardthausen, *Griechische Palaeographie*, 2te Auflage, I [Leipzig, 1911], 202).

[3] Dain, *op. cit.*, p. 22.

[4] In the second edition of Dain's *Les Manuscrits* (Paris, 1964), which was

One of the earliest representations of persons in the act of writing at a table is a relief dating from the end of the fourth Christian century found at Ostia (see Plate V). This shows two men seated at low tables on either side of a central figure who is standing on a platform or dias. Both seated figures hold a stylus in the right hand; one is busy writing in an open book lying on the table before him, while the other seems to be listening to the central standing figure. The books have the form of wax tablets, which are joined in codex fashion. In the background are five figures, of whom four are turned toward the central figure, and two are gesticulating. All the figures are dressed in tunics with long sleeves.

The interpretation of the scene is disputed. Is the central figure a teacher or preacher (either pagan or Christian), whose discourse, delivered within a hall (see the curtain at the top), arouses controversy among the listeners in the background? The scribes are, on this view, taking down stenographically the lecture or sermon. Or, does the relief represent an auction with two clerks who enter into their account books the bids made by several prospective buyers in the background?[1]

Another early representation of a person who is engaged in the act of writing on a table is a mosaic preserved in a fourth or fifth century chapel of martyrs found at Tabarka of North Africa (the ancient Thabraca of Numidia). This mosaic shows the figure of a bearded man, seated behind a massive table, and writing on what may be a papyrus roll, which lies on the top of the table (see Plate VI).[2] One can see clearly the letters which he has traced with his

published after an earlier form of the present study had been made available in *Akten des XI. internationalen Byzantinisten-Kongresses 1958* (Munich, 1960), Dain altered his statement so as to read: "... ce n'est que dans la seconde partie de Moyen Age que l'on trouve des représentations figurées de copistes écrivant sur un pupitre ... Du reste, la date de l'utilisation de table-bureau varie avec les différentes régions du monde médiéval" (p. 24).

[1] For discussions of the interpretation of the relief, see Guido Calza in *Le Arti*, I (1938-39), 388-393, Tav. CXX; *idem*, "Le Botteghe in Roma antica," in *Capitolium*, XIV (1939), 230; Heinrich Fuhrmann in *Jahrbuch des deutschen archäologischen Instituts*, LV (1940), 439, Abb. 18; and Raissa Calza and Maria Floriani Squarciapino, *Museo ostiense* (Rome, 1962), pp. 82f. and Pl. 43. Another relief, found at Porto, now in the Torlonia Museum (Visconti, *Catalogo*, no. 338), shows two porters unloading wine jars from a ship, while at one side sit three figures who, according to Meiggs, "may be a *tabularius* with two *adiutores*, recording the cargo on wax tablets in the form of a book" that rests on a table (Russell Meiggs, *Roman Ostia* [Oxford, 1960], plate XXVI, *a*).

[2] Paul Gauckler, "Mosaïques tombales d'une chapelle de martyrs à Tha-

pen, two uncials completely formed, and the vertical stem of a third, incomplete letter: MAI (the direction of writing is accomodated to the observer). Since the letters which are traced on the *volumen* are the same as those which begin the word MARtyr, it is tempting to conjecture that the unknown author may be writing the life of a martyr, perhaps one of those in whose honor the chapel itself was built.

Another piece of evidence which shows a person writing at a table comes from the fifth century (see Plate VII). On the right end of a sculptured sarcophagus, now in the Archaeological Museum of Milan, there is a male figure, writing while seated on a chair at a table.[1] Whether he is writing on papyrus or parchment cannot be determined, but it is probably the latter, for what may be a sheepskin is hanging from a rod over his head.

Of disputed age is the representation of the Evangelist, St. Matthew, on a purple leaf inserted as folio 17 in the Gospel Book of St. Victor in Xanten, now in the Royal Library of Brussels (no. 18723). Swarzenski is of the opinion that the leaf is a Roman original of the fourth century,[2] while Schapiro and others find in it reflections of Carolingian features.[3] The leaf in question depicts the Evangelist seated on a bench in the act of writing in a codex supported by a stand (see Plate VIII).

In the famous Lindisfarne Gospels[4] (c. A.D. 700) St. Mark is depicted (fol. 93ᵛ) seated and writing on a folio resting on a small circular stand.

During the latter part of the eighth century and throughout the ninth century the number of artistic representations of persons writing on desks or tables shows a marked increase. Miniatures of Sts. Mark and John in the Evangelistary of Godescalc,[5] which he copied between 781 and 783 on Charlemagne's orders, depict each evangelist writing in a codex that rests on a stand. Resembling the

---

braca," *Fondation Eugène Piot, Monuments et mémoires*, XIII (Paris, 1906), 197ff.

[1] Josef Wilpert, *I sarcofagi cristiani antichi*, II (Rome, 1932), plate CCXXXVII (4).

[2] Hanns Swarzenski, "The Xanten Purple Leaf and the Carolingian Renaissance," *Art Bulletin*, XXII (1940), 7-24; plate facing p. 8.

[3] Meyer Schapiro, *Art Bulletin*, XXXIV (1952), 162, note 122.

[4] For editions of the Lindisfarne Gospels, see above, p. 125, note 7.

[5] Wilhelm Koehler, *Die Karolingischen Miniaturen*; II, *Die Hofschule Karls des Grossen* (Berlin, 1958), folios 1 and 2.

purple leaf in the Gospel Book of Xanten, a miniature of St. Matthew (who in this case is nimbed) appears in the famous Charlemagne or Schatzkammer Gospels,[1] dated about A.D. 800 (see Plate IX, and compare Plate VIII).

From late in the eighth century is an ivory plaque, now in the Louvre, which was originally used as a book cover. The lower panel of this plaque shows Jerome holding a book while dictating to a scribe (see Plate X). The scribe is seated on a bench and is writing with a stylus in a book which rests on a stand.[2]

Examples dating from the ninth century include the following. The Ebbo Gospel Book, produced in the early part of the ninth century, has a miniature which presents certain features that are found in the purple leaf from the Gospel Book of Xanten and in the Charlemagne Gospels. On folio 18^v St. Matthew is depicted seated on a cushioned bench with a footstool (see Plate XI); he is holding an inkhorn in his left hand and writing with a pen in an open book which lies on the reclining top of a lectern or pedestal.[3] The characteristic features of the pedestal which appears in this miniature, as well as in several others, consist of a tripod base with a bead-and-reel shaft that supports a small platform or rack. Other ninth century representations of persons writing at a desk or table include Biblical personages, such as David,[4] John,[5] and Paul,[6] and Church Fathers, such as Ambrose of Milan,[7] Gregory the Great

---

[1] Amédée Boinet, *La miniature carolingienne* (Paris, 1913), plates 59 and 59. See also Florentine Mütherrich, "Die Buchmalerei am Hofe Karls des Grossen," in *Karolingische Kunst*, ed. by Wolfgang Graunfels and Hermann Schnitzler (Düsseldorf, 1965), pp. 9ff. (I owe this last reference to the kindness of Professor Nordenfalk, who also points out that in all such representations of persons writing in a bound codex the artist has taken certain liberties, for almost certainly the scribe had before him but a single leaf or folio at any one time).

[2] For a discussion, see Adolfo Venturi, *Storia dell'arte italiana*, II (Milan, 1902), 224ff. and fig. 156; and Adolf Goldschmidt, *Die Elfenbeinskulpturen*, I (Berlin, 1914), plate III, no. 4.

[3] The manuscript is now at Epernay in the Bibliothèque de la Ville, where it is no. 1.

[4] In a manuscript of John of Damascus's S. Parallela, Paris, Bibliothèque Nationale, gr. 923, fol. 257^v.

[5] *Ib.*, folio 147^r.

[6] *Ib.*, folio 304^r.

[7] In a manuscript of the Sermons of Egino, in the Staatsbibliothek, Berlin, Phill. 1676, fol. 24r. For a colored reproduction, see Joachim Kirchner, *Beschreibende Verzeichnisse der Miniaturen-Handschriften der preussischen Staatsbibliothek zu Berlin*, I (Leipzig, 1926), facing p. 6.

(see Plate XII),[1] Gregory Nazianzen,[2] and Nilus of Constantinople.[3]

By the end of the ninth century and throughout the tenth and eleventh centuries, examples of persons writing on desks, tables, and stands multiply noticeably. For example, a Psalter in the Landesbibliothek of Stuttgart (no. 23), dating from the ninth (or tenth) century, shows Isidore of Seville as a scribe (see Plate XIII), seated on an arc and writing with a pen in an inscribed book lying on a massive desk.[4] An inkpot is on a side table to the left of the desk. In the same manuscript (folio 47^v) a miniature which illustrates Psalm 37 depicts the Hand of God issuing from the arc of heaven to protect the righteous man, who is represented as a scribe seated on a bench with a footstool, writing with a pen in a book on a desk (see Plate XIV). An inkpot rests on a low stand in front of the writing desk. The Martyrologium of Wandalbertus of Prüm, of the ninth or tenth century, shows Wandalbertus as a scribe (see Plate XV A), tonsured and in a monk's habit, seated on a cushioned bench with a footstool, holding an inkpot in his left hand and writing (or illuminating) in an inscribed book on a stand.[5] Coming from the same period is a manuscript of the Psychomachia of Prudentius which shows (on folio 34^r) Prudentius nimbed and seated on a cushioned bench with a footstool; he is writing with a pen in a book that lies on a desk.[5] Dating from sometime during the eleventh century is a manuscript of the Lives of Paul the Hermit and Guthlac which on the verso of the first folio shows Jerome, tonsured and seated on a chair, writing in a book that rests on a lectern or stand (see Plate XV B).[7] From the eleventh century

---

[1] *Ib.*, fol. 25^v.

[2] In a manuscript of the Homilies of Gregory, in the Bibliothèque Nationale, Paris, gr. 510, fol. 424v, third register. For a reproduction, see H. A. Omont, *Miniatures des plus anciens manuscrits grecs de la Bibliothèque nationale* ... (Paris, 1929), plate 55.

[3] In the manuscript of the Sacra Parallela (see above, p. 129, note 4), fol. 238^r.

[4] It is on folio 1^v; a picture is in Ernest T. De Wald, *The Stuttgart Psalter* (Princeton, 1930). It is possible that the miniature is intended to represent an illuminator at work. (See addendum on p. 137 below).

[5] The Martyrologium is in the Vatican Library, Reg. lat. 438; the miniature is on folio 30^r. A picture appears in Joachim Prochno, *Das Schreider- und Dedikationsbild in der deutschen Buchmalerei* (Leipzig and Berlin, 1929), plate 17*.

[6] The manuscript is no. 264 in the Stadtbibliothek of Berne.

[7] The manuscript is no. 389 in the Library of Corpus Cristi College, Cambridge. A picture of the miniature on folio 1^v is given by Frances Wormald, *English Drawings of the Tenth and Eleventh Centuries* (London,

is a German Gospel Book now in the Fitzwilliam Museum, Cambridge, which has a fine portrait of St. Matthew. The Evangelist is seated and is in the act of writing on a scroll which is draped over a lectern or stand.[1] From the same century is a manuscript of the Satyrae of Persius which has a miniature representing the pagan author in a posture made familiar by the many examples of Christian authors. He is shown sitting on a bench, writing with his right hand in an open book which he holds with his left hand on the top of a lectern or stand (see Plate XVI).[2]

In seeking to discover when it was that scribes began to use a writing desk, one must not imagine that the habits of all scribes changed suddenly. The transition from the custom of writing on one's lap to the custom of using a desk or table must have taken place gradually, and is reflected in an interesting way in a scene found on an ivory plaque from the ninth or tenth century, now in the Louvre. The plaque depicts four scribes seated on benches; two are holding scrolls, while a third is writing in a codex held on his lap, and a fourth is writing in a codex that rests upon a stand (see Plate XVII).[3]

By way of further illustrating the manner in which the transition was effected, one can also point to several instances of the use of a lap-board which the scribe would hold on his knees and on which he would write. For example, a Latin manuscript of the Epistles of Paul from about A.D. 850, now in Düsseldorf at the Landesbibliothek,[4] shows St. Paul as a scribe, seated on a chair with a footstool, holding an inscribed scroll on a lap-board, on which are also a pen in an inkhorn and a knife (see Plate XVIII). From the latter half of the eighth century is the miniature of St. Matthew in the Vatican Gospels (Barb. Lat. 570, folio 11^v). This shows

---

[1952]), plate 36.

[1] The manuscript is McClean ms. no. 20. For a picture, see David Diringer, *The Illuminated Book, Its History and Production* (New York, [1958]), plate III-24, c.

[2] The manuscript is Cod. Leid. Bibl. Publ., lat. 82. See Stanisław Jan Gąsiorowski, *Malarstwo minjaturowe grecko-rzymskie i jego tradycje w średniowieczu* (Kraków, 1928), p. xxii and plate 57.

[3] The top of the plaque depicts David, seated on a throne and flanked on each side by two men of war; see Adolf Goldschmidt, *Elfenbeinskulpturen*, I (Berlin, 1914), plate LX (no. 141; see also 143). For another ivory showing scribes writing in various postures, see Robert Eisler, *Gazette des beaux-arts*, LXXIX, 2 (1937), 301, fig. 2.

[4] The manuscript is no. A.14; the miniature is on folio 120^r. See Adolf Goldschmidt, *Die deutsche Buchmalerei*, I (Firenze-München, 1928), plate 88.

the Evangelist seated on a chair holding on his lap a semicircular board; with his left hand he holds an open book on the lap-board.[1] He is in the act of dipping his pen, held in his right hand, into an inkhorn on his right side.[2]

In conclusion it will be appropriate to consider briefly what may have been some of the reasons for abandoning the ancient custom of holding on one's lap the scroll or codex in which one was writing.[3] It has been suggested that the explanation of the change is connected with the circumstance that "ancient society, being little concerned with the comfort or efficiency of slaves, provided no artifical support for the professional scribe, who was a slave; whereas the medieval scribe, usually a monk, was more likely to improve his means of writing."[4] This observation appears to be corroborated

---

[1] For a picture see Diringer, *op. cit.*, plate III-6, b.

[2] Though it represents an altogether different cultural tradition, reference may be made here to a paper fragment of a Manichaean miniature, dating from the eighth or ninth century A.D. Discovered in 1904 in Idiqut-Shahri (near Turfān, Eastern Turkestan), this miniature depicts nine Manichaean elders, seated in two rows, each with writing material in front of him, lying on what may be a lap-board or an extended table; see A. von Le Coq, *Die buddhistische Spätantike in Mittelasien*, II, *Die manichaeischen Miniaturen* (Berlin, 1923), p. 57 and plate 8b. Professor Arthur Vööbus of the Chicago Lutheran Theological Seminary has kindly called to my attention an enumeration of the typical writing equipment used by Manichaean scribes; see W. B. Henning's translation from the Sogdian in his edition of *Ein manichäisches Bet- und Beichtbuch* (= *Abhandlung der preussischen Akademie der Wissenschaften zu Berlin*, phil.-hist. Klasse, 1937, No. 10), pp. 33f.: "Wenn ich der Schreibkunst abgeneigt, sie hassend oder verachtend, einen Pinsel, eine Schreibtafel (?), ein Stück Seide oder Papier in den Händen gehalten (und dabei) viel Schaden und Beschädigungen angerichtet habe; wenn ich aus einer Wasserkanne ein Restschen vergossen habe, so dass es verlorenging— für all dieses: Verzeihung!" In view of the similarity between the word that Henning tentatively renders "Schreibtafel" (*t'š*) and the Sogdian verb "to cut" (see Ilya Gershevitch, *A Grammar of Manichean Sogdian* [Oxford, 1954], s.v.), the present writer ventures to suggest that *t'š* refers to the "knife" which scribes used for sharpening their writing instruments (see, e.g., Plate XIV). In reply to a query, Professor Richard N. Frye of Harvard University agrees (in a letter dated November 13, 1958) that this may be the meaning of *t'š*, and suggests that cognates of the Sogdian word may be attested in "Old Persian, Pahlavi, and even in New Persian *taš* 'axe.' Compare Kent's *Old Persian Lexicon*, s.v. *taxš*, with further remarks. MP *tāšitan* means 'to cut.'"

[3] This time-honored custom, however, has not been totally abandoned, for it is still the normal way of writing in the East; cf. Leonhard Bauer, *Volksleben im Lande der Bibel*, 2. Aufl. (Leipzig, 1903), pp. 79f.: "Der Orientale schreibt, anstatt einem Tisch als Unterlage benützend, das Papier oder die Tafel frei in der linken Hand haltend oder auf das recht Bein gestützt, welches über das linke Knie gelegt ist."

[4] So, for example, Professor Meyer Schapiro of Columbia University (in

by the fact that in the fellowship of the Christian monasteries the office of the scribe attained a special position of honor, and from the early Middle Ages the identity of the scribe came to be indicated through his signature, thus showing a greater interest in the personality of the workman.[1]

Another factor which must also have contributed to the altering of the ancient customs of scribes was involved in the growing popularity of large deluxe codices. According to the statistics collected by Diringer, in antiquity the average size of papyrus sheets used for literary works rarely, if ever, exceeded 13 × 9 inches, and apparently 10 × 7½ inches was the common size for books of moderate pretensions.[2] Sheets of these sizes would present no great difficulty to a scribe who was accustomed to write while holding them on his lap. On the other hand, obviously it would have been well nigh impossible to produce manuscripts of very large dimensions (such as, for example, the magnificent Codex Amiatinus, each bifolium of which measures about 20 inches by about 26 inches) without the use of some kind of support more firm than the scribe's knees. The splendid calligraphy so characteristic of such deluxe copies, even at the bottom of the columns of script, suggests that at the very least a lap-board must have been used by the scribe.

In this connection, however, what was said earlier regarding the transition from writing on one's lap to writing on a table or desk deserves to be reiterated; such a change probably took place neither quickly nor generally. The evidence presented by the ivory plaque referred to above (see Plate XVII) is what one would have expected. Even Codex Amiatinus itself, though it almost certainly was produced on a surface other than the scribe's knees, contains the well-known miniature of Ezra writing in a codex held upon his lap (see Plate IV B). In evaluating the significance of such iconographic evidence, one must always take into account the well-known conservatism in artistic representation, particularly of "sacred" scenes. Thus, it is not surprising that, after at least some scribes came to

---

a letter to the present writer dated January 8, 1956). He adds, however, to the sentence quoted above: "But I have not been able to confirm this by a comparative study of Greek, Latin, Hebrew, Islamic and other methods of writing."

[1] Cf. the remarks of Carl Wendel, *Die griechisch-römische Buchbeschreibung verglichen mit der des vorderen Orients* (Halle, 1949), p. 77.

[2] David Diringer, *The Hand-Produced Book* (London, 1953), p. 134. See also the statistics collected by Černý, *op. cit.*, pp. 14-17.

utilize writing desks, artists would continue to depict traditional motifs which called for representing scribes in the ancient posture of writing while holding the writing material on their knees. For example, the familiar scene of St. John dictating to Prochorus, who is writing in a codex held on his lap, is found as late as the fifteenth century in an Italian manuscript of the Apocalypse in the Venetian dialect (see Plate XIX A).[1]

By way of summary, evidence from various artistic media indicates that, except for sporadic earlier examples, it was during the eighth and ninth centuries that more and more scribes began to use a table or desk. The transition, however, from the customary practice of holding the writing material on one's lap was neither immediate nor absolute, and in subsequent centuries scribes continue to be represented in the traditional posture.

APPENDIX

JEWISH SCRIBES

Literary references to the equipment and customs of ancient Jewish scribes, so far as these relate to the present problem, are both meager and inconclusive. The statutes on uncleanness in the

---

[1] The manuscript is dated A.D. 1415; see Juliette Renaud, *Le cycle de l'apocalypse de Dionysiou* (Paris, 1943), p. 44 and plate XIII, I. For another example see the miniature of Mark in the twelfth or thirteenth century Greek Gospels Ms., Patmos 274 (Gregory 1385), reproduced in the *Harvard Theological Review*, xxv (1932), following p. 90. Cf. also A. M. Friend, Jr., *op. cit.* (see p. 126, note 1), and Hugo Buchthal, "A Byzantine Miniature of the Fourth Evangelist and its Relatives," *Dumbarton Oaks Papers*, xv (1961), 127-140.

According to the theory of Professor Friend (*op. cit.*) the stately seated figures of the Evangelists are derived from exemplars which were prefixed to the works of classical authors, such as the major tragic dramatists and the major philosophers, which have parallels in the plastic as well as the graphic arts. The area from which these Evangelist figures were diffused, Friend suggests, was Ephesus, an important center of production of works of art, such as ornamental tombs, upon which similar figures have been found. Representations of the Evangelists seated at their desks are often found in Gospel manuscripts of the period of the "Macedonian Renaissance" (ninth to eleventh century), when there was a great revival of art and scholarship in the Eastern Roman Empire. Friend's further suggestions that seated figures of the Evangelists, of Ephesian provenance, may originally have accompanied New Testament texts of the "Western" type, and that those with standing figures, which in his opinion are of Alexandrian provenance, may have originally accompanied texts of the "Alexandrian" type, remain interesting but unproved suppositions.

Mishnaic tractate Kelim include the following: "There are three kinds of בְּסָסִיּוֹת: that which lies before a bed or before scriveners, which is susceptible to *midras*-uncleanness; that of a side-table, which is susceptible to corpse-uncleanness; and that of a cupboard, which is not susceptible to any uncleanness" (24.6: Danby's translation). The crucial point here is the meaning of בְּסִיסָאוֹת (so Aruch). It is apparently derived from βάσις (cf. Syriac ܟܣܐ) and is defined in the lexica as *footstool, base, stand, step* (so Jastrow) and as *Basis, Gestell, Untersatz, Fundament* (so Krauss and Levy). In the context of this passage in Kelim, Danby renders the word by "dais," Blackman by "stands," and Slotki (in Epstein's edition) by "bases." The latter adds an explanatory footnote indicating that the scribe's "base" was used as a seat.

Another statute in Kelim refers to three kinds of writing tablets (פִּנְקְסִיּוֹת = πίνακες): "that of אֲפִיפוֹרִין, which is susceptible to *midras*-uncleanness; that which has a receptacle for wax, which is susceptible to corpse-uncleanness; and that which is polished, which is not susceptible to any uncleanness" (24.7; Danby's translation). Blackman regards אֲפִיפוֹרִין as an orthographic variant of אֲפוֹפּוֹדִין (i.e. ὑποπόδιον) and translates it, "[that which is used as] a foot-rest." Danby and Slotki read it as אֲפִיפְיָירוֹת (cf. παπυρεών) and translate "that of papyrus." The third variety of tablet, described as חֲלָקָה, is no doubt to be understood as a plain board, without a wax receptacle (so Jastrow and Blackman). Perhaps it was used as a lapboard on which the sheet of writing material was held.

Besides such testimony from literary sources of Jewish antiquity, there is available also the furniture of the Scriptorium at Khirbet Qumran, discovered in 1953. In an elongated room about 13 m. by 4 m. in dimensions,[1] brick and plaster fragments were found which, when put together, formed "une table étroite, longue d'environ 5 mètres, haute de 0 m. 50, et les morceaux d'une autres tables plus courtes. Ces tables étaient associées à des banquettes basses, courant le long des murs."[2] In the debris from the same room were two inkwells,[3] one of bronze and the other of terra cotta, still containing traces of dried ink. It is altogether likely that these and other

---

[1] J. T. Milik, *Dix ans de découvertes dans le désert de Juda* (Paris, 1957). p. 42.

[2] R. de Vaux, "Fouilles au Khirbet Qumrân: Rapport préliminaire sur la deuxième campagne," *Revue Biblique*, LXI (1954), 212.

[3] For a picture of the inkwells, see *Pictorial Biblical Encyclopedia*, ed. by Gaalyahu Cornfeld (Tel Aviv, 1964), p. 39.

artifacts[1] belonged to the scriptorium at Qumran, perhaps the one in which were produced some of the Dead Sea Scrolls (see Plate XIX b).

What is doubtful to the present writer, however, is the identification of the furniture of the scriptorium. Following de Vaux's original description, other scholars have likewise confidently referred to the furniture as a long, narrow "table" on which the scribes wrote, and a companion "bench" on which the scribes sat.

Such an identification, however, raises more questions than it answers. For one thing, the use of tables for writing purposes was, as we have seen above, extremely rare in antiquity. Furthermore, both the so-called table and the so-called bench are of quite unusual shape and dimensions to be used as desk and seat respectively. The sloping and rounded edge of the "bench," as well as its extremely low height (about nine inches) would appear to be ill-adapted for use as a seat. Likewise, the shape of the under part of the "table" is such as to make it impossible for a scribe to sit close enough in order to write comfortably on its top. Furthermore, the top of the "table" is not flat, as one would expect were it to be used as a writing surface, but is slightly concave. Moreover, the present height of the "table" as reconstructed in the Palestine Museum is deceptive, for it has been built higher than would appear to be warranted. In fact, careful measurements, made by Clark, reveal that the taller object is actually 44 cm. (17½ inches) high,[2] which is too low for convenient use as a writing desk.

In view of such considerations, at one time the present writer suggested that the "table" was in fact a bench on which the scribes sat, while using the lower object as a footrest so that their knees would be raised to a convenient height while holding the parchment on their laps.[3] After further consideration, however, in the light of Clark's experimentation with a dummy scribe, it appears that anatomical exigencies make such a theory improbable, and another must be sought. Whether the table was used for the preparation and repair of the skins and scrolls,[4] or whether it was used to hold

---

[1] The low, small platform with two shallow depressions hollowed out of the top surface, which was also found in the room, may have been used by the scribes for purificatory ablutions prior to copying the sacred Name.

[2] Kenneth W. Clark, "The Posture of the Ancient Scribe," *The Biblical Archaeologist*, xxvi (1963), 64.

[3] B. M. Metzger, "The Furniture of the Scriptorium at Qumran," *Revue de Qumran*, i (1958-59), 509-515.

[4] As suggested by Katharine Greenleaf Pedley, "The Library at Qumran,"

the necessary equipment for writing, such as the ink wells and perhaps the exemplar also,[1] in any case there is very little likelihood that it served as a writing desk.[2]

Revue de Qumran, II (1959-60), 21-41. Cf. also the general remarks of Bruce D. Rahtjen, "Library Procedures at Qumran," *Summary of Proceedings, Eighteenth Annual Conference, American Library Association* (1964), pp. 114-120.

[1] As suggested by Clark, *op. cit.*, p. 70.

[2] What light, if any, does Luke 16.6 shed upon the habits of writing in antiquity? The unjust steward says to his master's debtor, δέξαι σου τὰ γράμματα καὶ καθίσας τάχεως γράψον πεντήκοντα, that is, "Take from me your indenture (שטרך), which you delivered to me, and sit down quickly and write a new one for fifty measures only." Did the man sit on the ground or at the steward's desk or table? If the latter, was it a writing desk or a banker's table? Furthermore did τράπεζα come to mean "bank" because money lay on it or because accounts were written on it—or for both reasons? It is easier to ask such questions than to answer them.

Addendum to p. 130, footnote 3:

For representations of mediaeval artists at work illuminating manuscripts, cf. Virginia W. Egbert, *The Mediaeval Artist at Work* (Princeton, 1967): see especially Plate XI (facing p. 42) for a miniature from a Moralized Bible (ca. A.D. 1250) showing the illuminator's book resting on a draped stand supported by a moveable arm attached to his chair.

CHAPTER THIRTEEN

CODEX BEZAE AND THE GENEVA VERSION OF THE ENGLISH BIBLE (1560)

Although many studies have been published of the history and influence of Codex Bezae, textual critics have hitherto overlooked the contribution which it made to one of the most noteworthy of the earlier English versions of the Bible. This was the sixteenth-century translation prepared by a group of English exiles who had fled to the Continent in order to escape the persecution of Queen Mary Tudor, sometimes referred to as "Bloody" Mary. Published at Geneva in 1560 it was reprinted many times thereafter and became the family Bible of a very large number of English-speaking Protestants. It was the Bible of William Shakespeare, of John Bunyan, and the men of Cromwell's army. In the seventeenth century it was carried to America by the Pilgrims, who would have nothing to do with the more recently published King James version of 1611.

As is well known, the Geneva version was unique among English Bibles in several respects. It was the first English Bible to utilize numbered verses, each set off as a separate paragraph. It was the first to be printed with Roman type instead of the time-honored but clumsy-looking Gothic or black-letter type. It was the first to use italics for the words which the translators added in the interest of idiomatic English, but for which there was no distinct equivalent in the original.[1]

Of the group of English translators who prepared the Geneva version, the leader was William Whittingham, a fellow of All Souls College and senior student of Christ Church, Oxford. Since the Geneva Bible had the advantage of a certain amount of supervision given it by John Calvin and Theodore Beza, one is not surprised

---

[1] The use of a different font of type to distinguish such words added in the translation of the Bible as have no exact representatives in the original seems to have been first employed by Sebastian Münster in his Latin version of the Old Testament published in 1534, -35. In 1556 Theodore Beza adopted the same practice for his Latin New Testament. On its use in the King James version, see F. H. A. Scrivener, *The Authorized Edition of the English Bible* ... (Cambridge, 1884), pp. 61-81.

that this version possesses many scholarly excellencies.[1] One of these
marks of scholarship, which has not hitherto received the attention
which it deserves, is the presence in the margins of a number of
variant readings derived from Codex Bezae[2] and from several other
Greek manuscripts. These translations of variant readings are
printed in larger type[3] than that which is used for the numerous
marginal annotations on difficult passages and for the alternative
renderings, as though to suggest that the variants have almost equal
validity with the Scriptural text itself. The reader's attention is
drawn to each of them by the presence in the text of two vertical
parallel lines, which are repeated in the margin, after which the
variant reading is cited. No indication is given of the manuscript or
manuscripts which support the variant.

The following is a list of all the variant readings which are found
in the margins of the New Testament of the Geneva Bible of 1560.
In each case the location of the variant is indicated by quoting the
words of the text which immediately precede the two parallel lines.
The variant readings which have the support of Codex Bezae are
marked with an asterisk; those which had appeared in the margins
of Whittingham's earlier translation of the New Testament, published at Geneva in 1557, are marked with an obelisk.

1.*   Luke 17.35   the other shal be left. ‖ 36 And they answered. ....[4]
   ‖ Two shal be in the field: one shal be receiued, & another
   shal be left.

---

[1] The scholarly interest of the translators is shown in a number of ways.
In the Old Testament, for example, a point was made in returning to a more
precise spelling of proper names, and even in accenting them in accordance
with the original Hebrew. In the New Testament, marginal notes identify
the origin of the several quotations from pagan authors (namely the quotations at Acts 17.28; I Cor. 15.33; and Titus 1.12). The Geneva translators
were ahead of their times in observing that the Epistle to the Hebrews is
probably not by Paul, and in printing the title simply "The Epistle to the
Ebrewes." For other examples of the scholarship reflected in this version,
see the present writer's article, "The Geneva Bible of 1560," in *Theology
Today*, XVII (1960), 339-52.

[2] Nicholas Pocock called attention to several of these in his article, "Some
Notices of the Genevan Bible," published in the little-known journal, *The
Bibliographer*, VI (1884), 105-7.

[3] This is true of all the variants except that at I Cor. 15.51, where apparently the space in the margin was deemed to be too much crowded by
other comments to permit the use of the larger type for the variant reading.

[4] In Bibles current today what is given in the margin of the Geneva version
is assigned to verse 36, and the Genevan verse 36 is renumbered verse 37.

2.   John 8.59   went out of the Temple ||.
      || And he passed through the middes of them and so went his
      way.

3.   Acts 10.6   sea side : ||
      || He shal speake wordes unto thee whereby thou shalt be
      saued & all thine house.

4.*   Acts 10.48   the Name of the Lord ||.
      || Iesus Christ.

5.*   Acts 11.17   that I colde let God ||?
      || Not to giue them the holie Gost?

6.*† Acts 14.7   preaching the Gospel ||.
      || In so muche that all the people were moued at the doctrine.
      So bothe Paul & Barnabas remained at Lystra.

7.*† Acts 14.10   Said with a loude voyce, || Stand vpright
      || I say to thee in the Name of the Lord Iesus Christ.

8.†   Acts 14.18   had not sacrificed vnto them ||.
      || but that they shulde go euerie man home. And whiles they
      taried & taught, there came, etc.

9.†   Acts 14.19   they had persuaded the people, ||
      || And disputing boldely persuaded the people to forsake them :
      for, said thei, they say nothing true, but lie in all things.

10.*† Acts 15.29   and from fornication : ||
      || and whatsoeuer ye wolde not that men shulde do vnto you,
      do not to others.

11.*† Acts 15.34   to abide there stil ||.
      || and onely Iudas went.

12.† Acts 15.37   And Barnabas || counseled to take with them Iohn,
      called Marke.
      || wolde take Iohn, etc.

13.   Acts 16.7   but the Spirit ||
      || of Iesus.

14.*† Acts 16.35   when it was day, || the gouernours
      || The Gouernours assembled together in the market, & re-
      membring the earthquake that was, they feared and sent, etc.

15.*† Acts 19.9   in the schole of one Tyrannus ||.
      || From fiue a clocke vnto ten.

16.* Acts 20.23   afflictions abide me ||.
      || In Ierusalem.

17.   I Cor. 15.55 || O death, where *is* thy sting! ô graue where *is*
      thy victorie!

|| O death, where is thy victorie! o graue, where is thy sting!
18. Gal. 4.31 of the fre woman||. | CHAP. V. | Stand fast therefore
     in the libertie wherewith Christ hathe made vs fre,
     || By the libertie wherewith Christ hathe made vs fre.
19. I John 2.23 hathe not the Father||.
     || But he that confesseth the sonne, hathe also the Father.
20. I John 5.10 hathe the witnes|| in him self:
     || of God.
21. Jude 16 walking after their owne lustes||:
     || In vngodlines and iniquitie.

When one examines these twenty-one variant readings, a number of questions and observations present themselves. Since it was not until 1562, two years *after* the publication of the Geneva Bible, that Theodore Beza acquired from the monastery of St. Irenaeus at Lyons the famous codex which now bears his name,[1] a nice problem seems to be posed as to how Whittingham learned of the Bezan variants. In this connexion it is necessary to be reminded of the earlier history of the manuscript.

In 1546 William à Prato (Guillaume du Prat), bishop of the city of Clermont in Auvergne, came to the Council of Trent with an ancient manuscript having at John 21.22 the reading ἐὰν αὐτὸν θέλω μένειν οὕτως, on the basis of which he apparently argued that celibacy has dominical sanction.[2] Now, so far as is known, Codex Bezae is the only New Testament manuscript which has this reading. It was probably owing to the attention thus drawn to this manuscript that friends of the famous Parisian printer and editor, Robert Estienne, communicated to him from Italy a list of its noteworthy readings. In 1550 Estienne published the first Greek New Testament which had a critical apparatus. The margins of this handsome folio edition contain variant readings drawn from fifteen manuscripts and from the printed text of the Complutensian Poly-

---

[1] In an explanatory, handwritten statement prefixed to the codex, Beza indicates that he obtained the manuscript during the civil war of 1562, doubtless at the sack of Lyons by the Huguenot army under the infamous Des Adrets: "Est hoc exemplar venerandae vetustatis ex Graecia, ut apparet ex barbaris graecis quibisdam ad marginem adscriptis, olim exportatum, et in Sancti Irenaei monasterio, Lugduni, ita ut hic cernitur, mutilatum, postquam ibi in pulvere diu jacuisset, repertum oriente ibi Civili bello, anno Domini 1562" (quoted by F. H. [A.] Scrivener, *Bezae Codex Cantabrigiensis* [Cambridge, 1864], p. viii).

[2] See J. R. Harris, *Codex Bezae* (Cambridge, 1891), pp. 36-8.

glot Bible (see Plate XX). Here more than 350 Bezan variants are cited (with some inaccuracies) with the siglum β'.[1] At about the time of the publication of this edition Estienne sought refuge in Geneva, throwing in his lot with the Reformers, with whose thinking he had come to sympathize.[2] There is every reason to believe that in translating the Geneva version Whittingham and his associates made use of this edition and from its apparatus derived information regarding variant readings of Codex Bezae and other manuscripts.

There are, however, four variant readings in the margins of the Geneva version (nos. 2, 8, 9, and 17 in the list above) for which the apparatus of the 1550 edition supplies no Greek variant. Where then did Whittingham find these?

Here we must resort to conjecture. When Estienne moved to Geneva he undoubtedly brought with him his scholarly notes and manuscript studies. It appears that a copy of some of these passed into Beza's hands, for in the preface of Beza's bilingual Greek and Latin New Testament with annotations, which was published at Basel in 1559, he referred to an "exemplar ex Stephani nostri bibliotheca cum vigintiquinque plus minus manu scriptis codicibus, & omnibus penè impressis diligentissimè collatum." This statement was expanded in the edition of 1565 by the addition after *impressis* of the words "ab Henrico Stephano ejus filio, et paternae sedulitatis haerede, quam diligentissimè collatum." Whether this was a hand-written copy of the collations which Stephanus had accumulated (as Scrivener[3] and Gregory[4] believed), or a copy of the printed edition of 1550 with possibly a few additional notes entered in the margins (as Rendel Harris argued,[5] partly on the basis of an ingenious conjecture by Hug[6]), at any rate in 1559 Beza included in his annotations on Acts 14.18-19 two Greek variants found, he says, in four manuscripts. The fact that these variants do not appear in

---

[1] Estienne's statement in his "Epistle to the Reader" regarding the manuscript is τὸ δὲ β' ἐστὶ τὸ ἐν Ἰταλίᾳ ὑπὸ τῶν ἡμετέρων ἀντιβληθὲν φίλων. For the identity of the other fourteen manuscripts, all of them minuscules, see C. R. Gregory, *Textkritik des Neuen Testamentes*, II (Leipzig, 1902), 934.

[2] See Elizabeth Armstrong, *Robert Estienne, Royal Printer; an Historical Study of the Elder Stephanus* (Cambridge University Press, 1954), pp. 211ff.

[3] *A Plain Introduction to the Criticism of the New Testament*, 4th ed., II (1884), 191.

[4] *Op. cit.*, II, 935.

[5] *Op. cit.*, p. 6.

[6] J. L. Hug, *Einleitung in die Schriften des Neuen Testaments*, 4te Ausg. (Tübingen, 1847), §58.

Stephanus's apparatus of 1550 indicates that Beza had access to a larger body of manuscript evidence than that contained in the printed form of Stephanus's text.[1] We must assume that Beza made this information available to Whittingham prior to the publication of the latter's New Testament in 1557 (see items 8 and 9 in the list above). The other two variant readings in the Geneva Bible (numbers 2 and 17 above) are of a somewhat different nature. At John 8.59 the Geneva translators relegated to the margin the translation of the (longer) Greek text of Stephanus 1550 (διελθὼν διὰ μέσου αὐτῶν, καὶ παρῆγεν οὕτως) and printed as their text the English rendering of the (shorter) form of the Greek which Beza had adopted in his 1559 edition.[2] The latter expressed in his annotations his approval of the suggestion which Erasmus[3] had made to the effect that the words of the longer form of text are a scribal intrusion from Luke 4.30—a view to which present-day textual critics would subscribe. As regards I Cor. 15.55, the remaining passage for which the Stephanus 1550 apparatus supplies no Greek variant, in 1559 Beza included in his annotations a lengthy discussion of the variation in the sequence of the clauses in this verse, making comparison with the Hebrew and the Septuagint texts of Hos. 13.14, from which it is quoted, and expressing a strong preference for the sequence which the Geneva translators subsequently adopted in their marginal reading.[4]

---

[1] It has been debated whether Beza's mention of about twenty-five manuscripts (see above) was not much exaggerated, and whether, in fact, Beza had access to no more than two manuscripts in addition to the fifteen included in Stephanus's printed edition; see Isaac Newton in a letter to a friend dated 14 November 1690, in *The Correspondence of Isaac Newton*, III, ed. by H. W. Turnbull (Cambridge, 1961), 98f.

[2] This is one of fourteen passages in Beza's 1559 edition which differ from the text of Stephanus 1550 (so Eduard Reuss, *Bibliotheca Novi Testamenti Graeci* [Brunsvigae, 1872], p. 73); another passage is Luke 17.35-6 (see the first item in the list of Genevan variants).

[3] Bezae no doubt refers to Erasmus's *Annotationes*, ed. 1527, p. 238; ed. 1546, p. 249.

[4] It may be mentioned here that the Geneva version includes a conjectural emendation in the margin at Mark 16.2; opposite the difficult statement that the women "came into the sepulchre, when the sunne was yet rising," the margin reads "Or, not risen." (This variant is not mentioned in the list given above because it is introduced, not by the siglum of two parallel lines, but by "Or" as though it were like other alternative renderings, and because it is not printed in the large type characteristic of the alternative readings). Undoubtedly its presence is due to Beza's proposal that, since one manuscript known to him reads ἔτι ἀνατείλαντος, perhaps we should read οὐκ ἔτι ἀνατείλαντος, for, according to Luke 24.1 and John 20.1, the women arrive *before* the sun had risen.

In assessing the twenty-one variant readings presented in the margins of the Geneva Bible, we observe that many important readings are passed over in silence (for example, of the three variants from Codex Bezae listed on p. 243 of Stephanus's Greek New Testament [see Plate XX] only one is represented in the Geneva Bible) and several rather unimportant ones are included. At the same time, it must be remembered that in 1560 the textual criticism of the New Testament was still in its infancy, if indeed one can speak of the existence of such a discipline prior to Richard Simon's monumental *Histoire critique du texte du Nouveau Testament* (Rotterdam 1689; Eng. trans., London, 1689). In any case, when one compares the Geneva Bible with respect to variant readings with the King James or Authorized Version of 1611, the former comes off somewhat better than the latter, at least so far as the number of variant readings is concerned, for the margins of the 1611 Bible contain citations of only thirteen variant readings.[1]

---

[1] The New Testament passages in the 1611 Bible which are supplied with variant readings in the margin are Matt. 1.11; 26.26; Luke 10.22; 17.36; John 18.13; Acts 25.6; I Cor. 15.31; Eph. 6.9; Jas. 2.18; II Pet. 2.2, 11, 18; II John 8. The variants are introduced by a variety of formulas, such as "Many Greeke copies haue"; "Many ancient copies adde these words"; "Or, as some copies reade"; or, most frequently, "Some read." The only variant reading that is common to both the 1560 and the 1611 Bibles is that at Luke 17.36, which, in the latter version, reads, "This 36. verse is wanting in most of the Greek copies."

What amounts to conjectural readings are given at two passages in the 1611 Bible. In the margin opposite the close of John 18.13 there stand the words, "And Annas sent Christ bound unto Caiaphas the high Priest, ver. 24," a conjectured rearrangement which, according to information in the apparatus of the Nestle Greek New Testament, had been suggested also by Martin Luther. In the margin opposite Acts 13.18 the 1611 Bible gives the following alternative: "Gr. ἐτροποφόρησεν, perhaps, for ἐτροφοφόρησεν, *as a nurse beareth*, or, *feedeth her childe*, Deut. 1.31. 2 macc 7.27, according to the Sept. and so Chrysost."

CHAPTER FOURTEEN

RECENT DEVELOPMENTS IN THE TEXTUAL CRITICISM OF THE NEW TESTAMENT

A Brief Survey of Research, 1937–1967

During the years which have elapsed since the publication of F. G. Kenyon's useful volume, *The Text of the Greek Bible, A Students Handbook* (London, 1937), many significant advances have been made in the textual criticism of the New Testament. In the following pages the author has attempted to present a selective and concise report concerning several of the more notable (I) manuscript discoveries, (II) textual studies, and (III) editions of the Greek New Testament that fall within the third of a century extending from 1937 to 1967.

I. MANUSCRIPT DISCOVERIES

Greek manuscripts

The past thirty years have seen the acquisition and cataloguing of a considerable number of Greek witnesses to the text of the New Testament. The list of Greek papyri has gone from $\mathfrak{P}^{52}$ to $\mathfrak{P}^{81}$; the uncial manuscripts from 0208 to 0266; the minuscule manuscripts from 2401 to 2754; and the Greek lectionaries from l 1609 to l 2135.[1] Of the two dozen Greek papyri that have come to light the most important are those now in the possession of the Swiss bibliophile and humanist, M. Martin Bodmer, founder of the Bodmer Library of World Literature at Cologny-Geneva. The Bodmer Papyrus II, assigned the siglum $\mathfrak{P}^{66}$, preserves most of the first fourteen chapters of the Gospel of John and small fragments of the remaining chapters.[2] According to its editor, Victor Martin, Professor of Classical Philology at the University of Geneva, the manuscript dates from

---

[1] See Kurt Aland, *Studien zur Überlieferung des Neuen Testaments und seines Textes* (Berlin, 1967), p. 207.

[2] Victor Martin, *Papyrus Bodmer II: Évangile de Jean*, chs. 1-14 (Cologny-Geneva, 1956); *Supplément, Évangile de Jean*, chs. 14-21 (1958), new ed. by V. Martin and J. W. B. Barns (1962). The 1962 edition of the *Supplément* is accompanied by a photographic reproduction of the entire manuscript.

about A.D. 200,[1] and is thus one of the earliest witnesses to the Gospel of John (the oldest still seems to be the tiny scrap at the John Rylands Library, $\mathfrak{P}^{52}$, preserving a few verses from John 18, and usually dated A.D. 100-150). The text of $\mathfrak{P}^{66}$ contains elements which are typically Alexandrian and Western.[2]

One of the notable features of $\mathfrak{P}^{66}$ is the presence of approximately 440 alterations and corrections entered between the lines or in the margins. About two-thirds of these (approximately 260 instances) involve corrections made by the scribe of his own careless blunders.[3] Of the other alterations, in a few cases the scribe changed the text from an Alexandrian to a Western reading, in several more cases he changed from a Western to an Alexandrian reading, but in most cases it is difficult to ascertain any characteristic tendency, other than the evident desire to produce a smoother and more readily intelligible form of text.[4]

In several passages $\mathfrak{P}^{66}$ preserves unique readings not previously known from any other witness. In John 13.5 a picturesque word is used in the account of the Foot Washing scene; according to $\mathfrak{P}^{66}$ Jesus took not a "basin" (νιπτῆρα) but a "foot-basin" (ποδονιπτῆρα). In 7.52 the presence of the definite article in a difficult passage now provides added support for what some scholars had long thought was the required sense; namely, "Search [the Scriptures] and you will see that *the* Prophet does not arise from Galilee."[5]

---

[1] According to Herbert Hunger, however, who is the curator of the papyrological collections in the National Library at Vienna, $\mathfrak{P}^{66}$ should be dated earlier, in the middle if not even in the first half of the second century; see his article "Zur Datierung des Papyrus Bodmer II (P66)," *Anzeiger der österreichischen Akademie der Wissenschaften*, phil.-hist. Kl., 1960, No. 4, pp. 12-33.

[2] K. Aland, "Papyrus Bodmer II. Ein erster Bericht," *Theologische Literaturzeitung*, 1957, cols. 1-24.

[3] According to E. C. Colwell, "Wildness in copying is the outstanding characteristic of $\mathfrak{P}^{66}$" ("Scribal Habits in Early Papyri; a Study in the Corruption of the Text," *The Bible in Modern Scholarship*, ed. by J. P. Hyatt [Nashville, 1965], p. 386).

[4] See G. D. Fee, "The Corrections of Papyrus Bodmer II and Early Textual Transmission," *Novum Testamentum*, VII (1965), 247-257. Colwell concludes that "the relationship of $\mathfrak{P}^{66}$ to established text-types should be reconsidered with the nature and extent of $\mathfrak{P}^{66}$ corruption kept vividly in mind. $\mathfrak{P}^{66}$ might then look like a corruption of the Beta Text-type rather than like a mixed text" (*op. cit.*, p. 388).

[5] For other analyses of $\mathfrak{P}^{66}$ see J. Neville Birdsall, *The Bodmer Papyrus of the Gospel of John* (London, 1960), M.-E. Boismard in *Revue Biblique*, LXX (1962), 120-133, and E. F. Rhodes, "The Corrections of Papyrus Bodmer II," *New Testament Studies*, XIV (1967-68), 271-281.

The Bodmer Papyrus VII-IX, containing a miscellaneous assortment of biblical and patristic documents, is dated by the editor[1] in the third century; it is thus the earliest known copy of the Epistle of Jude and the two Epistles of Peter ($\mathfrak{P}^{72}$). Because of the relatively small size of the codex (it measures 6 by $5\frac{3}{4}$ inches), the editor concludes that it was made for private usage and not for reading in church services. In I and II Peter its affinities are with the Alexandrian type of text (in I Pet. it agrees with A 109 times, with Ψ 104 times, and with B 90 times,[2] and in II Pet. there is very frequent agreement with B).[3] In Jude its text has been described as "wild"[4] and analagous to the Western or Bezan text of the Gospels and Acts.[5]

Somewhat less noteworthy is the Bodmer Papyrus XVII ($\mathfrak{P}^{74}$) dating from the seventh century.[6] In a poor state of preservation, it contains, with many lacunae, portions of Acts, James, I and II Peter, I, II, and III John, and Jude. The type of text which it presents in Acts agrees more frequently with א and A than with B, especially as to order of words; it supports no truly Western reading.[7]

Of great importance is $\mathfrak{P}^{75}$, the Bodmer Papyrus XIV-XV, a single quire codex containing most of the text of the Gospels of Luke and John.[8] The editors date the codex between A.D. 175 and 225;[9] it is thus the earliest known copy of the third Gospel and one

---

[1] Michel Testuz, *Papyrus Bodmer VII-IX. VII, L'Épître de Jude; VIII, Épîtres de Pierre* ... (Cologny-Geneva, 1959).

[2] F. W. Beare, "The Text of I Peter in the Bodmer Papyrus ($\mathfrak{P}^{72}$)," *Studia Evangelica*, III (= *Texte und Untersuchungen*, LXXXVIII; Berlin, 1964), pp. 253-265. Cf. also Édouard Massaux, "Le Texte de la Iª Petri du Papyrus Bodmer VIII ($\mathfrak{P}^{72}$)," *Ephemerides theologicae Lovanienses*, XXXIX (1963), 616-671, and J. D. Quinn, "Notes on the Text of $\mathfrak{P}^{72}$," *Catholic Biblical Quarterly*, XXVII (1965), 241-249.

[3] M. A. King, "Notes on the Bodmer Manuscript," *Bibliotheca Sacra*, CXXXI (1964), 54-57.

[4] Éd. Massaux, "Le Texte de l'Épître de Jude de Papyrus Bodmer VII," *Scrinium Lovaniense. Mélanges historiques Étienne Van Cauwenbergh* (Louvain, 1961), pp. 108-125.

[5] J. Neville Birdsall, "The Text of Jude in $\mathfrak{P}^{72}$," *Journal of Theological Studies*, n.s. XIV (1963), 394-399.

[6] Rodolphe Kasser, *Papyrus Bodmer XVII. Actes des Apôtres, Épîtres de Jacques, Pierre, Jean et Jude* (Cologny-Geneva, 1961).

[7] Philippe-H. Menoud, "Papyrus Bodmer XVII," *Revue de théologie et de philosophie*, 3ᵉ sér, XII (1962), 112-116.

[8] Victor Martin and Rodolphe Kasser, *Papyrus Bodmer XIV-XV. Évangiles de Luc et Jean*, 2 vols. (Cologny-Geneva, 1961). With a facsimile of the entire codex.

[9] The date is supported by J. de Savignac, *Scriptorium*, XVII (1963), 50-55.

of the earliest of the fourth Gospel. The textual complexion of 𝔓⁷⁵
is definitely Alexandrian, being markedly similar to B.[1] Occasionally
it is the only known witness which agrees with the Sahidic version.
In Luke 16.19, in the account of the Rich Man and Lazarus, this
early witness inserts after πλούσιος the words ὀνόματι Νευης (i.e. the
scribe intended to write ὀνόματι Νινευης "whose name was Nine-
veh").[2]

Versional Manuscripts[3]

In connection with their monumental work of collecting patristic
evidence of the Vetus Latina (over a million slips of biblical quotations have been prepared and filed in scriptural sequence) the
monks at the Erzabtei of Beuron have discovered more than one
previously unknown manuscript of the Old Latin version. For example, the present director of the project, Fr. Bonifatius Fischer,
has published an interesting text of Acts from a Latin palimpsest
codex at the Cathedral of León.[4] The under-writing, which dates
from the seventh century, contains Acts 8.27-11.13 and 14.21-17.25
in alternating blocks of Old Latin and Vulgate text. Among its
Western readings are "the *Holy* Spirit *fell upon the eunuch, and the
angel* of the Lord caught away Philip" (8.39), the absence of καὶ
πνικτῶν and the presence of the negative golden rule in 15.29, and
the additional verse 34 in ch. 15.

Among important Coptic manuscripts which have been published
recently three may be singled out for special mention. One is a
papyrus codex belonging to M. Bodmer and containing the Gospel

---

[1] C. L. Porter, "Papyrus Bodmer XV (P75) and the Text of Codex Vaticanus," *Journal of Biblical Literature*, LXXXI (1962), 363-376; Kurt Aland,
"Neue neutestamentliche Papyri II," *New Testament Studies*, XI (1964), 5-21,
and XII (1966), 195-210; and Carlo M. Martini, s.j., *Il problema della recensionalità del codice B alla luce del papiro Bodmer XIV* (Rome, 1966).

[2] For bibliography concerning the name of the Rich Man in Luke 16.19
see B. M. Metzger, *The Text of the New Testament, its Transmission, Corruption, and Restoration* (Oxford, 1964), p. 42, note 1.

[3] For recent research on the ancient versions of the New Testament,
reference may be made to the present writer's surveys in *New Testament
Studies*, II (1955), pp. 1-16 (covers the five year period, 1950-54), and in
The Bible in Modern Scholarship, ed. by J. P. Hyatt (New York, 1965),
pp. 347-369 (covers 1955-64).

[4] Bonifatius Fischer, o.s.b., "Ein neuer Zeuge zum westlichen Text der
Apostelgeschichte," in *Biblical and Patristic Studies in Memory of Robert
Pierce Casey*, ed. by J. Neville Birdsall and R. W. Thomson (Freiburg, 1963),
pp. 33-63.

of John and the opening chapters of Genesis in Bohairic, dated by the editor in the fourth century.[1] When it is recalled that half a century ago several scholars were of the opinion that the Bohairic version was made in the seventh or even eighth century (such was the opinion, e.g., of Forbes Robinson, Burkitt, Leipoldt, and Baumstark), the importance of the Bodmer codex is hard to overestimate.

Since the Fayyumic version of the New Testament has hitherto been represented by only a relatively few documents,[2] scholars must be grateful to Elinor M. Husselman for her edition of a fragmentary fourth century manuscript of the Gospel of John (6.11-15.10) in that dialect.[3] In the format of a single quire codex, now in the Museum of Archaeology at the University of Michigan, the manuscript has some 25 readings peculiar to it alone; it agrees with the Sahidic against the Bohairic 68 times, and agrees with the Bohairic against the Sahidic 30 times.

Another manuscript in Middle Egyptian is even more noteworthy. This is a parchment codex from the fourth or fifth century that contains on 107 leaves the text of Acts 1.1-15.2. The manuscript, which is no. G67 in the Glazier Collection of the Pierpont Morgan Library in New York, is significant as an early witness to a Western type of text in Egypt.[4] Many typically Western readings, hitherto known from D, Old Latin ms. *h*, and the margin of the Harclean Syriac version, are now found to have been current also in Middle Egypt. Among many examples are the following: "claiming to be *a great* somebody" (5.36); "an angel *standing in their midst*" (6.15); "Herod ... made an oration to them, *and came to an agreement with*

---

[1] Rodolphe Kasser, *Papyrus Bodmer III. Évangile de Jean et Genèse I-IV,2 en bohaïrique* (Louvain, 1958).

[2] Concerning Middle Egyptian versions known in 1937 Kenyon wrote in his *Text of the Greek Bible*, "Of these dialects too little is known to be worth discussing here. The surviving fragments are too few and too small, and their interest is rather linguistic than textual" (p. 134).

[3] Elinor M. Husselman, *The Gospel of John in Fayumic Coptic (Mich. inv. 3521)* (Ann Arbor, 1962).

[4] A preliminary description of the manuscript is given by Theodore C. Petersen, C.S.P., "An Early Coptic Manuscript of Acts: An Unrevised Version of the Ancient So-Called Western Text," *Catholic Biblical Quarterly*, XXVI (1964), 225-241. See also Eldon J. Epp's discussion, "Coptic Manuscript G67 and the Rôle of Codex Bezae as a Western Witness in Acts," *Journal of Biblical Literature*, LXXXV (1966), 197-212. Unfortunately Father Petersen died before completing his edition of the manuscript; his work, however, is to be finished under the expert guidance of Fr. Paul Bellet of the Catholic University of America.

the Tyrians" (12.21-22); "against the brethren; *but the Lord gave peace speedily"* (14.2); and at the end of 14.7 *"and the whole multitude was shaken* (?) *at the teaching; and Paul and Barnabas remained in Lystra."*

Among the so-called minor versions of the New Testament, the Armenian version deserves at least a brief comment. It is not generally realized how abundant are the manuscripts of this version; contrary to a rather widespread impression of their rarity,[1] many more manuscripts are extant of the Armenian version than of any other ancient version of the New Testament, with the exception only of the Latin Vulgate. Several years ago an invaluable catalogue listing 1244 Armenian manuscripts of the New Testament was published by Erroll F. Rhodes.[2] In addition to identifying the manuscripts by their library and museum numbers, Rhodes also supplies information concerning their contents, physical description, scribes, place and date of writing, as well as references to previous lists and monographs in which the manuscripts are cited. With such a useful tool available it is to be hoped that Western scholars will pay far greater attention to this, the "Queen of the versions," than has been true in the past.

Patristic manuscripts

Undoubtedly one of the most noteworthy patristic acquisitions during the past third of a century is the recovery of about three-fifths of the Syriac text of Ephraem's Commentary on Tatian's Diatessaron, previously known only through an Armenian translation of Ephraem (preserved in two manuscripts that were copied in A.D. 1195) and in brief quotations made by other Eastern Fathers.[3] The manuscript, which is of parchment and in two distinct parts, is in the possession of Sir Chester Beatty. The part that contains Ephraem's work, which is dated by its editor, Dom Louis Leloir, in the late fifth or early sixth century, has been published recently in a handsome edition with a Latin translation.[4] A comparison of the

---

[1] Reflected, for example, even in Kenyon's *Our Bible and the Ancient Manuscripts*, 5th ed. rev. by A. W. Adams (London, 1958), p. 237.

[2] *An Annotated List of Armenian New Testament Manuscripts* (Tokyo, 1959).

[3] For a survey of the dozen or so secondary and tertiary witnesses to the Diatessaron, see the present writer's *Chapters in the History of New Testament Textual Criticism* (Leiden and Grand Rapids, 1963), pp. 96-102.

[4] *Saint Éphraem, Commentaire de l'Évangile concordant, text syriaque (manuscrit Chester Beatty 709)* (Dublin, 1963).

Syriac and Armenian texts discloses that the latter is, on the whole, a reliable rendering of the original. It apparently, however, was not made from a form of text identical with that preserved in the Beatty manuscript, for occasionally the latter presents supplementary paragraphs (containing both quotations from the Diatessaron as well as Ephraem's comments on it) and occasionally the Syriac text lacks material (in addition to the approximately two-fifths that has been lost) that is present in the Armenian.

Among noteworthy readings of the Diatessaron, now available in Syriac, is the curious expansion of the Johannine account of Jesus' healing of the blind man (9.6): "He spat upon the ground, and formed clay of his spittle, and made eyes from the (*lit.* his) clay (ܩܡܝܗ ܡܢ ܐܝܢ̈ܐ ܘܥܒܕ)."[1]

II. TEXTUAL STUDIES

The stage at which New Testament textual studies had arrived in the 1930's was characterized by a general approval given to the view that most New Testament manuscripts fall into one of four major text-groups, the α-text or Byzantine group, the β-text or Alexandrian group, the γ-text or Caesarean group, and the δ-text or Western group. It was widely acknowledged that the α-text was the latest and most debased form of the New Testament, which, having accumulated the transcriptional errors of scribes and the deliberate emendations of editors, was finally embalmed in print during the sixteenth century and remained the dominant "Textus Receptus" until the rise of critical scholarship in the nineteenth century. Textual critics were less certain, however, whether the original text was preserved chiefly in the Alexandrian, the Caesarean, or the Western type of text. Thus, in 1926 James Hardy Ropes, in a magisterial edition of the book of Acts in codex Vaticanus and codex Bezae, usually favored the Alexandrian text, whereas in 1933 Albert C. Clark, in an equally painstaking edition of Acts, just as consistently preferred the Western text.

Today a somewhat different mood prevails. Instead of arguing that a single text-type represents most nearly the original text, scholars are much more likely to practice what can be called impartial eclecticism. Despairing of ever succeeding in drawing up a detailed stemma of New Testament manuscripts, textual critics

---

[4] Eph. *Com.* xiv.28 (p. 186).

today seek to ascertain in each set of textual variants the reading that is most nearly in accord with the style of the author and that accounts best for the origin of the other variants, irrespective of textual families. At the same time, most scholars also seek to give adequate consideration to the weight of external evidence, involving questions of age, geographical distribution, and the like. As practised by a few textual critics, however, a reading which is attested by only versional or patristic evidence may be preferred, on the basis of internal or transcriptional considerations, to a reading supported by the entire Greek tradition.

Noteworthy developments in the investigation of special topics and areas of textual study include those relating to the Caesarean and Byzantine texts, the corpus Paulinum and the book of Revelation, and the effect of the discovery of $\mathfrak{P}^{75}$ on textual theory.

The Caesarean Text

Although the discovery of $\mathfrak{P}^{45}$ seemed at first to confirm the existence and unity of the Caesarean text (which had been isolated in 1924 by B. H. Streeter as one of the several "local texts" of the principal ancient sees), subsequent study has led to its being divided into the pre-Caesarean text and the Caesarean text proper. In a painstaking study entitled "¿Texto cesariense o precesariense?"[1] the late Teófilo Ayuso Marazuela, professor in the Roman Catholic Seminary at Segovia, came to the following conclusions: (*a*) At Caesarea Origen and Eusebius used a "Caesarean" text. This text, however, did not originate at Caesarea but was carried there from Egypt. (*b*) It appears to have originated, not in Alexandria, where a "Neutral" text was current, but in a locality off the beaten track so far as ancient scholarship was concerned; it came from the region of Gizeh and the Fayyum. (*c*) The witnesses which today preserve the primitive, pre-Caesarean text are $\mathfrak{P}^{45}$, W^{Mk}, *fam.* 1, *fam.* 13, and ms. 28. On the other hand, Θ, 565, 700, the Sinaitic Syriac, the Old Armenian and Old Georgian versions, and Origen and Eusebius are witnesses to a subsequent recensional text, which may be called the Caesarean text proper.

At about the time that Ayuso published his research, a student of F. C. Burkitt's at Cambridge University was finishing a M. Litt. thesis which, though not widely known at the time, was the harbin-

---

[1] *Biblica*, XVI (1935), 369-415.

ger of further dissolution of Streeter's Caesarean text. Under the title "The Caesarean Text *Inter Pares*"[1] James E. McA. Baikie concluded that "the Caesarean witnesses did not agree in one family preference for types of variant," but were, in fact, "in greater absolute agreement with outsiders than with the majority of their fellows." ... "Further evidence of Caesarean diversity was afforded by Inter-Familiar Variation, i.e. cases where, when two or more variants occur, the family witnesses are divided against themselves and united with those of other families." It thus appears that "the Caesarean unity is one of influences rather than origin, and that the Caesarean text, in a measure at least, is really a Textual Process."

The Byzantine Text

Recent studies of minuscule manuscripts of the New Testament and ecclesiastical writers of the Byzantine period have served to correct a one-sided tendency which, sometimes associated with the views of Westcott and Hort, had too much depreciated the value of later witnesses. For example, the analysis of the New Testament quotations in the writings of Photius, the ninth-century scholar, statesman, and theologian, has brought to light surprising data. Contrary to what might have been expected of a patriarch of Constantinople, Photius did not, according to J. Neville Birdsall, make use of the current Byzantine text, but in the Gospels quoted one which (in John) had close affinities with the Caesarean text and which (in Matthew and Mark, and perhaps Luke) had a pre-Caesarean type of text.[2] In the Acts and Epistles, Photius habitually quoted, not the Κοινή-type of text, but "texts akin to those isolated by von Soden and classified in his various I-groups, and denominated 'mixed texts' by Ropes in his study of the text of Acts. ... It is noteworthy that Photius should conserve so many ancient and good readings in his text. This may at least suggest that ... the investigation into the Byzantine text and lectionaries may not be without value for the establishment of the original text and for the tracing of earlier epochs of textual development."[3]

---

[1] See *Abstracts of Dissertations Approved for the Ph.D., M.Sc. and M.Litt. Degrees in the University of Cambridge during the Academic Year 1935-1936* (Cambridge, 1936), pp. 53f.

[2] "The Text of the Gospels in Photius," *Journal of Theological Studies*, n.s. VII (1956), pp. 42-55, 190-198.

[3] "The Text of the Acts and the Epistles in Photius," *ibid.*, n.s. IX (1958), 278-291. The quotation is from pp. 290f.

The mention of lectionaries in the previous sentence leads one to comment that this extensive group of witnesses to the text of the New Testament, so long neglected by textual scholars, at last seems to be receiving attention more nearly in accord with their importance. In his *Text of the Greek Bible* (pp. 108ff.) Kenyon called attention to the preliminary work on lectionaries by two American scholars, Colwell and Riddle,[1] and suggested that these manuscripts deserve further investigation. Over the past two or three decades several doctoral dissertations accepted at the University of Chicago and, more recently, at Princeton Theological Seminary have resulted in the publication of six monographs and many articles dealing with Greek Gospel lectionaries.[2] In a summary of such publications Allen Wikgren concludes that, though the lectionary text is essentially Byzantine in character, the presence of occasional early readings indicates that lectionaries "are important for a reconstruction of the history of the text, and may also serve as valuable supporting witnesses to readings found in the earliest pre-recensional documents."[3]

Textual Analyses of Paul and Revelation

Amid many significant textual analyses published during the past third of a century it is difficult and somewhat invidious to single out for special mention only one or two. In any case, however, the Schweich Lectures delivered in 1946 by Günther Zuntz deserve more than a passing notice.[4] Paying primary attention to philological considerations, Zuntz made a detailed examination of variant readings in I Corinthians and the Epistle to the Hebrews. He was concerned to recover the original text of the *Corpus Paulinum* rather than that of the autographs of the separate epistles, for all of the extant evidence reflects this collection of letters, which was made about A.D. 100. In Zuntz's opinion the editor who brought together

---

[1] E. C. Colwell and D. W. Riddle, *Prolegomena to the Study of the Lectionary Text of the Gospels* (Chicago, 1933).

[2] The most recent monograph is by Ray Harms, whose Princeton dissertation, *The Matthean Weekday Lessons in the Greek Gospel Lectionary*, was published as vol. ii, no. 6, of *Studies in the Lectionary Text of the Greek New Testament*, ed. by Allen Wikgren (Chicago, 1966).

[3] "Chicago Studies in the Greek Lectionary of the New Testament," in *Biblical and Patristic Studies in Memory of Robert Pierce Casey*, ed. by J. N. Birdsall and R. W. Thomson (Freiburg, 1963), pp. 96-121. The quotation is from p. 121.

[4] *The Text of the Epistles. A Disquisition upon the* Corpus Paulinum (London, 1953).

the several epistles had perforce to rely upon copies that already contained faults and interpolations, which henceforward infected all strands of manuscript tradition. For example, Zuntz cites I Cor. 6.5 "to judge between his brother" as "an unintelligible corruption due to *homoioarcton* of 'to judge between a brother and a brother' "— the latter being preserved today only in two Old Latin manuscripts and in the Peshitta Syriac because their translators made the obvious conjecture to remove the primitive error.

In his examination of variant readings Zuntz naturally pays most attention to the testimony of 𝔓⁴⁶, B, 1739, and manuscripts of the Western text. Manuscript 1739, copied in the tenth century by a monk named Ephraim, has a textual importance hardly less than that of 𝔓⁴⁶ and B, for, according to a colophon, the text of the Pauline corpus was copied from an ancient archetype which, investigation shows, was made about A.D. 400 by a scholar, perhaps at Caesarea, whose text reveals links with the text used by Origen of the previous century.

Among Zuntz's conclusions the following may be singled out:

(*a*) Western readings (i.e. those supported by the Greek archetype of D F G, Tertullian, and the archetype of *d* and the pre-Vulgate quotations of the Latin Fathers) which are not shared by 𝔓⁴⁶ B 1739 are usually found to be wrong.

(*b*) The Alexandrian witnesses have nearly always preserved the right reading against the rest of the evidence when 𝔓⁴⁶ sides with them, and very often they are wrong when the papyrus is in the opposite camp. It even happens, Zuntz finds, that 𝔓⁴⁶ alone with one Western witness can be right against the entire bulk of other witnesses.

(*c*) In the Epistles one should reserve the use of the term Caesarean text for the Euthalian recension; 𝔓⁴⁶ B 1739 represent not a Caesarean text but a proto-Alexandrian group of manuscripts.

(*d*) There was, in Zuntz's view, a second century "reservoir" of variant readings from which the stream of tradition flowed in two main courses, one the remarkably pure Alexandrian tradition and the other the "muddy Western tradition." (This metaphor is illustrated by an illuminating graph at the end of the book). Thus, the text of Clement of Alexandria, described by Hort as "Neutral" and by Burkitt as "mainly Western," belongs, in fact, to the earliest stage of the Alexandrian tradition, but is Western in the sense that it contains a number of readings recurring in Western witnesses but absent from most of the later Alexandrians.

(e) "A reading peculiar to average late manuscripts or, on the other hand, to Western witnesses will require an overwhelming amount of intrinsic probability in order to be accepted. As soon, however, as any members of these two groups agree with each other, we must acknowledge a second-century tradition. This may still be wrong, and often it is wrong. Where Western witnesses are joined by a member, or some members, of the Alexandrian group, the authority of the relevant reading is powerfully increased: such a reading is likely to have been approved by Alexandrian critics who relied upon evidence such as we can never hope to recover. Thus the probabilities rise with the accession of authoritative witnesses. In these calculations the Byzantine text is by no means *quantité négligeable.*" At the same time, however, Zuntz acknowledges that *"recensio* [consideration of external evidence] alone can no longer settle any really problematical point. There is no *règle de fer*, no divining-rod to save the critic from the strain of labour and thought."

Another important analysis of the text of a book of the New Testament is Josef Schmid's monograph on the book of Revelation.[1] Beginning with a thorough study of the textual tradition of the Commentary on the Apocalypse written between A.D. 563 and 614 by Archbp. Andreas of Caesarea (in Cappadocia), preserved in about fifty manuscripts, Schmid analyzed the textual families of the Greek witnesses of the book of Revelation. On the basis of an examination of about two hundred manuscripts of Revelation (most of them available in the careful collations of H. C. Hoskier), Schmid found that the textual tradition of Revelation falls into four main families of texts.

(a) The most important family is that represented by manuscripts A and C and the text of Oecumenius (particularly MS. 2053).

(b) Next in importance is the text represented by $\mathfrak{P}^{47}$, א, and several minuscules. According to Schmid these two families stand closer to each other than to the following two groups, and closer than the following stand to each other.

(c) The minuscule manuscripts preserving the Commentary of Andreas of Caesarea.

(d) The so-called K(οινή)-text.

---

[1] Josef Schmid, *Studien zur Geschichte des griechischen Apokalypse-Textes.* I. Teil: *Der Akpoalypse-Kommentar des Andreas von Kaisareia. Text* (München, 1955). *Einleitung* (1956). 2. Teil: *Die alten Stämme* (1955).

Especially noteworthy in Schmid's investigations is the attention given to the usage of the article, pronouns, verbs, prepositions, stereotyped expressions, and Hebraisms in the Apocalypse. On the basis of such stylistic considerations, Schmid chooses among variant readings, particularly where the external evidence is more or less evenly divided. Among Schmid's conclusions concerning the relative importance of individual manuscripts and groups of manuscripts of the book of Revelation, the following deserve to be mentioned. Among all witnesses codex A is the most weighty except for matters of orthography. The Chester Beatty Papyrus, $\mathfrak{P}^{47}$, though earlier in date, is less valuable than either A or C. Indeed, Schmid is prepared to say that "when $\mathfrak{P}^{47}$ stands alone it never preserves the original reading; in company with ℵ, it preserves the original in several passages." According to Schmid, each of the four basic groups of witnesses, mentioned above, is important; for, in different passages, each of the four preserves, alone, the original reading.

The Significance of $\mathfrak{P}^{75}$

Until the publication of $\mathfrak{P}^{75}$ in 1961 the earliest witnesses to a pure form of the Alexandrian type of text (Hort's "Neutral"; von Soden's "Hesychian") were B and ℵ of the fourth century. It was customary to regard the type of text preserved in B ℵ as the result of editorial supervision, undertaken perhaps in the third century.[1] Now, however, a copy of Luke and John ($\mathfrak{P}^{75}$) has turned up which presents a text like that of B and which is about a century and a half older than B—that is, $\mathfrak{P}^{75}$ is contemporary with Clement of Alexandria (*d.* 212) and earlier than Origen (*d.* 254).[2] In fact, the degree of close relationship between $\mathfrak{P}^{75}$ and codex Vaticanus can be gauged from the presence of numerous readings for which the only Greek support is $\mathfrak{P}^{75}$ and B.[3]

Thus proof is now available that the text of codex Vaticanus was not the product of deliberate revision in the third century. Since B

---

[1] In 1943, for example, it was possible for G. D. Kilpatrick to describe the Alexandrian text as a revised text which "cannot be traced back beyond the third century" (*Journal of Theological Studies*, XLIV, p. 35).

[2] See C. L. Porter, "Papyrus Bodmer XV (P75) and the Text of Vaticanus," *Journal of Biblical Literature*, LXXXI (1962), 363-376, and Carlo M. Martini, s.j., *Il problema della recensionalità del codice B alla luce del papiro Bodmer XIV* (Rome, 1966).

[3] For a list of readings in Luke supported only by $\mathfrak{P}^{75}$ and B, see Martini, *op. cit.*, pp. 181-183.

is not a lineal descendent of $\mathfrak{P}^{75}$, the common ancestor of both carries the Alexandrian type of text to a period prior to A.D. 175-225, the date assigned to $\mathfrak{P}^{75}$. Of course, such an early date does not mean that the readings of $\mathfrak{P}^{75}$ B in Luke and John must in all cases be preferred, but it does mean that the scribe of codex Vaticanus, so far from creating the Alexandrian type of text, transmitted it with only the most minor alterations from the form in which it circulated toward the end of the second century. Whether this form was produced by editorial revision is perhaps still an open question, but in any case the general lineaments of the textual theory of Westcott and Hort have been confirmed rather than weakened by the discovery.[1]

III. EDITIONS OF THE GREEK NEW TESTAMENT

Current editions of the Greek New Testament reflect wide differences in textual complexion. Not all editions that carry on the title page a twentieth-century date represent twentieth-century scholarship. For example, Alexander Souter's handsomely printed volume (Oxford, 1910; 2nd ed., 1947) presents an utterly antiquated text; it is, in fact, the text drawn up in 1881 by Archdeacon Edwin Palmer as that which inferentially lies behind the English Revised Version of 1881. Taking as his basic text the third edition of Stephanus (1550), Palmer altered it only where the Revisers had clearly expressed a preference for a reading different from the discredited Textus Receptus. There were, of course, many passages where the order of words, the presence or absence of the article, the spelling of proper names, and similar features were taken over without alteration from the sixteenth-century edition. In fact, Palmer states in his Preface that "even peculiarities of Stephanus, which appeared to be typographical errors" were retained![2]

The well-known and convenient Nestle edition (now in its 25th

---

[1] A somewhat similar evaluation has been reached in a recent analysis of the textual affinities of $\mathfrak{P}^{72}$ (which also is dated about A.D. 200). In a monograph entitled *P72 and the Codex Vaticanus* (*Studies and Documents*, vol. XXVII; Salt Lake City, 1965), Sakae Kubo concludes that in I and II Peter and Jude where $\mathfrak{P}^{72}$ and B agree "their common text is almost always superior to any other opposing combinations" (p. 154).

[2] It was this edition, as reprinted by Souter, that the translaters of the New English Bible regarded, along with the editions of Westcott and Hort and of Nestle, as "a standard text" (!), entirely suitable for use in making a draft translation; see below, pp. 160f.

ed., 1963), prepared originally by Eberhard Nestle and carried on since his death by his son Erwin Nestle and, more recently, by Kurt Aland, also reflects, in the main, nineteenth-century scholarship. It reproduces, with few exceptions, the text of Tischendorf (1869-72) and of Westcott and Hort (1881), and where these differ it follows whichever of the two agrees with Bernhard Weiss's edition (1892-1900). The few exceptions are a limited number of readings that, from the 17th ed. onward (1941), have been introduced into the text on the basis of scholarly consensus favoring their originality. The excellence of the Nestle editions depends more on the apparatus than on the text, for important variant readings from the most recently discovered manuscripts have been periodically introduced into the apparatus, while the text remains substantially that preferred by the scholarship of a preceding generation.

In connection with its one hundred fiftieth anniversary (1954), the British and Foreign Bible Society issued in 1958 a second edition of its 1904 edition of the Greek New Testament. (The 1904 edition, it should be mentioned, presented the mechanically-produced Nestle text). The second B.F.B.S. edition of 1958 was prepared by the collaboration of Dr. Erwin Nestle of the Württemberg Bible Society and Professor G. D. Kilpatrick of The Queen's College, Oxford. Except for several orthographic and typographic modifications the 1904 text remains substantially unchanged; in fact, according to information provided by the B.F.B.S. itself, in only about a score of passages was the Nestle text (namely, the older form of the Nestle text, prior to the alterations introduced into the 17th edition of 1941) modified.[1] The apparatus of the 1958 edition is a condensation of the evidence offered in the current editions of Nestle, with the incorporation of a certain amount of manuscript evidence derived from the researches of British scholars. Thus, though the apparatus reflects mid-twentieth-century scholarship, the text is essentially a nineteenth-century text.

Three Roman Catholic editions are in current use: those of H. J.

---

[1] According to information contained in a leaflet circulated by the British and Foreign Bible Society, the text and punctuation of the 1958 edition of the Greek New Testament differs in only "some twenty passages" from the 1904 edition (the present writer is indebted for this information to the Prof. T. Francis Glasson). The identity of fourteen of the changes is disclosed in the Preface to the second edition (pp. vii sq.). According to Glasson, six other changes were made in Mark 1.1; 10.35; Luke 7.39; 10.1, 17; and Acts 9.12.

Vogels (1920; 4th ed., 1955), A. Merk (1933; 9th ed., 1964), and J. M. Bover (1943; 4th ed., 1959). Their textual complexion, in comparison with the medieval Textus Receptus and the Souter and the Nestle texts, can be gauged from the following statistics based on an analysis of eleven sample chapters:[1] Nestle's text differs from the Textus Receptus in 233 cases, Merk's differs in 160 cases, Bover in 111 cases, Vogels in 67 cases, and Souter in 47 cases. That is, the (Palmer-) Souter text is by far the most archaic of all five widely used editions.

Shortly after the publication of the New Testament of the New English Bible of 1961, requests were received by the Oxford and Cambridge University Presses to issue an edition of the Greek text which inferentially lies behind the new English version. R. V. G. Tasker, professor emeritus of New Testament Exegesis, University of London, and a member of the Panel of Translators of the N.E.B., was entrusted with the task of preparing the edition, which was published in 1964. In evaluating this edition one must differentiate between Tasker's work, which was chiefly a mechanical process, and the text-critical decisions of the panel of British translators.

The Greek text underlying the New Testament of the New English Bible is a curiously eclectic one. Part of the eclecticism was deliberate and part was fortuitous. The directive which guided the individual translators responsible for preparing the first draft of the English rendering was as follows: "The translator shall start with a standard text (e.g. Westcott and Hort, Souter, or Nestle); he shall be free to depart from it where he considers it desirable, but every such departure shall be open to challenge by any member of the Panel, and the reading finally adopted shall be determined by the Panel as a whole." Though most of the draft translators probably made use of the Nestle text, some did not. For example, J. A. T. Robinson, now Bishop of Woolwich, told the present writer that he refused to use the Nestle text because he disliked the Teubner font of type with which it is printed!

In making the basic textual judgments the Panel seems to have given primary consideration to intrinsic and transcriptional proba-

---

[1] The statistics, which were collected by J. Harold Greenlee, are quoted by Kurt Aland in his article, "The Position of New Testament Textual Criticism," *Studia Evangelica*, ed. by Aland, F. L. Cross, *et al.* (= *Texte und Untersuchungen*, LXXIII; Berlin, 1959), p. 719. For more elaborate statistics, see Aland, *Studien zur Überlieferung des Neuen Testaments und seines Textes* (Berlin, 1967), pp. 59ff.

bility, and only meager attention to the weight of external evidence. Occasionally the Panel abandoned all Greek manuscripts and adopted a reading witnessed only by versional and patristic evidence. Thus, in the last verse of the New Testament (Rev. 22.21) according to Tasker the N.E.B. translators regarded the reading *cum omnibus vobis*, found in some manuscripts of the Latin Vulgate, as original and rendered it into English. In this case Tasker had to "invent" a Greek text to represent the reading adopted by the Panel.[1] Since the English translators have advised the reader in a footnote in the N.E.B. concerning the several variant readings in this verse, Tasker could at least set forth in his apparatus the precarious state of the evidence supporting the text that he was compelled to print.

In other cases, however, even this information is withheld from the reader. More than once the N.E.B. translators adopted a reading supported by what many scholars would regard as insufficient evidence without appending a footnote—and in such cases Tasker of course provides no apparatus. For example in Matt. 10.19 the Panel, following *a, b, ff*[1], *k*, syr[s], Cyprian, Augustine, Epiphanius, omitted πῶς ἤ, and in Luke 19.37 it followed syr[s,c] in omitting δυνάμεων. Here, because the N.E.B. contains no footnote mentioning the variant readings, the Greek edition provides no indication of the exceedingly slender evidence supporting the text.

The freedom exercised by the Panel in translating the Greek makes it difficult to correlate Tasker's Greek text with the N.E.B. Thus, in the Fourth Gospel Tasker prints the Johannine ἀμὴν ἀμήν twenty times, whereas the Panel rendered the idiom in four different ways, only one of which requires the geminated expression. Not a few times in Mark, Tasker prints εὐθύς where the English rendering has no corresponding word. It appears that in these instances Tasker has followed the Nestle text.

The most recently published edition of the Greek New Testament is that which was issued by five Bible Societies[2] in 1966. Twelve years earlier Dr. Eugene A. Nida, Secretary for Translations of the American Bible Society, conferred with the present writer about the selection of an international and interdenominational committee of scholars to produce an edition that would reflect twentieth-

---

[1] Apparently unknown to the Panel, there is, as it happens, one Greek manuscript which reads μετὰ πάντων ὑμῶν; it is MS. 296, dating from the sixteenth century!

[2] They are the American, British and Foreign, Dutch, Scottish, and Württemberg Societies.

century text-critical scholarship. The members of the committee included a German, Prof. Kurt Aland, then of Halle now of the University of Münster; a Scotsman, Principal Matthew Black of St. Mary's College, University of St. Andrews; and two Americans, Prof. Allen Wikgren of the University of Chicago, and the present writer. For the first four years of its work, the committee included also an Esthonian scholar, Prof. Arthur Vööbus.[1]

The following are several of the noteworthy features of the new edition. (1) For the first time in the history of Christendom an edition of the Greek New Testament was produced by an international committee. (2) A special set of footnotes provides information concerning more than six hundred differences of punctuation. Since the early manuscripts of the New Testament contain no marks of punctuation, it is necessary that editors supply them, and in these six hundred passages a systematic attempt was made to provide meaningful alternative punctuation. (3) The most important features of the new edition involve the manuscript basis of the Greek text. All 76 of the then known papyri were utilized, as well as 169 of the 250 then known uncial manuscripts; a selection from more than 600 minuscule manuscripts; 150 Greek lectionaries, including 50 of which are cited systematically in the apparatus; nine ancient versions (Old Latin, Vulgate, Syriac, Coptic, Gothic, Armenian, Georgian, Ethiopic, and Nubian); and more than 200 Church Fathers. From these witnesses 1,400 sets of alternative readings were selected for the critical apparatus on the basis of: (a) importance for translation and exegesis; and (b) inclusion of all marginal readings of the English Revised Version, the American Standard Version, the Revised Standard Version, and the New English Bible.[2]

---

[1] For additional information concerning the making of the edition, reference may be made to the pamphlet issued by the five sponsoring Bible Societies and written by Robert P. Markham and Eugene A. Nida, entitled *An Introduction to the Bible Societies' Greek New Testament* (1966).

[2] The present writer was asked by the Committee to prepare a supplementary volume setting forth the reasons that led the Committee to select certain variant readings for inclusion in the text and to relegate certain other readings to the apparatus. The volume, to be entitled *A Textual Commentary on the Greek New Testament*, is expected to be ready toward the end of 1968.

INDEX

NEW TESTAMENT TOOLS AND STUDIES

EDITED BY

BRUCE M. METZGER, PH.D., D.D., L.H.D.

Vol. I

INDEX TO PERIODICAL LITERATURE ON THE APOSTLE PAUL, compiled under the direction of Bruce M. Metzger. 1960. xv + 183 pages.

Vol II

CONCORDANCE TO THE DISTINCTIVE GREEK TEXT OF CODEX BEZAE, compiled by James D. Yoder, Th.D. 1961. vi + 73 double column pages.

Vol. III

GREEK PARTICLES IN THE NEW TESTAMENT, LINGUISTIC AND EXEGETICAL STUDIES, by Margaret E. Thrall, PH.D. 1962. ix + 107 pages.

Vol. IV

CHAPTERS IN THE HISTORY OF NEW TESTAMENT TEXTUAL CRITICISM, by Bruce M. Metzger. 1963. xi + 164 pages.

Vol. V

THE EARLIEST CHRISTIAN CONFESSIONS, by Vernon H. Neufeld, Th.D. 1963. xiii + 166 pages.

Vol. VI

INDEX TO PERIODICAL LITERATURE ON CHRIST AND THE GOSPELS, compiled under the direction of Bruce M. Metzger. 1966. xxiii + 602 pages.

Vol. VII

A Classified Bibliography of Literature on the Acts of the
Apostles, compiled by A. J. Mattill, Jr., Ph.D., and Mary Bed-
ford Mattill, M.A. 1966. xviii + 513 pages.

Vol. VIII

Historical and Literary Studies, Pagan, Jewish, and Christian, by Bruce M. Metzger. 1968. X + 170 pages.

Vol. IX

Studies in Methodology in Textual Criticism of the New
Testament, by Ernest Cadman Colwell, Ph.D., Litt.D., LL.D.,
S.T.D. *in preparation*

PLATES

PLATE I A

Bilingual Stela from Armazi in Georgia (see pp. 36-37).
From Giorgi Tseret'eli, *Armazis bilingva* . . . .
(Tiflis, 1942).

PLATE I B

Papyrus Amulet for Curing Fever (see p. 108).
From the Princeton University Collections, no. 159.
Actual size 2 3/8 × 5 1/4 in.

PLATE II

Berlin, Kgl. Bibl. Ms. Or. Quart. 1019, pp. 106 and 109. The best preserved double leaf of Nu
Lectionary for Christmastide (see p. 119). From F. Ll. Griffith, *The Nubian Texts of the Christian P*
(Berlin, 1913).

PLATE III

Ivory diptych of Rufius Probianus, vicarius urbis Romae, A.D. 399-402,
showing two notarii writing in wax tablets held in their left hands
(see p. 124). From Richard Delbrueck, *Die Consulardiptychen und verwandte
Denkmäler* (Berlin, 1929).

PLATE IV b

PLATE IV a

PLATE V

Relief from Ostia (Museo ostiense, no. 130), dating from the end of the
fourth century A.D. (see p. 127).

PLATE VI

Mosaic from the Chapel of Martyrs at
Tabarka, the ancient Thabraca of Numidia
(see pp. 127f.). Fourth or fifth century.

PLATE VII

Milan, Archaeological Museum, Sculptured Sarcophagus, fifth century
(see p. 128).

PLATE VIII

Brussels, Royal Library, no. 18723, Gospel Book of St. Victor in Xanten.
Purple leaf showing St. Matthew the Evangelist (see p. 128).

PLATE IX

Vienna, Imperial Treasury, Cod. no. 7621 the Schatzkammer or Charlemagne
Gospels, dating about 800. St. Matthew the Evangelist (see p.129).

PLATE X

Ivory plaque of late eighth century, in the Louvre. Lower panel shows
St. Jerome dictating to scribe (see p. 129).

PLATE XI

Ebbo Gospel Book, early ninth century. St. Matthew the Evangelist
(see p.129).

PLATE XII

Berlin, Staatsbibliothek, Cod. Phill. 1676, early ninth century. St. Gregory
the Great (see pp. 129f.).

PLATE XIII

Stuttgart Landesbibliothek, Psalter of ninth or tenth century. Isidore of
Seville (see p. 130).

PLATE XIV

Stuttgart Landesbibliothek, Psalter of ninth or tenth century. Miniature
for Ps. 37 (see p. 130).

PLATE XV A

Vatic. Reg. lat. 438, Martyrologium of Wandelbertus of Prüm, dating from the ninth or tenth century (see p. 130).

PLATE XV B

Corpus Christi College, Cambridge, ms. 389, Lives of Paul the Hermit and Guthlac, dating from the eleventh century. St. Jerome (see p. 130).

PLATE XVI

Leiden, Bibl. Publ. lat. 82, eleventh century. Persius
(see p. 131).

PLATE XVII

Ivory plaque in the Louvre, showing four scribes (see p. 131).

IAM DUDUM SAULUS PROCERĀ
PRECEPTI SECUTUS

paulus

PLATE XVIII

Düsseldorf, Landesbibliothek, Lat. Ms. A 14, from about A.D. 850.
St. Paul (see p. 131).

PLATE XIX B

Furniture from Scriptorium at Qumran (see pp. 135f.).

PLATE XIX A

Apocalypsis S. Johannis italice, dated A.D. 1415. St. John and St. Prochorus (see p. 134).

κ̀ Σίλας ᴨροσευχόμυοι ὑμνουν (τ) Θεόν· ἐπηκροῶντο ὴ αὐτῶν οἱ δέσμιοι. Ἄφνω ὴ σͱσμὸς ἐγͱύετ μέγας, ὥστε σαλͱθͱ-
ναι τͰ Ͱεμͱλια τͱ δεσμωτειου· ἀͱεώχθησαν τε ᴨαραχͱῆμα
αἱ θύραι πᾶσαι, κͱ πάντων τͱ δεσμͱ ἀͱέθη. Ἔξυπν(ͱ) ὴ γε-
νόμͱυος ὁ δεσμοφύλαξ, κͱ ἰδͰν ἀͱεωͳμένας τͱς θύρας τῆς
φυλακῆς, ͱᴨασάμͱυος μͱχαιραν ἔμͱͱͱͱ ἑαυτ̀ ἀναιρεῖν, νο-
μίͳων ͱκπεφͱͱͱͱͱͱτͱͱς δεσμίοις. Ἐφώνͱσε ὴ φωνῇ μεγά-
λͱ ὁ ΓαͰλͱς, λέγων, Μηδὲν ᴨράξͱς σεαυͱͰ κακόν· ἅπαντες
γαρ ἔσμεν ͱνθάͱε. Αἰτͱσας ὴ φͰτα, εἰσεπͱδͱσε, κͱ ἔντͱμος
ͳͱόμͱυ(ͱ) ᴨροσέπεσε Τͱ Παύλͱ ͱ τͰ Σίλͱ· κͱ ᴨρο-
ͳαγͱν αὐτͱς ἔξω, ἔφη, Κύͱͱοι, τͱ με δεῖ ποιεῖν ἵνα σωθͰ;
Οἱ ὴ εἶπον, Πίͳευσον Ͱᴨι (τ) Κύͱͱον ἸησοͱͰ Χͱιͳόν, κͱ σω-
θͰσͱ σὺ κͱ ὁ οἶκός σου. Κͱ ͱͰλͱσαν αͱτͰ τὸν λόͳον τ̀ Κυͱͱ̀
κͱ πͱͳι τ̀ͱς ͱν τῆ οἰκίͱ αͱτ̀. Κͱ ᴨαραλαβͰν αͱτͱς ͱν ͱ-
κͱͰνͱ τͱ ῶͱͱ τͰς νυκτὸς ͱλευσεν Ͱπὸ τͰͰ πλͱͳͰν, κͱ ͱͱͱπͳͱ-
θͱ αͱτὸς κͱ οἱ αͱτ̀ πͱντες ᴨαραχͱͰμͱ · ͱͱαͳαͳͰͱ τε αͱ-
τ̀ς εἰς τὸν οἶκον αͱτ̀, ᴨαρέθͱκε τͱͱͱͱͱ῱, κͱ ͱͳͱͱͱͱͱτͱ,
ᴨανͱͱκͱ πεπιͳͱͱͱ τͰ ΘεͰ. Ἡμέρας ὴ ͳͱͱͱͱͱ · ͱͱͱͰ-
λͱͱ οἱ ͳͱͱͳͱͱ τͱͱς ͱͱͱͰͱͰͳͱͱͱ, λέͳͱτͱ, ἈͱͰλͱͱͱ τͱͱς ͱ-
ͳͱͱͱͱͱ ͱͱͱͱͱͱ. ἈͱͰͱͱͱͱ ὴ ὁ δεσμοφύλαξ τͱͱς λόͳͱͱ
τͱͱͱͱ ᴨρὸς (τ) ΓαͰλͱͱ, Ὅτι ͱͱͱͳͱͱͱͱͱͱ οἱ ͳͱͱͳͱͱ, ἵνα
ͱͱͱͱͱͰͱͱ· νͱͰ ͱͱ ͱͱ̀ͱͱͱͱͱ πͱͱͰͱͱͱ ͱν εἰͱͱͱ. Ὁ ὴ ΓαͰ-
λͱͱ ἔφη ᴨρὸς αͱτͱͱͱ, Δͱͱͱͱͱͱ ͱͱͱͱ ͱͱͱͱͱͰͱ, ἀͱͱͱͱͱͰ-
τͱͱͱ, ͱͱͱͱͱͱͱͱ Ῥͱͱͱͱͱͱ ͱͱͱͱͱͱͱͱͱ ͱͱͱͱͱ εἰς φυλͱͱͰͱ,
ͱ νͱͰ λͱͱͱͱ ͱͱͱͱ ͱͱͱͱͱͱͱͱ; ͱͱ ͳͱ̀ ͱͱͱͱ ͱͱͱͱͱͱ αͱ-
τͱͱ ͱͱͱͱ ͱͱͱͱͱͱͱͱͱ. ἈͱͰͱͱͱͱ ὴ τͱͰ ͳͱͱͳͱͱͱ οἱ ͱͱͱͱͱͱͱ τͱ ͱͱͰͱͱͱ ͱͱͱͱ · κͱ ͱͱͱͱͰͱͱͱ ͱͱͱͱͱͱͱ ͱͱ
Ῥͱͱͱͱͱ εἰͱ, κͱ ͱͱͱͱͱͱͱ ᴨαρεͱͱͱͱͱ αͱͱͱͱ, κͱ ͱͱͱͱͱ-
ͱͱͱͱͱ ͱͱͱͱͱ ͱͱͱͱͱͱ τͰͱ πͱͱͱͱͱ. Ἐͱͱͱͱͱͱ ͱ ͱͱ τͰͱ φυλͱͱͰͱ εἰͱͰͱͱͱ εἰͱ τͰͰ Λυͱͱͱ· κͱ ἰͱͱͱͱ τͱͰͱ ͱͱͱͱͱͱͰͱ,
ᴨαρεͱͱͱͱͱͱ αͱͱͱͱ, κͱ ͱͱͰͱͱͱͱ.

αͱͱͱͱ ͱͱͱͱͱͱ, εἰͱͱͱͱͱ, Πͱͱͱͱͱͱͱ ͱͱ κͱ̀ ͱͱͱͱ, ͱͱ εͱ ͱͱͰͱͱ ͱͱͱͱͱͱ. Κͱ ͱͱͱͱͳͱͱͱ ᴨαρεͱͱͱͱͱ αͱͱͱͱ, λέͳͱͱͱ, Ἐͱ τ
ᴨͱͱͱͱ ͱͱͱͱͱ ͱͱͱͱͱ, ͱͱͱͱ ᴨͱͱͱ ͱͱͱͱͱͱͱͱ ͱͱͱ, ͱͱͱͱͱͱͱͱ κͱ̀ ͱͱͱ. Ἐͱͱͱͱͱ ὴ ͱͱ τ φυλͱͱͱ, ͱͱͱͱͱ ᴨͱͱͱ τͰͱ
Λͱͱͱͱ ͱ ἰͱͱͱͱ τͱͱͱ ͱͱͱͱͱͱͱ, ͱͱͱͱͱͱͱ ͱͱ ͱͱͱͱͱ Κͱͱͱͱ αͱͱͱͱ, ᴨͱͱͱͱͱͱͱͱ αͱͱͱͱ. β

q.ii.

PLATE XX
Robert Stephanus's third edition of the Greek New Testament (Paris, 1550),
the first printed Greek Testament with a critical apparatus. Lower portion
of p. 243, showing three variant readings from Codex Bezae for Acts 16. 35
and 38-40 (see pp. 142 and 144). Actual size of page is 12 7/8 in. x 8 1/2 in.